Q&A

Routledge Questions and Answers Series

Intellectual
Property Law

Routledge Q&A series

Each Routledge Q&A contains 50 questions on topics commonly found on exam papers, with comprehensive suggested answers. The titles are written by lecturers who are also examiners, so the student gains an important insight into exactly what examiners are looking for in an answer. This makes them excellent revision and practice guides. With over 500,000 copies of the Routledge Q&As sold to date, accept no substitute.

Other titles in the series:

BUSINESS LAW

CIVIL LIBERTIES & HUMAN RIGHTS

COMMERCIAL LAW

COMPANY LAW

CONSTITUTIONAL & ADMINISTRATIVE LAW

CONTRACT LAW

CRIMINAL LAW

EMPLOYMENT LAW

ENGLISH LEGAL SYSTEM

EQUITY & TRUSTS

EUROPEAN UNION LAW

EVIDENCE

FAMILY LAW

JURISPRUDENCE

LAND LAW

TORTS

For a full listing, visit www.routledgelaw.com/revisionaids

Routledge Questions & Answers Series

Intellectual Property Law

JANICE DENONCOURT

Routledge
Taylor & Francis Group

LONDON AND NEW YORK

Second edition published 2010 by Routledge
2 Park Square, Milton Park, Abingdon, Oxon, OX14 4RN

Simultaneously published in the USA and Canada
by Routledge
270 Madison Avenue, New York, NY 10016

Routledge is an imprint of the Taylor & Francis Group, an informa business

© 2007, 2010 Routledge

Typeset in Garamond by
RefineCatch Limited, Bungay, Suffolk
Printed and bound in Great Britain by
TJ International Ltd, Padstow, Cornwall

British Library Cataloguing in Publication Data
A catalogue record for this book is available from the British Library

Library of Congress Cataloging-in-Publication Data
Denoncourt, Janice.
Q&A intellectual property law / Janice Denoncourt.—2nd ed.
p. cm.
Includes bibliographical references and index.
1. Intellectual property—Great Britain.
I. Title. II. Title: Q and A intellectual property law.
KD1269.D46 2010
346.4104'8076—dc22
2009048237

ISBN10: 0–415–55297–4 (pbk)
ISBN13: 978–0–415–55297–4 (alk. paper)

ISBN10: 0–203–85635-X (ebk)
ISBN13: 978–0–203–85635 -2 (ebk)

CONTENTS

Preface   *vii*
Exam Question Methodology   *ix*
Table of Cases   *xiii*
Table of Legislation   *xxi*

	Introduction	1
1	General Themes in IP Law	3
2	Intellectual Property Litigation – Enforcement and Remedies	21
3	Copyright and Moral Rights	31
4	Computer Technology and Copyright Law	57
5	Registered Design and Design Right	73
6	Patents	85
7	Registered Trade Marks	115
8	Passing Off	139
9	Geographical Indications	147
10	Confidential Information and Know-How	155
11	Character Merchandising and Malicious Falsehood	171
12	Image Rights	179

13   Franchising and Intellectual Property Rights   183

14   IP Law Exam Technique   187

15   Intellectual Property Exam Cram Guide   191

16   Useful Websites   195

Index   197

PREFACE

The law of intellectual property is now a standard option on most qualifying law degree courses and continues to increase in popularity, especially with students who regard the subject as exciting 'new law' at the centre of the creative economy. This second edition of *Questions & Answers Intellectual Property Law* is designed to make preparing for law exams easier, by focusing on typical intellectual property exam questions students may face when they are assessed. It has been revised and updated and the new content reflects the latest trends and developments in intellectual property law. Fifty problem and essay questions have been arranged topically, followed by an answer plan and a comprehensive suggested answer. New questions deal with, for example, the recently introduced 'Green Channel' for patent applications relating to environmentally friendly subject matter as well as certain House of Lords and European Court of Justice decisions published in early 2009.

As a result of feedback from students, it is clear many find problem questions the most difficult form of assessment. Bearing this in mind, this second edition includes additional problem questions to assist students in this regard. There is advice on intellectual property law exam technique, an 'Exam Cram' feature and a list of weblinks to additional resources for those students who wish to take their exam preparation further.

There is no doubt that the sheer volume of material relating to intellectual property law and the ever-increasing rhythm of change in this area of law challenges even the best student. My hope is that this Q&A text provides students with a good basis for tackling a good range of topics to enable them to succeed in their intellectual property law exams.

I wish to thank my colleague Dr Rebecca Wong, Professors Paul Torremans (University of Nottingham), Ruth Soetendorp (Bournemouth University) and Jonathan Black-Branch (University of Brighton) who have all provided me with continued support for my academic endeavours over the years.

I have attempted to state the law as it stands on 20 June 2009. I apologise if inadvertently any sources remain unacknowledged and will be glad to make the necessary arrangements at the earliest opportunity.

Janice Denoncourt
Senior Lecturer in Law
Nottingham Law School
Nottingham Trent University
20 June 2009

EXAM QUESTION METHODOLOGY

Law exams commonly contain three types of questions: essay, problem and mixed topic.

ESSAY QUESTIONS

An essay question is often a short statement of law contained in a quote from a court judgment or an academic article, which requires the student to answer the query or proposition within it. Essay questions are designed to test the student's depth of understanding of intellectual property law and issues as well as their ability to critically analyse the law. The best approach is to adopt a succinct style, following an answer plan that covers the basic principles. Set out below are three examples of typical essay question terminology.

'Critically analyse'

You may be asked to 'critically analyse. . . .'. In this case, a useful approach is to provide an objective assessment of the positive and negative points of the subject. Ensure that your answer is clearly structured to signpost the progression of your argument(s).

'Discuss'

Another commonly used instructing word is 'discuss'. This is an instruction to discuss the keywords identified in the essay question.

'Subdivided' questions

Some essay questions are broken down into subsections, for example, (i), (ii) . . . or (a), (b) . . . etc. The best approach to this type of question is to answer each sub-question in turn, clearly identifying the separate parts of the essay. Unless you are told otherwise, it is reasonable for you to assume that each subdivision carries equal marks. This means you may want to allocate equal time to each subsection.

In general, when dealing with an essay question, the following approach is suggested:

Step one

What is the widest possible classification of the specific topic? For instance, copyright law, design law, etc.

Step two

Identify the focus within that topic – for example whether the fair dealing provisions in the **Copyright Designs and Patents Act 1988** provide the public with sufficient access to copyright works.

Subject	Copyright Law
Topic	Defences
Focus	Whether the fair dealing defences provide the public with sufficient access to copyright works.

Step three

Identify the key words in the title and explain and define them in the course of your essay. Refer to relevant statutes and case law which support your thesis. There is no excuse for not citing cases accurately. Use the correct name for an Act (the short title).

Step four

Attempt to weave analysis, constructive criticism and evaluation of the law into your essay. There are always two sides to an issue and it is important to engage in a balanced discussion.

Step five

Review and proofread your essay to ensure that everything mentioned in it is relevant to the title. This is how to attract marks. End your essay with a brief summary and reach a sensible and reasoned conclusion.

PROBLEM QUESTIONS

Problem-solving questions contain a set of hypothetical facts and read like a short story. The facts may be based on or similar to a decided case or may be completely made up. The difficulty lies in recognising the areas of law from the factual circumstances. In answering the problem question, in essence, you put yourself in the position of the judge. Judges try to evaluate the strength of each party's position and arrive at a logically reasoned decision through the application of the relevant law. A problem question is NOT an invitation to write an essay. The facts of the case are important and should be specifically referred to in your answer. Most intellectual property law problem questions can be dealt with by adopting the following methodology:

IP law problem question checklist

- Classify the key facts (for example items of property, relevant dates, significant events, etc.).
- Identify the area(s) of intellectual property law concerned.
- Identify the author, inventor and/or owner of the right concerned.
- Note all the elements that need to be proved for the right to subsist, be registered, be granted, etc. In other words, explain the applicable law and conclude as you progress.
- Assess whether the alleged infringer has infringed by setting out all the elements that need to be proved. Deal with the facts as you progress.
- Consider whether the alleged infringer is able to rely on any defences.
- If the cause of action is established, consider what remedies are available.
- Advise the party(s) as to the strength of their case.

Examiners differ in their preferred practice for answering problem questions. The above checklist is general guidance. There are also two acronyms that may help when dealing with problem questions:

IRAC	Issues	**IDEA**	Identify the legal issue
	Rules		Define the legal rule
	Apply		Explain how the rule works
	Conclude		Apply the rule to the facts

▌MIXED TOPIC QUESTIONS

A mixed topic question includes two or more topics on the syllabus in the same question. This type of question is often used both to increase the level of difficulty and to ensure that students cannot study topics in an overly selective manner. Typical combinations of intellectual property topics involve:

> Copyright + Moral Rights
> Copyright + Design
> Trade Marks + Passing Off
> Trade Marks + Geographical Indications
> Patents + Design
> Patents + Remedies

Note however, that any form of intellectual property right that arises in the syllabus can be combined with:

- 'traditional justifications for intellectual property';
- 'international themes in intellectual property';
- enforcement;
- remedies; or
- law reform.

The key answering a mixed topic question is to engage in a balanced discussion of each of the main issues.

GRAMMAR, SYNTAX AND SPELLING

Developing a good writing style is crucial for law students because the law is all about communicating through words. Keep sentences relatively short to avoid grammar and syntax errors. Do not adopt an overly journalistic or casual style of writing. On the other hand, avoid grandiose and flowery language. Use plain English where possible and write succinctly. Well-written answers have more authority and will attract better marks.

From your experience of exams so far, you know that beginning to write is difficult, so do not start writing until you have an idea of what you want to say. Creating a brief answer outline will help you to plan the beginning, middle and end of your answer. Each example in this text contains a short 'Answer Plan' for you to emulate.

TABLE OF CASES

Note: Where recent cases have not been widely reported, it is possible to read the judgment on the ECJ website. Go to *www.curia.eu.int*, select 'Proceedings' and 'case law'. Use the case number to search for the case you want to read.

A v B and C plc [2003] QB 195 .... 25, 27, 182

AD2000 Trade Mark [1997] RPC 168 116

Adam v Opel AG v Autec AG (2007) Landgerick Nurnberg-Furth Case C-48/05 125

American Cyanamid v Ethicon [1975] 1 All ER 504 .... 25, 26, 27

Antec International Ltd v South Western Chicks (Warren) Ltd
[1990] EWHC Patents 330 142

Anton Piller KG v Manufacturing Processes Ltd [1976] RPC 719 .... 29, 163

Argyll v Argyll [1967] Ch 302 163

Arsenal Football Club Plc v Reed [2001] All ER (D) 67;
(No. 2) [2003] 1 CMLR 13; [2004] EIPR 479 .... 123, 124, 125, 180–1

Associated Newspapers v News Group [1986] RPC 515 43

Atkins v Perrin (1862) 175–6

Attorney-General v Blake (1990) 160

Attorney-General v Guardian Newspapers Ltd [1990] AC 109 .... 159, 163

Auchinloss v Agricultural and Veterinary Supplies [1997] RPC 649 101

Australian Children's Television Workshop Inc v
Woolworths (NSW) Ltd [1981] RPC 187 132

Baby Dan AS v Brevi SR [1999] FSR 377 .... 74, 75

Balden v Shorter [1933] Ch 427 175

Barclays Bank v RBS Advanta (1996) RPC 307 .... 128, 129

BBC v Precord Ltd [1992] 3EIPRD-52 26

BBC v Talksport [2001] FSR 53 141

BBC Worldwide Ltd v Pally Screen Printing Ltd [1998] FSR 665 79

Beloff v Pressdram Ltd [1973] 1 All ER 241 41

Bollinger v Costa Brava Wine Co Ltd [1960] RPC 16 141

Bonnard v Perryman [1891] 2 Ch 269 176

Boscobell Paints v Bigg [1975] FSR 42 176

BP Amoco plc v John Kelly Ltd [2001] FSR 21 142

Bristol Conservatories Ltd v Conservatories Custom Built [1989] RPC 455 139

British Airways plc v Ryanair Ltd [2001] FSR 541 .... 128, 129, 176

British Horseracing Board Ltd and Ors v William Hill Organization Ltd
    [2001] CMLR 12 71

British Horseracing Board Ltd and Ors v William Hill Organization Ltd
    [2005] EWCA (Civ) 863 71

British Leyland Motor Corp Ltd v Armstrong Patents Co Ltd [1986] 2 WLR 400 74

British Steel Plc's Patent [1992] RPC 117 107

Byrne v Statist [1914] 1 KB 622 43

Cable & Wireless plc v British Telecommunications plc [1998] FSR 383 .... 128, 129

Caird v Sime (1887) 12 App Cas 326 42

Cantor Fitzgerald International v Tradition (UK) Ltd [2000] RPC 95 .... 58, 65

Catnic Components Ltd v Hill & Smith Ltd [1982] RPC 183 .... 98, 99

Celanese International Corporation v BP Chemicals Ltd [1999] RPC 203 23

Chelsea Man Menswear Ltd v Chelsea Girl Ltd [1987] RPC 189 .... 140, 142

Chiron v Murex Diagnostics [1996] FSR 153 .... 88, 104

Ciba-Geigy plc v Parke Davis and Co Ltd [1994] FSR 124

Clark v Associated Newspapers [1998] RPC 261 .... 39, 56

Coco – AN Clark (Engineers) Ltd [1969] RPC 41 156–9

Confetti Records v Warner Music [2003] EMLR 35 .... 39, 54, 55

Consorzio del Prosciutto di Parma v Asda Store Ltd [2002] FSR 3 .... 141, 150, 151

County Sound plc v Ocean Sound plc [1991] FSR 367 141

Cream Holdings and other v Banerjee and others (2004) Ch 650 27

Danish Mercantile v Beaumont [1950] 67 RPC 111 176

'Das Prinzip Der Bequemlichkeit' "[The Principle of Comfort"] C-64/02 P 118

De Maudsley v Palumbo and Others (1996) FSR 447 158

Designers Guild Ltd v Russell Williams (Textiles) Ltd (No 2)
    [2001] 1 All ER 700 43

Donoghue v Allied Newspapers [1938] 1 Ch 108 50

Dowson v Mason Potter [1986] 2 All ER 418 160

DSG Retail Ltd v Comet Group plc [2002] FSR 899 174–5

Dunlop Pneumatic Tyre Company v Maison Talbot (1904) TLR 579 175–6

Dyson Ltd v Qualtex (UK) Ltd [2004] EWHC 2981 (Ch) 74, 75, 76

Electronic Techniques v Critchley Components [1997] FSR 401 .... 29, 39, 43

Emaco v Dyson Appliances (1999) *The Times*, 8 February 176

EPI Environmental Technologies Inc v Symphony Plastic Technologies plc
[2004] EWHC 2945 (Ch); [2005] 1 WLR 3456 159
Exxon Corporation v Exxon Insurance Consultants International Ltd
[1981] 3 All ER 241 51

Faccenda Chicken v Fowler [1985] 1 All ER 617; [1986] Ch 117 .... 161, 162
Farmer's Build Limited v Carrier Bulk Materials Handling Ltd [1999]
RPC 461 .... 74, 75, 76
Fixtures Marketing Ltd v OPAP (2004) C-444/02 72
Francis Day and Hunter v Twentieth Century Fox [1940] AC 112 .... 42, 50, 51
Fraser-Woodward v BBC and Brighter Pictures Limited
[2005] EWHC 472 (Ch) 43

Gartside v Outram (1856) 26 LJ Ch 113 167
Gary Flitcroft (A v B plc and Another) [2002] 3 WLR 542 ....
GEC Avionics Ltd' Patent [1992] RPC 107 107
General Tire v Firestone Tyre Co Ltd [1975] RPC 457 23
Graver Tank & Manufacturing Co Inc v Linde Air Products Company
339 US 605, 607 (1950) 100

Harrods v Harrodian School (1996) unreported 143
Harvard College v Canada (Commissioner of Patents) (2002)
21 CPR (4th) 417 (SCC) 95, 97, 105
Harvard ONCO Mouse (T-19/90) (1990) EPOR 501 .... 95, 96, 105
Hawkes & Sons v Paramount Film Services [1934] Ch 593 45
HFC Bank v HSBC Bank plc [2000] FSR 176 142
Hivac Ltd v Park Royal Scientific Instruments Ltd [1946] 1 Ch 169 162
Hubbard v Vosper [1972] 2 QB 84 .... 34, 35, 42
Hubbuck & Sons Ltd v Wilkinson, Heywood & Clerk Ltd [1899] 1 QB 86 176
Hyde Park Residence Ltd v Yelland [2000] RPC 604 .... 34, 36

Ibcos Computers v Barclays Mercantile High Finance [1994] FSR 275 .... 58, 59, 60, 65
Independent Television Publication v Time Out Magazine [1984] FSR 64 35
Intel Corporations Inc v CPM United Kingdom Ltd
[2008] WLR (D) 371 .... 130, 131
IPC Magazines Ltd v MGN [1998] FSR 431 51
IPC Media Ltd v Highbury – SPL Publishing Ltd (2004) 51
Irvine v Talksport [2002] EMLR 32 .... 144, 146, 179–81
Island Records Inc v Tring International plc [1995] FSR 560 80

J Bollinger v Costa Brava Wine Co Ltd [1960] Ch 262 Chancery Division 152
James Duncan Kelly, Kwok, Wai Chiu v GE Healthcare Ltd
    [2009] EWHC 181 (HL) 106
Jeanette Winterson v Mark Hogarth (2000) WIPO Case No.D2000–0235 136
JH Coles Pty Ltd v Need [1934] AC 82 184
John Richardson Computers Ltd v Flanders and Chemtech Ltd
    [1992] FSR 497 .... 59, 65, 66
John Wyeth & Bros Ltd Application [1985] RPC 545 104
Joyce v Sengupta [1993] 1 All ER 897 175
J&S Davis (Holdings) Ltd v Wright Health Group (1988) 38, 47

Kelly and Chiu v GE Healthcare Limited [2009] EWHC 181 (Pat) HL 106, 107, 110
Kenrick & Co Ltd v Lawrence & Co [1890] 25 QBD 99 .... 33, 59, 65
Khodaporast v Shad [2000] All ER (D) 21 177
Kirin-Amgen Inc and others v Hoechst Marion Roussel Ltd and others
    [2004] UKHL 46 .... 98, 99, 100, 101, 102
KWS Saat AG v OHIM [2002] ECR II-3843 120

Ladbroke (Football) Ltd v William Hill (Football) Ltd [1964] 1 WLR 273 .... 41, 42, 52
Lambretta Clothing Co Ltd v Teddy Smith (UK) Ltd [2005] RPC 88 .... 77, 78
Lawson v Dundas, *The Times*, 13 June 1985 45
Leland Stanford Modified Animal [2002] EP 2 104
Libertel Group BV v Benelux –Merkenbureau [2004] FSR (4) 65 .... 118, 120, 121
Lion Laboratories Ltd v Evans [1985] QB 526 .... 167, 168
L'Oreal SA and others v Bellure NV and others
    [2009] WLR (D) 203 .... 123, 126, 130, 133
Lock International plc v Beswick [1989] 3 All ER 373 147
London Evening Mail v Express Newspapers [2003] EWHC 1322 (Ch) 142
London Regional Transport v Mayor of London [2003] EMLR 88 167
Ludlow Music Inc v Robbie Williams (No 2) [2002] EWHC 638,
    [2002] EMLR 29 .... 42, 45
Lyngstad v Anabas Products [1977] FSR 62 132

Mail Newspapers v Express Newspapers [1987] FSR 90 56
Mark Wilkinson Furniture v Woodcraft Designs [1998] FSR 63 78
Mawman v Tegg (1826) 2 Russ. 385 42
Mayne Pharma Pty Ltd and Mayne Pharma Plc v Pharmacia Italia SpA
    [2005] EWCA Civ 137 .... 98, 101, 102

McCulloch v Lewis A May (Produce Distributors) [1947] 2 ALL ER 845 145

Memco-Med's Ltd's Patent [1992] RPC 403 107

Microdata v Rivendale (1984) unreported, 11 September 176

Mirage Productions v Counter-Feat Clothing Co Ltd [1991] FSR 135 .... 172, 173

Morning Star Co-operative Society v Express Newspapers [1979] FSR 113 142

Morrison v Moat (1851) 9 Hare 241 157

Mothercare UK Ltd v Penguin books Ltd [1988] RPC 113 27

MS Associates Ltd v Power [1988] FSR 242 59

Naomi Campbell v Mirror Group Newspapers
    [2002] EWHC 499 (QB) and (2004) 157, 182

Navitaire Inc v Easjet Airline Company [2004] EWHC 1725 .... 58, 60, 65

Navitaire Inc v Easyjet Airline Company (2006) RPC 111 .... 58, 60, 66, 67

Nestle SA's Trade Mark Application (Have a Break) v Mars Ltd Case C-35 (2005) 118

Neutrogena Corpn v Golden Ltd [1996] RPC 473 142

Newspaper Licensing Agency Ltd v Marks & Spencer plc (1999) *The Times*, 15 June 36

Niema Ash v Loreena McKennitt [2006] EWCA Civ 1714 Court of Appeal 180–1

Nottinghamshire Healthcare NHS Trust v News Group Newspapers Ltd
    [2002] EWHC 409 23

02 Holdings Ltd & anor v Hutchinson 3G UK Ltd [2008] WLR (D) 193 130

02 Ltd v Hutchinson 3G UK Ltd [2006] ETMR 54 128

Ocular Sciences Ltd v Aspect Vision Care Ltd [1997] RPC 289 .... 74, 76

Parke-Davis & Co v H.K. Mulford & Co (1911) 189 F 95 113

Pasterfield v Denham and Another [1998] FSR 168 .... 39, 54

Perry v Truefitt (1842) 6 Beav 66 .... 139, 141

Phillips Electronics NV v Remington Consumer Products Ltd (1998) 117

Phones 4u Ltd v Phones4u.co.uk Internet Ltd [2007] RPC 5 141

PLG Research Ltd v Ardon International Ltd [1995] FSR 116 88

Prince Albert v Strange (1894) 2 De G & Sm 293 157

Produce Records Limited v BMG Entertainment International UK and
    Ireland Limited (1999) 44, 45

Pronuptia de Paris v Schillgalis Case 161/84 ECR 353 185

Pro Sieben Media AG v Carlton UK TV Ltd [1999] FSR 610 36

R v Chief Constable of the North Wales Police, ex p AB [1998] 3 All ER 167–8

Ralf Sieckmann v Deutsches Patent und Markenamt
    [2002] ECR I-11737 .... 118, 119, 120, 122

Ratcliffe v Evans [1892] 2 QB 524 174

Reckitt and Coleman Products v Borden Inc
   [1990] All ER 1873 HL 79, 141, 142, 167, 173

Reddaway & Co Ltd v Banham & Co Ltd [1896] AC 199 141

Redwood Music v B Feldman & Co Ltd [1979] RPC 385, CA 44

Robb v Green [1895] 2 QB 315 157

Saltman Engineering Co Ltd v Campbell Engineering Co Ltd
   [1963] RPC 203 .... 157, 158, 163

Schering and Wyeth's Application [1985] RPC 545 93

Schulke & May UK Ltd v Alkapharm UK Ltd [1999] FSR 161 174

Seager v Copydex Ltd (No 2) [1969] RPC 349 .... 157, 159, 160, 163

Series 5 Software Ltd v Philip Clarke and Others [1996] FAS 273 ...... 25, 26, 27

Shell/Blood Flow [1993] EPOR 320 .... 93, 103, 104

Sieckmann [2003] RPC 38 .... 118, 119, 120, 122

Sinanide v La Maison Kosmeo (1928) 44 TLR 371 51

Smith Kline and French's Trade Mark [1975] 2 All ER 57 120

Sony Computer Entertainment v Ball [2004] EWHC 1738 .... 61, 63

Sony Computer Entertainment Inc v Edmunds [2002] EWHC 45 (CH) 61, 63

Spalding & Bros AW Gamage Ltd [1915] 32 RPC 273 141

Stafford-Miller's Application [1984] RPC 239 93

Stannard v Reay [1967] RPC 589 142

Stewart Brady v Express Newspapers (1994) 176

Stilltoe v McGraw Hill Books [1983] FSR 545 .... 34, 36, 42

Stringfellow v McCain Foods (GB) Ltd [1984] FSR 175

Terrapin Ltd v Builders Supply Co (Hayes) Ltd [1967] RPC 375 159

Tolley v JS Fry and Sons Ltd [1930] 1KB 467 180

Unilever (Davis's) Application [1983] RPC 219 .... 93, 120

Universal Thermosensors Ltd v Hibben [1992] 3 All ER 257 30

University of London Press Ltd v University Tutorial Press Ltd
   [1916] 2 Ch 601 .... 38, 41, 47, 50, 51, 52, 58, 65

Upjohn's Application [1976] RPC 324 93

Vodafone Group Plc v Orange Personal Communications Service Ltd
   [1997] FSR 34 .... 128, 129

W v Edgell [1990] Ch 359 167–9

Warnink BV v Townend & Sons (Hull) Ltd [1980] RPC 31 HL 141, 143

Wheatly v Drillsafe Ltd [2001] RPC 133 100

Whelan Associated Inc v Jaslow Dental Laboratory Inc [1987] FSR 1 .... 59, 65

William Edge & Sons Ltd v William Nichols & Sons Ltd [1911] AC 693 79

Windsurfing International Inc v Tabur Marine (GB) (1985) RPC 59 .... 86, 88

Wombles Ltd v Wombles Skips Ltd [1975] RPC 99 50

Wrigley/Light Green [1999] ETMR 214 Board of Appeal of the OHIM 120

TABLE OF LEGISLATION

STATUTES

Copyright, Designs and Patents Act 1988

s 1(1)	38, 41, 44, 47, 50, 58, 65
s 3(1)	40, 44, 53, 58, 65
s 3(2)	42, 44, 59, 65
s 3(3)	42
s 4	172
s 4(1)	38, 39, 46–7, 51, 66
s 4(2)	37, 47
s 6(3)	69
s 9(1)	38
s 9(2)	23
s 9(3)	41
s 9(5)	33
s 11	59
s 12	41
s 14(2)	23
s 16(1)	28–9, 32, 38, 39, 42, 44, 45, 182
s 16(2)	29, 44, 47
s 16(3)	42
s 17	28, 39, 58
s 17(2)	43
s 17(3)	39, 42
s 18	29, 58
s 21	28, 58
ss 22–27	43–4
s 28	34,-35
ss 28–76	42, 48
s 29	35, 69
s 30(1)	35, 38, 43
s 30(2)	35, 52
s 31	35, 48

s 50 68

s 58 43

s 60BA 69

s 62 .... 39, 47, 48

s 76 35

ss 77–79 .... 33, 53–5

ss 80–83 .... 33, 39, 53–5

s 84 .... 33, 39, 54

s 85 .... 33, 39, 54

s 86 .... 39, 56

s 87 55

s 94 .... 38–39, 54

s 96(2) 23

s 99 39

s 100 .... 24, 29

ss 107–110 24

ss 153–155 41

s 178 43

s 196ZB 24

s 201 24

s 213 .... 74–8, 80, 83

s 215 79

s 226 79

s 277 79

ss 229(2)-231 .... 23, 80

s 263(3) 79

s 296 62

s 296(2) 62

s 296(4) 62

ss 296ZA-ZF 61–4

s 297 24

s 297 A 24

s 297ZE 61

Competition Act 1998 185

Defamation Act 1952 176

s 5 176

s 6 176

Data Protection Act 1998 182

Freedom on Information Act 2000 166

Human Fertilization and Embryology Act 2008 104
Human Rights Act 1998 .... 25, 27, 176

London Olympic Games and Paralympic Games Act 2006 .... 13–14, 16, 115

Olympic Symbol etc (Protection) Act 1995 .... 13–14, 16, 115, 121, 122
  s 3(1)(a) 115

Patents Act 1977 .... 7, 23, 24, 85–90, 92–98, 104–7, 109, 163
  s 1(1) 86, 104–5, 111
  s 1(2) 87, 95–97, 102–4
  s 1(3) 103–5, 111
  s 1(4) 96
  s 2 87
  s 2(2) 88
  s 3 .... 86–8, 104
  s 4 87
  s 4(1) 88
  s 4A 93–4, 103
  s 5(1) 88–9
  s 16(1) 88
  s 17 89
  ss 39–41 106–7
  s 43 107
  s 61(1)(c) 23
  s 76A 108–9
  s 9(2) 23
  s 17 89
  s 61(1)(d) 23
  s 109 24
  s 110 24
  s 125 98
  Sch A2 .... 95, 97, 103–5

Patents Act 2004 85
  s 1 105
  s 4A 92–3
  s 10 109
  s 12 107
Plant Varieties Act 1997 105
  ss 4–7 105
  Sch 2 105

Registered Designs Act 1949 .... 8, 23–4, 73–4, 80–3, 180
  s 1(3) 80–1
  s 1B 81–2
  s 9(1) 23
  s 35 24
  s 35A 24

Trade Descriptions Act 1968 179
Trade Marks Act 1994 .... 7, 23, 24, 115, 116, 117–20, 123–5, 128–9, 147, 174, 184
  s 1 .... 115, 117–20, 124
  s 3 116–18
  s 4 117
  s 5 .... 115, 117, 119, 124–5
  s 9 124
    s 10 .... 123, 125, 128–9, 174
    s 14 23
    s 25 184
    s 28 184
    s 29 184
    s 59 24
    s 60 24
    s 92 24

STATUTORY INSTRUMENTS

Artist's Resale Right Regulations 2006 .... 34, 54, 56

Block Exemption Regulations 185–6

Control of Misleading Advertisements (Amendment) Regulations 2000 128
Copyright (Computer Programs) Regulations 1992 67–8

Copyright and Related Rights Regulations 2003 69
Copyright and Rights in Databases Regulations 1997 70
    reg 13(1) 70
    reg 16 71
    reg 17 70

Patent Regulations 2000 110–11
Plant Breeders/ rights (Naming and Fees) Regulations 2006 105

Registered Designs (Fees) Rules 2006 82
Regulatory Reform (Registered Designs) Order 2006 81–2
Regulatory Reform (Patents) Order 2004 105

EUROPEAN COMMUNITY AND EEA LEGISLATION

Regulations (listed in date order)

Council Regulation 3295/94 concerning customs action against goods
    suspected of infringing certain IPRs 24

Protected Designations of Origin Regulation 1992 149
    Art 2(1) 149

Traditional Foods Regulation 1992 150
    Art 2(1) 150

Directives

Biotech Directive 98/44/EC 97, 105, 110–11

Comparative Advertising Directive 97/55EC 128–31
    Art 3a 131

Database and Information Society Directive 69
    Art 7 71
Directive 40/94 115
Directive 91/250/EEC of 14 May 1991 67

Legal Protection of Designs Directive 98/71/EC 80–1
    Art 6 67
    Art 6(3) 69

Resale Right Directive 34, 56

Software Directive 1991 .... 67, 69

Trade Marks Directive 89/104/EEC 115–116, 122, 124–5, 129–33
    Art 4.4(a) 132
    Art 5.2 133

INTERNATIONAL AGREEMENTS, CONVENTIONS AND TREATIES
Australia-EU Agreement on Wine 1994 152

Berne Convention for the Protection of Literary and Artistic Works 1886 .... 34, 53, 54
    Art 6 .... 53, 54
    Art 14 34

Convention Establishing the World Intellectual Property Organization 1967 103
Convention on Biological Diversity 1992 11

EU-Chile Association Agreement on Wine, Spirit Drinks and
    Aromatised Drinks 2002 152
EU-Mexico Agreement on Spirits 1997 152
European Convention on Human Rights 181–2
    Art 8 181–2
    Art 10 181–2
European Patent Convention 1973 .... 91, 95, 96, 98
    Art 53(a) 95–6
    Art 69 98
European Patent Convention 2000 93
    Art 52(4) 106
    Art 53 .... 93, 96, 104
    Art 54(4) 106
    Art 54(5) 106

Lisbon Agreement for the Protection of Appellations of Origin and their
    International Registration 149, 151
    Art 2 139

Madrid Agreement for the Repression of False or Misleading Indications of
    Source on Goods 151

Paris Convention for the Protection of Industrial Property 1883 .... 74, 131, 139–40, 151
    Art 10bis 131, 139, 152

Patent Cooperation Treaty 1970 .... 86–7, 91, 103

Substantive Patent Law Treaty (SPLT) 102, 104–5

TRIPS Agreement (Trade Related Aspects of Intellectual
  Property Rights) 5, 7, 10, 19, 33, 74, 91, 137, 141–2, 147–8, 150–1
  Art 2 33
  Art 2(3) 91
  Art 4 5
  Art 7 10
  Art 22 .... 7, 147–8, 151
  Art 23 .... 137, 141–2, 151–2
  Art 23(4) 142, 151–2
  Art 24 .... 137, 141, 151
  Art 67 19

Universal Declaration of Human Rights 1948 .... 4, 5, 54
  Art 27 .... 4, 38, 54

World Intellectual Property Organization on Copyright Treaty 1996 .... 57, 61, 62
  Art 4 57
  Art 11 62
World Intellectual Property Organization Performers and Phonograms Treaty 61, 62
  Art 18 62

INTRODUCTION

The term 'intellectual property' is used to describe the various rights that protect innovation and creative endeavour. An optional law subject, intellectual property law arises in the curriculum towards the end of a law (LLB) degree. This is because it is regarded as an advanced and specialist subject due to its diverse content and the fact that it draws on core legal subject knowledge including contract, tort, land, common law and equity. The discipline became popular in the late 1980s and early 1990s and was included in the curricula as a standalone course to accommodate the changing demands of the legal professional bodies and business.

Typically, at the undergraduate level, an intellectual property law course will cover copyright, moral rights, patents, trade marks, passing off, confidential information, remedies and enforcement. Occasionally, if the syllabus is not too crowded, undergraduate courses will also include design law, geographical indications, franchising and, more rarely, plant breeders' rights and chip topographies. Common themes across the different forms of intellectual property include authorship or inventorship, ownership, requirements for the right to subsist, the extent and duration of the statutory monopolies granted, remedies and enforcement.

Fortunately, the number of books and online resources on the subject of intellectual property law has grown to support the increased level of study of the subject. In 2003, the UK Government introduced the teaching of basic intellectual property concepts to primary and secondary schools via the UK Patent Office's 'Think Kit' to encourage the key skill of entrepreneurship.

In late 2006, the Gower's Review of Intellectual Property Report recommended that all judges receive training in the subject. The emergence of the knowledge-based economy means that judges are increasingly asked to adjudicate on intellectual property issues and may not have had the opportunity to study the subject while they were university students. In the future, however, most law students will begin their undergraduate law courses having developed intellectual property law awareness at primary or secondary school. This means that modern law teachers will be able to devote more teaching time to analysing the way in which social, economic and political conditions affect the intellectual property landscape. According to Professor Ruth Soetendorp, a pioneer in intellectual property law education at Bournemouth University, 'there is growing evidence of criticality in the intellectual property law syllabus'. In addition, with globalisation, cross-border issues and the

1

harmonisation of some of the administrative aspects of international intellectual property regimes, the focus of the intellectual property curricula is increasingly international.

Although this book is aimed at helping students to successfully deal with their written exams through a selection of problem, essay, and mixed topic questions, it is hoped that they will retain some knowledge of this fascinating subject – even once the exam is over!

CHAPTER 1

GENERAL THEMES IN IP LAW

Essay questions are commonly used to invite the student to discuss a variety of themes in intellectual property law. We are surrounded in our everyday lives by intellectual property, but defining or describing it is no easy feat. The range of matter which falls within the scope of intellectual property is diverse and extensive.

Examples of things that can be protected by intellectual property include inventions, novels, works of art, photographs, musical scores, sound recordings, films, computer software, bio-engineered living organisms, trade secrets, know-how, invented characters and brand names. Examiners often set questions relating to the rationales or traditional justifications for the existence of intellectual property protection.

Another theme running through intellectual property law is that the systems are constantly adapting, whether in response to advances in technology or as a result of shifting perceptions about the appropriate reach of intellectual property protection.

Finally, a popular topic with examiners relates to the most important international agreement on the subject of intellectual property, the **Agreement on Trade-Related Aspects of Intellectual Property (TRIPS)**. Another topical subject is the forthcoming 2012 London Olympics and its associated intellectual property.

Question 1

Critically analyse the traditional justifications for the existence of the systems of intellectual property protection.

Answer plan

This question requires the student to demonstrate an appreciation of the various theories for justifying the granting of monopolistic intellectual property protection rights:

- 'Natural rights'; John Locke's Labour theory (1632–1704);
- Art 27(2) of the Universal Declaration of Human Rights;
- Hegel's Personality theory (1770–1831);
- Economic justification and the Utilitarian theory;
- Consumer protection.

Answer

Legal and political philosophers have often debated the status and legitimacy of intellectual property. They ask, 'Why should we grant intellectual property rights?' The answer to this question is important, because society has a choice as to whether it chooses to grant such rights. It is also important because the decision to grant property rights in intangibles impinges on traders, the press and media and the public.

Intellectual property rights have three key features. First, they are property rights. Secondly, they are property rights in something intangible. Thirdly, they protect innovation and creations and reward innovative and creative activity. All intellectual property rights have one common feature: for any subject matter to be protected by an intellectual property right, the minimum criteria for that form of property must be met.

On the one hand, the grant of private property rights in land and tangible resources is premised on the scarcity or limited availability of such resources and the impossibility of sharing. However, how can we justify the grant of exclusive rights over ideas and information – that are not scarce and can be replicated without any direct detriment to the original possessor of the intangible (who continues to be able to use the information)?

A central characteristic of intellectual property rights is that they are negative monopolistic rights. They exclude others from the use and exploitation of the subject matter of the right. However, all intellectual property rights expire at some point in time, except for confidential information, trade marks and geographical indications, which can be perpetual.

Intangible property rights are fundamentally different from rights attaching to tangible property such as a house, a car or a piece of jewellery. The subject matter of intellectual property rights, creative endeavour and inventions, necessarily has a link with knowledge and ideas. In economic terms, such matter is a public asset not easily owned by one person or group. The ability to exclude others from use or copying arises due to an artificial legal regime which grants an intangible property right to the inventor or creator.

As we will see, philosophers have not always found intellectual property rights to be justified in the form they currently take. Why are intangible property rights created? The existence of intellectual property rights is usually justified by reference to one or more of the following grounds.

(1) Natural rights

One of the most basic justifications for intellectual property is that a person who puts intellectual effort into creating something should have a natural right to own and control what he creates. This is derived from the 'Labour theory' by the seventeenth-century philosopher John Locke. He argued that everyone has a property right in the labour of his own body, and that the appropriation of an unowned object arises out of the application of human labour to that object. There must remain objects of similar quality in sufficient quantity to supply others. In other words, 'He who sows shall also reap'. Such an entitlement is recognised in Art 27(2) of the **Universal Declaration of Human Rights**, which states:

> Everyone has the right to the protection of moral and material interests resulting from any scientific, literary or artistic production of which he is the author.

In addition, according to Georg Hegel's Personality theory, 'Creation is an extension of its creator's individuality or person, belonging to that creator as part of his or her selfhood'.

(2) To encourage and reward innovation and creation

Intellectual property rights serve as an incentive for the investment of time and capital in the research and development which are required to produced inventive and creative works. By providing the owner with exclusive property rights, he enjoys the benefit of the stream of revenue generated by exploitation of his intellectual property.

(3) To encourage dissemination of information and ideas

The existence of intellectual property laws encourages the disclosure and dissemination of information and widens the store of knowledge available in the community. This justification is commonly given for patents. The specification of patented inventions are published by patent offices around the world and form a valuable source of advanced technical information.

(4) Economic efficiency

Economic theorists justify the recognition of property rights in creative endeavour on the basis that it leads to more efficient use of resources. Innovation is an essential element in a competitive free market economy. Economists argue that if everyone was freely allowed to use the results of innovative and creative activity, the problem of 'free riders' would arise. Investors would be reluctant to invest in innovation. Competitors would just wait for someone else to create a product, which they would then copy at little upfront cost. Legal protection of intangible property rights creates a climate in which investors are stimulated to invest in research and development, as they will be guaranteed a competitive 'first to market' advantage for a period of time.

(5) Consumer protection

Some intellectual property rights offer protection for consumers by enabling them to make informed choices between goods and services from different sources (for example trade marks and geographical indications).

(6) Technology transfer

Intellectual property systems facilitate the transfer of technology through foreign direct investment, joint ventures and licensing.

In conclusion, intellectual property law attempts to strike a balance between:

- the conflicting interests of society as a whole in economic and cultural development;

and

- the interest of the individual to secure a 'fair' value for its intellectual effort or investment of capital or labour.

This continual tension leads scholars to constantly evaluate the philosophical, economic and ethical justifications of the systems for granting intellectual property rights.

Question 2

There are few legal regimes that are so firmly involved with the promotion of investment and innovation as the laws governing the creation and exploitation of intellectual property. Yet, as a society, we are blissfully unaware of the significance of these laws and take little, if any, time or effort to consider how they might be made to work better . . . [T]he law of intellectual property has a pivotal role in providing both incentive and security for those engaging and investing in the innovative process.

Sam Ricketson, 'The Future of Australian Intellectual Property Law Reform and Administration' (1992) 3 AIPJ 1 at 3, 5.

Discuss.

Answer

The term 'intellectual property rights' (IPRs) is used to describe the various rights that afford legal protection to innovative and creative endeavour. The main rights that fall within the field of intellectual property include:

(1) Patents. A patent is a statutory property right governed by the **Patents Act 1977** that gives the patent owner the exclusive right to use certain inventions.

(2) Copyright. Copyright is a statutory right governed by the **Copyright Design and Patents Act 1988** subsisting in original literary, dramatic, musical, artistic works, sound recordings, films, broadcasts, cable programs and the typography of published editions. Owners of copyright have several economic rights in their works, including the right to prevent unauthorised copyright and adaptations.

(3) Moral rights. Moral rights are statutory rights under the **Copyright Design and Patent Act 1988** that authors retain in their works, irrespective of who owns the economic rights.

(4) Trade marks. Registered trade marks are statutory rights, as provided by the **Trade Marks Act 1994**. This gives the owner the exclusive right to use a distinctive sign (for example a name, symbol, tune etc) in relation to a product or service.

(5) Geographical indications (or indications of source or appellations of origin). These are signs assuring consumer that produce comes from, or has been processed in a particular region renowned for the quality of such produce. Familiar examples include Champagne, Scotch whisky and Parma ham. The UK is bound by art 22(2) of **TRIPs** to prevent the use of any means in the designation or presentation of a good that indicates or suggests that the good in question originates in a geographical area other than the true place of

origin in a manner which misleads the public as to the geographical origin of the good.

(6) Design. A registered design is a statutory right under the **Registered Designs Act 1949** that gives the exclusive right to use certain features of the appearance of a range of products. The unregistered design right is the right under the **Copyright Designs and Patents Act 1977** to prevent copying of aspects of the shape or configuration of an article.

The common law and equity also continue to feature in the protection of intellectual property:

(7) Passing off. Goodwill is a form of intangible property consisting of the market's perception of the quality and value of a business and its products, which can be protected by the common law tort of passing off. Passing off is a common law tort or cause of action used to prevent a third party from making misrepresentations which damage the goodwill of another.

(8) Breach of confidence. The equitable doctrine of breach of confidence is used to protect certain confidential information which does not fall within the scope of the other intellectual property law systems set out above, against unauthorised disclosure or use.

Some intellectual property rights come into existence automatically (for example copyright, the design right), while others take effect only upon completion of registration (patents, registered trade marks and designs).

Over the centuries, various rulers of the United Kingdom and its governments have recognised that protecting creative endeavour is crucial to the promotion of innovation and entrepreneurship. Not only does it provide an incentive to engage in the innovation process, it also provides security for investment in innovation. It does so by providing exclusive rights or a monopoly, in some cases for a limited duration. Following the Industrial Revolution, the United Kingdom derived the greater part of its wealth from exports of manufactured goods, and this led to a strengthening of the 'industrial' property law system. There is a correlation between industrialisation and patent protection. The 'industrial property' system has since been transformed into an 'intellectual' property system with advances in technology.

However, the goalposts have moved. The modern industries of the twenty-first century – information technology, biotechnology, pharmaceuticals, communications, education and entertainment – are all knowledge-based, requiring the system to be updated to work better. TV formats, image rights, character merchandising and franchising all have significant commercial value which the traditional intellectual property system is struggling to adequately protect. If the United Kingdom is to successfully participate in the global information economy of the new millennium, the importance of the role of intellectual property in addressing the needs of these modern forms of intangible property will need to be better understood and greater attention accorded to ensuring that the intellectual property laws are indeed effective in promoting innovation. In some cases, new *sui generis* legislation is required to grant statutory rights to promote certainty for the investment community to engage in the innovative process.

The extension of intellectual property protection is also occurring at the international level. The seven forms of intellectual property outlined above are included in the **Agreement on Trade-Related Aspects of Intellectual Property Rights** (the **TRIPS Agreement**) which was finalised at the end of the Uruguay Round of world trade negotiations in 1993. The **TRIPS Agreement** draws attention to the fact that the various systems of intellectual property protection developed independently of each other and are not based on any shared underlying principle. There is, however, a common thread running through the intellectual property systems that justifies grouping them together and studying them as a whole. Intellectual property is concerned with protecting applications of ideas and information that are of commercial value. This is reflected in the legal definition of intellectual property, which focuses on the rights or bundles of rights given for the protection of creative output. Most of the intellectual property systems give the creator exclusive rights over the use of his creation (for example a painting or invention) for a limited period of time, and delineate conduct for which the right-owner's permission is required.

A central theme running through the entire field of intellectual property is the necessity of striking a balance between the interests of right-owners on the one hand and those of users and the general public on the other. Intellectual property law systems are concerned not only with providing incentive and reward to authors and inventors, but also aim to promote dissemination and use of new ideas, information and technology for the benefit of society as a whole. If the appropriate balance is struck, the flow of new and innovative ideas will be optimised, whereas protection which is either too broad or inadequate will not be conducive to optimal levels of innovation. The attempt to balance the interests of innovators and the broader community is evident in the exceptions provided in the various intellectual property regimes.

In conclusion, the extension of legal protection to intellectual creations is not without its critics. Arguments against the recognition of intellectual property rights have been made with renewed force in the context of debates about the regulation of the Internet, methods of business and biotechnological inventions. The government has a responsibility to its people to adequately consider supplementing the existing intellectual property law systems to deal with modern forms of intangible property in consultation with the relevant stakeholders.

Question 3

Explain the UK Government's new Green Channel for environmentally friendly patent applications and critically analyse the impact of the 'green' agenda on patent law? Are there any other 'green' patent initiatives afoot?

Answer plan

This essay question requires the student to consider the UK's green policy as it affects intellectual property and how this has resulted in new developments to the patent registration procedure, providing patent applicants with a new option.

- Explain the impetus and background for the new 'Green Channel' for environmentally friend patently applications which results in fast-tracking through the system.
- Set out the criteria patent applicants need to demonstrate in order to qualify to use the 'green channel'. In other words, discuss which kind of inventions are eligible to use the system.
- Critically analyse the potential advantages and disadvantages of using the system.
- Note that other 'green' initiatives exist in relation to patents, in particular, the 'Eco Patent Commons' that is administered and overseen by the Geneva-based World Business Council for Sustainable Development.

Answer

Since 12 May 2009 the UK Intellectual Property Office (UK IPO) has allowed patent applications to be made via the new 'Green Channel'. This means that environmentally friendly patent applications can be fast-tracked and granted in as little as nine months from the date of filing. This is less than half the current average processing time of two to four years.

There have been critics of the patent system who hold the view that it takes too long to secure patent rights making it difficult to exploit important new technologies swiftly in order to deal with global warming and climate change.

The UK IPO statistics are that in the past ten years the number of green technology patent applications has increased by 500 per cent which is a startling increase. In real terms, this translates to the UK IPO receiving approximately 23,500 patent applications per week of which 150–200 of these are said to be for green technologies.

To access the new 'Green Channel' patent applicants must be able to demonstrate that their invention relates to green or environmentally-friendly technology when applying for a UK patent.

While it had always been an option to either accelerate or expedite the patent application process through the Accelerate Search and/or Examination stages, the applicant had to demonstrate to the UK IPO why a quicker path to grant was significant. For example, the applicant had to argue that a patent had to be granted quickly due to a potential infringement in the UK or for commercial reasons such as to secure an investor or licensee.

What is an eligible 'green' invention'? The patent applicant must be able to make a reasonable assertion that the invention has a degree of environmental benefit, only then can the applicant request that the Search and/or Examination stages be stepped up without any further explanation. Once accepted on the 'Green Channel', the patent application will be fully searched and examined by an appropriately qualified patent examiner.

The key issue is how the UK IPO will determine which inventions have a suitable degree of environmental benefit to warrant the privilege of accessing the 'Green Channel'. It could be argued for example that many inventions are more efficient than their known equivalents. Other inventions may be formed from biodegradable materials rather than plastics. Other inventions may be part of main-stream 'green' technology focusing on renewable energy systems, solar power or wave energy.

The new 'Green Channel' is available for pending as well as new applications. The patent application must make a request to the UK IPO in writing stating:

(1) that the patent application in question relates to a 'green' or environmentally-friendly technology; and

(2) which actions they wish to accelerate: Search, Combined Search and Examination, Publication, and/or Examination.

The 'Green Channel' is an optional feature of the UK patent system and it is not necessary to accelerate a patent application simply because it relates to 'green' technology.

The key advantage of the 'Green Channel' is that the owner obtains a granted patent quicker and this is a valuable right enabling the patent owner to take action against infringers, a right which a pending patent application does not provide. A granted patent is also more valuable in that it is better security when raising finance from investors and lenders.

However, there are a few disadvantages to consider when determining whether to fast-track a patent application:

(1) A UK patent application cannot be granted until three months following the date upon which the application has been published. If a 'green' patent is granted nine months from its filing date, it is a requirement that the patent be published to the world at a very early point in time. This can have serious implications in relation to protecting future developments to the invention.

(2) Although in some cases a prospective investor may feel more at ease investing in a project supported by a patent, a favourable Search Report can give investors a similar indication of the chances of the application proceeding to grant. A Search Report can usually be achieved around three to six months from the patent application filing date. So if one chooses not to use the 'Green Channel', one retains the option of keeping the invention confidential for about eighteen months from the filing date. This will assist in keeping competitors from knowing the extent of the final claims that support the patent application. A side effect of this is that the competitor may well be more wayward in terms of how close to the claims they try to work. A granted patent necessarily defines a clearer boundary for competitors to circumvent.

The new 'Green' initiative forms part of the Government's wider programme of measures designed to tackle climate change. The underlying aim is to foster and encourage the development of low-carbon technology to benefit the environment and ensure the UK's future economic competitiveness.

In practice, the 'Green Channel' initiative will provide innovative UK business working in the field of green technologies the chance to secure their patent rights faster in order to ultimately exploit them commercially and bring them to the market. It is envisaged that this will benefit business and consumers, as well as the environment. The UK IPO is confident that it now has one of the quickest schemes in the world for granting green and clean technology patents. It also hopes that other countries, including the US and China, will consider adopting a similar scheme.

Other international 'green' initiatives afoot include a project launched in 2008 by a number of high profile technology firms including IBM, Sony, Nokia, Pitney Bowes, DuPont, Ricoh, Xerox and Bosch. It involves a patent-sharing plan, known as the Eco-Patents Commons. The project was born of an idea from IBM, the company that owns the largest number of patents in the world. The Eco-Patents Commons encourages companies to donate environmentally friendly intellectual property into the public domain, particularly those that do not represent a source of business advantage for them. For example, patents donated so far include a recyclable protective packaging material for electronic components from IBM and mobile phones recycled into calculators and personal digital assistants from Nokia.

The Eco-Patents Commons will be overseen by the Geneva-based World Business Council for Sustainable Development whose membership includes 200 of the world's largest companies. It is envisaged that the free exchange of valuable patented technology will support the resolution of environmental challenges. However, the sharing of patented technology is not a new phenomena. One of the earliest instances occurred in early 1856 when the four major sewing machine producers (who had spent decades suing each other over alleged intellectual property infringement) jointly formed the Sewing Machine Combination and pooled their patents. Other manufacturers not involved in the Combination had to secure a licence to use the patents and pay a fee for every sewing machine they built using the patented technology. The Eco-Patent Commons is one that unites business across a diverse range of sectors, but with a purely environmental aim. The patents are listed and searchable at www.wbcsd.org. Any business can freely use the pledged patents without having to register or notify anyone of their use.

In conclusion, it is clear that there are indeed positive intellectual property initiatives, particularly in the field of patents, aimed at promoting and advancing green and clean technologies for the benefit of the environment.

Question 4

Critically analyse the impact of the **London Olympics Games and Paralympic Games Act 2006** on the intellectual property rights of the London 2012 Olympic Games and its sponsors.

Answer plan

This essay question requires students to consider intellectual property in the context of a major international sporting event, namely the forthcoming Olympic Games 2012 to be hosted by London. Several types of intellectual property rights and associated legislation are relevant and should be included in the discussion.

- Introduce the background to the **London Olympics Games and Paralympic Games Act 2006** (the 2006 Act);
- **Olympic Symbol etc (Protection) Act 1995 (OSPA)**;
- The Games' Marks and other intellectual property;
- The London Olympic Association Right;
- Defences.

Answer

In 2005, London was selected to host the 2012 Olympics. The London Organising Committee of the Olympic Games and Paralympic Games (LOCOG) has stated that it will protect its London Olympic brand by registering trade marks and relying on the laws of copyright, design right and passing off. In addition, Parliament has granted LOCOG special legal rights under the **London Olympic Games and Paralympic Games Act 2006** (the 2006 Act) and the **Olympic Symbol etc (Protection) Act 1995 (OSPA)**.

OSPA protects the Olympic and Paralympic symbols, mottos and various words. Sched 3 to the 2006 Act also amends **OSPA** resulting in a significant extension of the previous protection which is discussed further below. Additional protection is provided by the 2006 Act which creates the new 'Association Right' in Sched 4. This prevents the creation of an unauthorised association between people, goods or services and London Olympics 2012.

The Games' Marks and intellectual property

All of the names, phrases, marks, logos and designs related to the 2012 Games and the Olympic and Paralympic Movements are collectively known as the Games' Marks. The following are the current items that comprise the Games' official registered trade marks:

- the London 2012 logo and word mark;
- the words 'London 2012';
- British Olympic Association logo;
- Team GB logo;
- Paralympics GB logo.

In addition, **OSPA** prevents the use, in the course of trade, of any of the following words, mottos and symbols:

- the Olympic symbol;
- the Paralympic symbol;
- the words 'Olympic', 'Olympiad', 'Olympian' (and their plurals, translations and anything similar to them);
- the words 'Paralympic', 'Paralympiad', 'Paralympian' (and their plurals, translations and anything similar to them);
- the Olympic motto: 'Citius Altius Fortius'/'Faster Higher Stronger';
- the Paralympic motto: 'Spirit in Motion'.

OSPA does not just apply to the London 2012 Games, but relates to any activity which uses the words, mottos or symbols protected by the Act. **OSPA** also protects words and symbols similar to those listed above. For example, sound-a-like word 'Olympix' and variations of the Olympic rings would infringe.

In addition, copyright protects intellectual property in all film, musical works, artistic works and designs (for example the Games' emblems, mascots and posters created by Official Olympic and Paralympic bodies in connection with the Games).

By way of background, as a condition of hosting the Games, the International Olympic Committee (IOC) required London to guarantee that it would pass specific legislation to effectively reduce and provide sanctions against ambush marketing. The IOC wanted to ensure that only official sponsors are linked to the Olympic Games. The requirement to enact specific legislation is not new. Both the 2000 Sydney Olympics and the 2004 Athens Olympic Games enacted new domestic legislation to regulate the use of indicia and images associated with the Games for commercial purposes. To raise the necessary revenue to run the games, LOCOG must be able to give sponsors an exclusive association to London 2012; they will only invest if they are given such an exclusive association. If anyone could create an association with the Games for free, there would be no point in becoming a sponsor.

A key purpose of the LOPGA 2006 is to protect the 'Games Marks' and prevent people using the London 2012 brand without authorisation. The unauthorised use of any of the Games' Marks, or any other marks or logos that are confusingly similar to, or likely to be mistaken for, them is strictly prohibited. For example, without the London 2012 Organising Committee's written consent, it is unlawful to use the Olympic symbol, the London 2012 logo or the mark 'London 2012' in the course of trade. Such symbols, logos or marks cannot be used on goods, in business names, on business papers or in advertising.

The London Olympic Association Right

The **2006 Act** grants LOCOG the London Olympic Association Right. This gives LOCOG the exclusive right to grant its sponsors and licensees authorisation to create an association between their business, goods or services and London 2012. It is unlawful, whether through the use of the Games' Marks or otherwise, to falsely represent any association, affiliation, endorsement, sponsorship or similar relationship with London 2012, the British Olympic and Paralympic teams, or any other part of the Olympic and/or Paralympic Movements. The question of whether or not an association with London 2012 has been created in any particular case will depend on the overall impression given by the advertisement, marketing material or goods etc in question.

An association with London 2012 can be created by the use of any words, images or marks, or, more likely, a combination of these. For example, athletic images, representations of an Olympic-style torch and flame, the colours of the Olympic rings and other representations relating to the Games may each contribute to the creation of an association with the Games. The **2006 Act** also includes certain 'Listed Expressions' and states that a court may take these into particular account when determining if an association has been created with London 2012. The Listed Expressions are any two of the words in list A below or any word in list A with one or more of the words in list B below.

List A	List B
List A	*List B*
Games	London
Two Thousand and Twelve	medals
2012	sponsors
Twenty-Twelve	gold
	silver
	bronze

The Games' Marks can be used with the authorisation of the London 2012 Organising Committee; however, authorisation will only be given to official sponsors and broadcasters, official merchandise licensees and licensed non-commercial partners. There are very few instances when the Games' Marks can be used without consent. The words protected by OSPA can, however, be used in editorial news pieces without authorisation. And, for example, businesses which have traded under an 'Olympic' name for many years may also benefit from an exception to the rules which will allow them to continue to do this. The **OSPA** and **2006 Act** also allow exceptions for editorial and journalistic use. Defences allow for honest statements of fact to be made, provided this is in accordance with honest commercial practices and not made gratuitously for purely marketing purposes.

Question 5

One of the most significant modern intellectual property (IP) issues is the clash between the developing and the developed countries. Discuss whether or not the international intellectual property frameworks of the developed countries lean to protecting the interests of the rich rather than the poor.

Answer plan

This essay question enables the student to consider the impact of the current IP regime from a policy point of view. The student should write a composition in continuous prose demonstrating the depth of his or her knowledge of the wider IP global policy issues. The discussion should adopt a two-sided approach and present arguments for and against each particular view. The arguments should be based on evidence such as key treaties and legislation.

- Explain how the international IP framework tends to promote the interests of the developed countries and in particular **TRIPS**.
- Set out the issues of concern of the developing countries.

- Consider the merit of possible solutions or policy responses to the issues identified.
- Reach a reasoned conclusion.

Answer

The control of knowledge is a key concern in relation to the international intellectual property law framework. Will knowledge be monopolised by the commercial interests of the developed countries, or will knowledge be within the public domain, readily able to be used to overcome poverty, hunger and disease? The **World Trade Organisation's Agreement on Trade-related Aspects of Intellectual Property Rights (TRIPS)**, introduced in 1994 after intense lobbying by developed countries, is at the centre of this controversy. It is the main international treaty determining rights over intellectual property (IP), which includes patents, copyright and trademarks among other forms of IP. **TRIPS** established enforceable global minimum standards for most intellectual property rights (IPRs).

Global minimum standards of legal protection

TRIPS requires all member states to implement relatively high minimum standards of protection, irrespective of a particular state's level of development or social needs. It is felt that this one-size-fits-all approach may damage social welfare in the developing countries. Has the balance shifted too far towards the private interests of corporations in the developed countries, and away from the users of knowledge?

Many non-governmental organisations such as OXFAM fear that the damaging effects of international IP rules will be felt most acutely in poor countries, in that high standards of intellectual property protection will exclude poor people from access to vital 'knowledge goods'. They claim that **TRIPS** will result in higher prices for knowledge-rich goods, further excluding poor people from access to vital medicines, seeds, computer software and educational materials. The high price of HIV/AIDS medicines has illustrated graphically the iniquitous effect that the temporary twenty-year monopolies created by patents can have. Higher prices also limit the ability of developing-country governments to meet people's basic rights to food, health and development. Supporters of **TRIPS** say that short-term welfare losses caused by higher prices are offset by longer-term benefits through increased innovation and technology transfer for poor countries. In addition, the developed countries argue that higher levels of IP protection in developing countries will prompt greater foreign direct investment or licensing by transnational companies, even in pharmaceuticals and chemicals.

The technology divide

There is a wide technological gap between rich and poor countries. Although developing countries are rich in informal knowledge, for example traditional medicine, they are net importers of the kinds of high-tech goods and know-how protected by **TRIPS**. Developed industrialised countries, on the other hand, account for 90 per cent of global research and development (R&D) spending, an even higher share of patents, and are the main exporters of IP.

Developing countries are concerned that the **TRIPS** provisions will exacerbate this divide by increasing the cost of knowledge-rich goods they import. Royalties and licence fees paid by developing countries to patent holders in the industrialised world have been increasing rapidly over the last two decades. Typically, for example the US receives a net surplus of billions of pounds from its IP exports.

Research and development

Developing countries argue that global research and development is targeted at the markets of rich consumers, rather than at the basic needs of the poor. Less than 10 per cent of global spending on health research addresses 90 per cent of the global disease burden. Similarly, much agricultural research aims to improve the appearance and taste of produce for consumers in rich markets, rather than to support the sustainable farming of staple foods such as sorghum and cassava, on which many poor farmers depend. Developing countries are concerned that global IP rules will worsen this problem by further concentrating R&D into profitable areas such as cures for obesity or impotence.

Developing countries are very concerned that the biological resources and traditional knowledge of their farmers and indigenous people are the subject of piracy by the developed world. **TRIPS** was designed to prevent so-called piracy by developing countries of the inventions and products of rich countries. However, the agreement does not deal with the systematic appropriation of biological knowledge and informal forms of traditional knowledge from developing countries by the corporations of the developed countries.

TRIPS and essential medicines

Another concern of developing countries is their ability to access essential medicines subject to patent rights. Fortunately, however, the developed countries have taken positive steps in this regard beginning in 2001, when a declaration was reached to the effect that the **TRIPS Agreement** does not and should not prevent member states from taking measures to protect public health. In 2002, the European Union member states met to try to assist the TRIPS Council find a solution to help countries with little or no manufacturing abilities in the pharmaceutical sector, make effective use of compulsory licensing, as agreed in the declaration on **TRIPS** and public health. In 2003, the WTO member states agreed to allow the making of medicines under compulsory licences for export to developing countries within the terms set out in the decision. Finally, in 2005, WTO members agreed changes to the **TRIPS Agreement** to reflect this decision. This new General Council decision means that for the first time, a core WTO agreement will be changed.

Technical assistance provided to developing countries by the UK

Article 67 of **TRIPS** requires developed country members to provide technical and financial cooperation to developing and least-developed country members. The UK Government's White Paper, 'Eliminating World Poverty: Making Globalisation Work for the Poor', published in 2000, pointed to the need for IP regimes to work better for poor people. In addition, the UK Government's response to the 2002 Report of the Commission on Intellectual Property Rights confirmed the need to tailor IP regimes to individual country's circumstances within the **TRIPS** framework.

Current initiatives to assist developing countries with IP issues

A number of international programmes and resources currently exist to assist developing countries:

- World Intellectual Property Organisation's (WIPO) Cooperation for Development Programme;
- World Health Organisation's Commission on Intellectual Property Rights, Innovation and Public Health;
- Integrated Framework for Trade-Related Assistance to Least Developed Countries;
- recent research reports from the World Bank, 'Intellectual Property and Development' and 'Poor People's Knowledge';
- the World Trade Organisation/Organisation for Economic Co-operation and Development Trade Capacity Building Database;
- the United Nations Conference on Trade and Development (UNCTAD) and the International Centre for Trade and Sustainable Development (ICTSD) are implementing a capacity-building project on IP rights and sustainable development;
- United Nations Economic Commission for Europe IP Advisory Group.

Issues for reform of TRIPS

Several NGOs have come together to form the TRIPS Action Network (TAN), with a view to campaigning for further reforms of **TRIPS** and to lobby the Group of Eight (G8) developed countries.

The G8 is an informal but exclusive body founded in 1975 whose members set out to tackle global challenges through discussion and action. With no headquarters, budget or permanent staff, the G8 comprises eight of the world's leading industrial-ised nations (France, Germany, Italy, Japan, UK, US, Canada and Russia). The leaders of these countries meet face-to-face at an annual summit that has become a focus of media attention and protest action. The G8 IPR experts group has also agreed that technical assistance plans are needed to help developing countries strengthen their efforts to combat trade in pirated and counterfeit goods. G8 members can agree on policies and can set objectives, but compliance with these is voluntary. The G8 has clout with other world bodies because of the economic and political muscle of its members.

In conclusion, the two ends of the spectrum in relation to the IP global frame-work established by **TRIPS** are: (1) reinterpretation and incremental changes to the articles of **TRIPS** versus (2) outright abolition of the agreement. It appears that the former approach to **TRIPS** is slowly achieving long-term change, as evidenced by the progress with essential medicines and public health issues. These concrete gains have largely legitimised the **TRIPS Agreement** for developing countries. Despite it being an inherently pro-IP and protectionist agreement that currently favours the developed countries, in order to promote their own knowledge economy, the devel-oping countries must think more deeply about the validation of the IP regime from the perspective of 'balance' rather than the IP theories put forward by the developed countries. The developing countries therefore shall have more rights to design their own IP regime reflecting some internationally workable common grounds. Finally, the reality in today's international IP policymaking is that too often the voices of the powerful industries and companies in the developed countries dominate in the evolu-tion of IP policy, but as there is no coherent alternative to the **TRIPS Agreement** the developing countries have no real choice and must continue to call for reform.

CHAPTER 2

INTELLECTUAL PROPERTY LITIGATION – ENFORCEMENT AND REMEDIES

This topic requires the student to identify and apply the range of court orders, statutory, common law and equitable remedies that are available to an intellectual property rights owner to enforce their rights.

A knowledge of remedies is important for answering essay questions or indeed to answer problem questions which require the student to advise a party as to their 'rights and remedies'. The methods of enforcing intellectual property rights are of great practical importance as rights that cannot be enforced are ultimately worthless.

Essentially, intellectual property infringement can be described as tortious in nature and as a wrong committed against property. Civil actions are normally brought before the Chancery Division of the High Court of England and Wales. Actions involving smaller monetary sums can be brought in the county court and there is also a specialised Patents County Court in London.

The most important civil remedies for the victim of an infringing action are:

- injunctions (an equitable discretionary remedy which needs to be considered in almost every situation); and
- damages or an account of profits.

The purpose of awarding damages is to compensate the intellectual property owner for the loss caused by the defendant's infringement. In claiming damages, the intellectual property owner will need to establish that:

- the claimed method for assessing damages is appropriate (measure); and
- the damages are not too remote (remoteness).

Sometimes, the remedy of damages will be inadequate. Equity therefore developed a number of remedies, discretionary in nature, directed towards ensuring that a claimant was not unjustly treated by being confined to a remedy in damages. An injunction is an example of a remedy that seeks to restrain the defendant from committing infringement(s). Another example is an account of profits, which seeks to take back from the defendant profits made through the unauthorised use of the claimant's intellectual property. An account of profits is usually accompanied by an injunction and it is granted at the discretion of the court.

In addition to civil remedies, UK law provides criminal sanctions for a variety of infringing acts. Moreover, intellectual property rights are increasingly exploited internationally, giving rise to transnational litigation.

Question 6

According to the UK Patent Office (an Executive Arm of the Department of Trade and Industry) there is evidence that intellectual property piracy and counterfeiting crime is increasingly well organised. Are the current remedies available to enforce intellectual property rights adequate or is there a need for further measures? Discuss.

Answer plan

The question expects the student to demonstrate a knowledge of the range of civil remedies and criminal sanctions available for intellectual property infringement and whether or not they are fit for the purpose of enforcing an intellectual property owner's rights in combating organised crime.

- Clarify and distinguish between piracy and counterfeiting.
- Evaluate the range of civil remedies.
- Discuss the Department of Trade & Industry's National Intellectual Property Crime Report and TellPat database.

Answer

While it is important to ensure that the various intellectual property regimes offer appropriate and adequate protection for the results of creative effort, the other side of the coin is the availability of measures to enforce those rights. A frequent criticism of the operation of the intellectual property laws in practice has been the difficulties encountered when it comes to enforcement of those rights. Such arguments have particular force in relation to combating organised crime, given that litigation is invariably so expensive and time-consuming that it is likely to be out of reach of all but large corporations. Enforcement has become an increasingly challenging area in the fight against the importation of fake goods as well as due to the rise of the digital environment. Historically, crime has always followed the economy and as the knowledge-based economy provides more opportunities, that is where the criminal element has moved.

Piracy and counterfeiting are a real threat to intellectual property owners both domestically and internationally as well as for consumers and the government. Counterfeiting refers to wilful trade mark infringement, for example: fake replica rock band or football shirts; trainers and clothing branded with fake marks. Piracy refers to wilful copyright infringement such as fake digital versatile discs (DVDs) and compact discs (CDs), or unauthorised downloading of music from the Internet, and so on.

There are a range of civil remedies and criminal sanctions provided in order to enforce intellectual property rights. These are interim and final injunctions, damages, account of profits, search orders, orders for delivery up and destruction, and declarations of infringement. Usually, an IP owner will focus on obtaining civil remedies, but some criminal sanctions are also available. Four types of action are possible:

- civil proceedings;
- criminal proceedings;
- administrative action by giving notice to UK HM Revenue & Customs, or the UK Advertising & Standards Authority;
- self-help by IP owners.

Final pecuniary remedies are remedies such as damages or an account of profits. These remedies provide financial compensation for losses caused by infringement. However, an intellectual property right owner cannot enjoy both damages and an account of profits. They have to make an informed choice to elect one or the other.

The most common award is for damages and these are calculated on the basis of compensating for lost profits or on a royalty basis: *General Tire v Firestone Tyre (1975)*. See **Patents Act 1977**, s 61(1)(c); **Trade Marks Act 1994**, s 14(2)); **Copyright Designs and Patents Act 1988**, s 9(2); **Registered Design Act 1949**, s 9(1). Aggravated damages may be available, for example, to include a restitutionary element: *Nottinghamshire Healthcare NHS Trust v News Group Newspapers Ltd (2002)*.

Account of profits is an equitable remedy (**PA 1977**, s 61(1)(d); **TMA 1994**, s 14(2)); **CDPA 1988**, ss 96(2) and 229(2)) for infringement of registered designs. The case of *Celanese International Corporation v BP Chemicals (1999)* provides guidance as to how to calculate an award under account of profits.

Non-pecuniary remedies include:

(1) declaration of infringement or non-infringement;

(2) delivery up and destruction;

(3) court order for a party to reveal relevant information (**CPR 31**)/*Norwich Pharmacal* order;

(4) injunction.

Interim remedies include:

(1) interim injunctions;

(2) *ex parte* orders;

(3) search orders.

Criminal sanctions are sometimes available:

* patents (**PA 1977**, ss 109 and 110);
* trade marks (**TMA 1994**, ss 59, 60, 92);
* copyright (**CDPA 1988**, ss 107–110, 198, 297, 297A, 196ZB and 201; and
* registered designs (**RDA 1949**, ss 35 and 35A).

In relation to 'self-help', s 100 of the **CDPA 1988** gives the copyright owner an additional right. This is the only example of self-help in the IP field. Section 100 enables the copyright owner or his agent to seize and detain infringing copies. However, a series of restraints applies to this far-reaching right:

* the infringing copy must be exposed or otherwise immediately available for sale or hire;
* no force may be used, and advance notice of the time and place of the proposed seizure must be given to a local police station;
* nothing may be seized from what appears to be a normal place of business; and
* only premises to which the public has access may be entered in the exercise of this right, for example a market stall, a car boot sale.

Self-help is increasingly popular and several intellectual property owner organisations have been established to assist to enforce IP rights. These include:

* FAST – Federation Against Software Theft;
* FACT – Federation Against Copyright Theft;
* IFPI – Represents the Recording Industry;
* ACID – Anti-Copying in Design.

The above organisations are active in enforcing their members' interests by providing advice on interim measures and initiating civil proceedings to deter and ultimately prevent infringement.

In relation to administrative proceedings, customs officers, trading standards authorities and the Advertising Standards Association play an ancillary role in the enforcement of intellectual property rights. The most important role belongs to the customs officers who, at the request of the rights holder, may arrest infringing imports at their point of entry in the United Kingdom. These measures operate together with an EU Regulation (**Council Regulation 3295/94**) to stop the release of counterfeit goods into free circulation. The EU Regulation gives the rightholder 10 days from notification of seizure to start full-scale infringement proceedings and counterfeit goods are normally destroyed.

In the UK, the Department of Trade and Industry (DTI) (which includes the

Patent Office) is responsible for government policy on intellectual property rights enforcement. At an international level, WIPO has created an Advisory Committee on Enforcement. In 2006, the DTI launched the second National Intellectual Property Enforcement Report. The Report states the answer to tackling intellectual property crime is the continuing cooperation between government, industry and enforcement agencies. In support of this partnership, the UK Patent Office is in the process of creating a new 'TellPat' database to collect the intelligence gathered by industry and enforcement agencies in order to track illegal infringement activities and the criminals involved.

The traditional remedies to enforce intellectual property infringement normally granted at trial have their place in the intellectual property system. However, intellectual property infringement often requires immediate action or a pre-emptive strike. This is where the interim injunctions and self-help play an important role. Finally, gathering evidence which is vital for the full trial is not easy, but it is hoped that the 'TellPat' database and increased cooperation between government, industry and enforcement agencies will ensure that more and more counterfeiters and pirates do not escape justice.

Question 7

When granting an interim injunction, what issues and principles must a court consider? Discuss with reference to recent case law.

Answer plan

This question focuses specifically on the interim equitable remedy of an injunction and requires a thorough discussion of the relevant case law and legislation.

- *American Cyanamid (1975)*;
- *Series 5 Software v Clarke (1996)*;
- Impact of the **Human Rights Act 1998**;
- *A v B and C plc (2002)*.

Answer

The modern law on the practice of granting an interim injunction is the result, in some measure, of the role intellectual property litigation has played over the last thirty years. The claimant's first concern in cases of intellectual property infringement is that the infringing act stops. Even today, it is rare for an intellectual property case to go all the way to trial. This is largely because wilful disobedience of an interim injunction will amount to contempt of court, and contempt is punishable by fine, imprisonment or sequestration of assets. Typically, an interim injunction is the only order that a claimant needs to prevent further infringement by the defendant. The sooner this happens, the easier it will be to limit the damage to his business, rights and reputation. The remedy is also known as an 'interlocutory' or 'temporary' injunction.

Accordingly, an interim injunction is designed to give preliminary relief in circumstances where allowing on-going infringement, while the substantive merits of the case are determined, would cause irreparable damage to the intellectual property rights owner. An interim injunction may be used to prevent imminent infringement, preserve evidence (where there is sufficient evidence that key evidence relating to the infringement would be destroyed or otherwise concealed) or to preserve the assets of the infringer. The order to award an interim injunction is made at the court's discretion; therefore it is an equitable remedy.

The principles governing the grant of an interim injunction were first laid down by the House of Lords in *American Cyanamid v Ethicon (1975)*. This case sets out the standard principles on which interim injunctions will be granted:

- the claimant should have a prima facie (arguable) case;
- damages would not provide an adequate remedy in the circumstances; and
- the court will consider the balance of commercial convenience. If this is equal, then the courts should act to preserve the status quo.

Justice Laddie reviewed the principles in the *American Cyanamid* decision in the case *Series 5 Software v Clarke (1996)*. The *American Cyanamid* principles were criticised because it was felt that interim injunctions were being awarded too easily. Laddie J held that when considering whether to grant interim relief, the court should bear in mind the following:

1. the grant of an interim injunction is a matter of discretion and depends on all the facts of each case;
2. there are no fixed rules; and
3. the court should rarely attempt to resolve difficult questions of fact and law.

Nevertheless, *American Cyanmid* is still good law and the preferred judicial approach. Improved court efficiency in hearing cases at trial more quickly than in the past appears to have resulted in less interim injunctions being awarded in recent years.

An example of an appropriate case for interim relief was that of the *BBC v Precord Ltd (1992)*. In this case, the defendants proposed to make a rap record featuring illicitly obtained extracts from an unbroadcast interview in which the then Opposition leader had famously lost his temper.

In contrast, in *Mothercare UK Ltd v Penguin Books Ltd (1988)*, a complete lack of confusion meant that no interim relief was permitted in the passing-off claim. The defendants were allowed to continue publishing a serious sociological study entitled 'Mother Care/Other Care'.

Overall, the post-*Cyanamid* approach to the award of interim injunctions shows the courts are generally able to react in a sensible way.

However, the **Human Rights Act 1998 (HRA 1998)** has made an impact on the award of interim injunctions. The **HRA 1998** has reduced the availability of interim injunctions in respect of breach of confidence cases and issues relating to freedom of expression. In light of the **HRA 1998**, the *American Cyanamid* principles can be re-stated as follows:

• The claimant should have a prima facie (arguable) case, as per *A v B and C plc (2002)*, except in breach of confidence cases where issues of freedom of expression are raised – here a higher standard should apply.

  More recently, in *Cream Holdings and other v Banerjee and others (2004)* the House of Lords held that the court should consider whether the applicant's prospects of success at trial are sufficiently favourable to justify the order.

• Whether damages would provide an adequate remedy in the circumstances and the ability of the parties to pay *(Series 5 Software v Clarke (1996))*; and

• The court will consider the balance of commercial convenience. If this is equal, then the courts should act to preserve the status quo.

In breach of confidence cases, where an issue of freedom of expression arises, the court should weigh up the claim based on freedom of expression as against the claimant's position. If the claimant invokes a claim of privacy, the court should weigh the claim to privacy as against that of the claim of freedom of expression. An injunction should be granted only when justified.

Generally in the UK, the applicant for an injunction must provide:

• documentation to prove validity of the intellectual property right it seeks to enforce, for example a patent or trade mark certificate and certificates of payment of renewal or annuity fees;

• evidence relating to the alleged infringement – for patents, this shall include the alleged infringing product, a description of the technical features of the patented process/product and a comparison thereof; for trade marks, a sample of the product bearing the alleged infringing trade mark should be produced;

• where a licensee is applying for relief, evidence of the licence – copy of the licence, certificate of recordal of licence with appropriate authorities (a non-recorded licensee may never enforce licensed intellectual property rights against a third party);

• where a sole licensee is applying for relief, in addition to the evidence above, evidence that the patentee or trade mark registrant itself has abandoned its right to apply for relief;

- where a legal heir is applying for relief, evidence that the legal heir has inherited or is in the process of inheriting the patent or trade mark right.

- The applicant may be ordered to pay a monetary bond against possible damage caused to the injuncted party if the injunction is subsequently found to be unwarranted. However, the injuncted party cannot seek to have the injunction lifted by pledging a counter-bond.

In conclusion, in order to obtain an interim injunction, it is important to remember that an injunction is an equitable remedy and is thus subject to equity's ever-present requirement of conscionability. A final injunction can be granted after the conclusion of the trial in which the infringement of the claimant's right is established.

Question 8

In January 2007, Universal Films released a 60-minute DVD re-living Jennifer Tarvill and Craig Dane's most magical ice-dancing routines entitled *Tarvill & Dane's Golden Moments*. Through a tip-off from an informer at a Manchester street market, followed up by private investigators, Universal discovers that a young man, Rodney Racket, has based his operation at his flat in Manchester. The informer confirms that Rodney has stored 100 crates of pirate *Golden Moments* DVDs at his flat. Advise Universal Films as to how to enforce their intellectual property rights.

Answer plan

This question requires a knowledge of self-help measures and search orders.

- The nature of a copyright owner's exclusive rights;
- Potential infringement of those rights by Racket;
- Enforcement and search orders;
- **Civil Procedure Rule 25.**

Answer

It appears that Rodney Racket is engaging in producing pirate DVDs, which amounts to wilful copyright infringement. A DVD is a copyright work protected by the **Copyright Designs and Patents Act 1998.** Under s 16(1) **CDPA 1988,** only

Universal Films has the exclusive right to authorise copies of the *Golden Moments* DVD and to issue these to the public. Section 16(2) of the Act provides that to make copies and issue copies to the public in the UK without authorisation infringes copyright. Infringement takes two forms, primary infringement and secondary infringement.

Restricted acts/primary infringement are carried out without the permission of the copyright owner regardless of the defendant's mental state. Intention by the defendant is not relevant to finding infringement: Laddie J in *Electronic Techniques v Critchley Components (1997)*. See **CDPA 1988** ss 16–18, 21.

Secondary infringement is concerned with large-scale infringements taking place with actual or constructive knowledge, that is forms of piracy. Secondary infringement is committed only if the defendant knew or had reason to believe there was a defined state of affairs relating to infringement. Nevertheless, most secondary infringements will be based on an earlier primary infringement. For example, dealing in infringing copies such as Rodney Racket's dealing in pirate DVDs, will usually be based on an earlier infringement of the primary reproduction rights.

The gathering of evidence is crucial in intellectual property infringement cases. It is vital that Universal has the opportunity to discover this evidence. It would be relatively easy for a *mala fides* defendant such as Racket to move or destroy the incriminating DVDs once he had been served with a claim. All that is required to copy a DVD are blank DVDs, labels and a machine. Universal needs to acquire the evidence without giving Racket any advance warning to reduce the risk that the evidence will be lost. Racket is unlikely to comply with the normal process of discovery in civil proceedings.

Unfortunately, although s 100 of the **CDPA 1988** enables the copyright owner or his agent to seize and detain infringing copies, this is not available to Universal because only premises to which the public has access may be entered in the exercise of this self-help right. In this case, Racket has based his operation in his own private residence, a flat.

Accordingly, the appropriate remedy for Universal is to seek an *ex parte* search order against Racket. Proceedings without notice (*ex parte* hearings) occur when only one side is represented at the hearing. This means that Universal would be under a duty of full and frank disclosure. An *ex parte* order preserves the status quo pending a full hearing of the matter at trial.

Search orders were first introduced by Ormrod J of the Court of Appeal in the case of *Anton Piller KG v Manufacturing Processes Ltd (1976)*. They are granted to allow a claimant to enter the alleged infringer's premises for the purpose of search and seizure of relevant documents and articles. Applications for a search order should be made *ex parte* to a patents judge in the High Court or to the Patents County Court. They can eventually also be made to a Chancery judge (**CPR 25; r 25 Practice Direction**). The essential pre-requisites for granting a search order require that:

- there must be a strong prima facie case;
- the damage, potential or actual, must be very serious for the applicant;
- there must be clear evidence that the defendants have in their possession incriminating documents or things and that there is a real possibility that they may destroy such material before any application *inter partes* can be made.

The order will be drawn up so to extend no further than necessary to preserve the evidence. The *Universal Thermosensors v Hibben (1992)* case established standard guidelines for the exercise of a search order, which must be carried out by an experienced solicitor who acts in the capacity as an officer of the court, not as a member of the firm acting for the applicant. The supervising solicitor must also explain the terms of the search order to Racket in plain English and he must advise him of his rights. Racket would be obliged to permit the inspection, otherwise he would face proceedings for contempt of court. Where documents or items are removed, they must be returned within days where possible.

The three key aims of the search order will be to seize the infringing DVDs, obtain information on the distribution and sale of the infringing DVDs and to obtain the names and addresses of any other conspirators involved in the chain of distribution. The search order should be worded to require Racket to disclose the names and addresses of any of his associates.

If Racket tries to obstruct entry this will be a contempt of court, and he could be committed under **Order 52** or receive a fine. This type of act would also be highly prejudicial evidence at trial against Racket.

In the unlikely event that the court does not grant Universal Films a search order, they are advised to seek an injunction as an alternative remedy to stop the pirate DVDs being copied and issued to the pubic by Racket.

CHAPTER 3

COPYRIGHT AND MORAL RIGHTS

The purpose of copyright is to allow creators to gain financial rewards for their efforts with a view to encouraging future creativity and developing new material. Copyright material is usually the result of creative skill, significant labour and judgement. Without legal protection such material would often be relatively easy for others to exploit without paying the creator.

In the UK, there is no official copyright registry or fees to pay as in some other countries. Copyright protection is automatic as soon as there is: (1) a permanent record in any form of the newly created material; and (2) the material conforms with the criteria set out in the **Copyright Designs and Patents Act 1988 (CDPA 1988)**.

Copyright is a partial monopoly and the law allows a number of exceptions whereby a copyright work may be lawfully copied without infringing the rights of the author. The wide range of permitted acts, exceptions and the fair dealing defences limit the copyright owner's rights.

As copyright is statute-based, in every answer students should refer to the relevant sections of the **CDPA 1988** as well as to case law authorities. The majority of questions will deal with literary, dramatic, musical or artistic (LDMA) works under Part I of the Act.

Question 9

What are the benefits of copyright and moral rights protection?

Answer plan

This is a mixed topic question that requires the student to describe the key features of the copyright protection system as well as the range of moral rights that exist. It is important to critically analyse how such protection assists author/creators.

- Briefly summarise the origins and nature of copyright: the variety of subject matter afforded protection;
- Part I of the **CDPA 1988**;
- Exclusive economic rights;
- Automatic protection – no need to register;
- Duration of the monopoly;
- Personal property;
- Moral rights.

Answer

Although copyright protection has existed in the UK for several centuries, in modern times the scope of copyright has expanded incrementally to encompass new forms of creative material as well as new ways of disseminating material, made possible by technological advances. Modern copyright law gives the creators the benefit of protection over a wide range of material, such as literature, drama, art, music, sound recordings, films, broadcasts, cable programmes, typographical arrangement of published editions, computer software and databases. In the United Kingdom, copyright law is governed by the **Copyright Designs and Patents Act 1988 (CDPA 1988)**. Copyright protection provides benefits in the form of economic rights which entitle the creators to control use of their material in a number of ways, such as by making copies, issuing copies to the public, performing in public, broadcasting and use on-line: s 16 **CDPA 1988**. Copyright also enables creators to obtain an appropriate economic reward such as royalties and licensing fees. In other words, copyright allows an author to protect his original material and stops others from using that work without permission. However, in order to balance the rights of copyright owners with the interests of the general public, the **CDPA 1988** permits certain uses to be made of works and subject matter without the permission of the copyright owner. The wide range of permitted acts, exceptions and the fair dealing defences limit the copyright owner's rights (ss 28–76 **CDPA 1988**).

Another economic benefit afforded to authors of copyright works is that they are entitled to compensation where their works are loaned by public libraries. This 'public lending right' compensates them for lost revenue from sales. This right is administered via a Public Lending Rights Scheme.

A further benefit of the copyright system is that in the UK there is no need for an author to register or deposit the copyright work or pay a fee in order to obtain protection. Copyright protection is automatic once the criteria set out in the Act are met.

Nor is it necessary to put a copyright notice (© name of the copyright owner, year of publication) on a work, although it is advisable to do so.

The duration of copyright protection varies according to the material protected. But for published literary, dramatic, musical and artistic works, protection lasts for 70 years following the end of the calendar year in which the author dies. The length of copyright protection is a key benefit for author/creators, as they are able to continue to financially control their work for a long period before coypright expires and the work falls into the public domain and is free to copy. It is interesting to note that even unknown authors are recognised by the **CDPA 1988**. An unknown author is one whose identity cannot be ascertained by 'reasonable enquiry' (s 9(5)). The copyright work is known as an 'orphan' copyright.

Copyright works are like any other form of personal property: all or part of the rights in a work may be transferred or assigned by the owner to another. This means that copyright can be inherited, so that the author's beneficiaries will continue to benefit from the author's economic rights after his or her death.

However, one of the fundamental concepts of copyright law is that copyright does not protect ideas, information or facts, but instead protects the form in which those ideas, information or facts are expressed. The idea–expression distinction has been accepted and applied by the courts in the UK throughout the history of copyright, although it is not explicity stated in the **CDPA 1988**. This concept is, however, explicit in Art 2 of the **Agreement on Trade Related Aspects of Intellectual Property (TRIPS)**, which states that copyright protection extends to 'expressions and not to ideas, procedures, methods or operation or mathematical concepts as such'. Where an idea can only be expressed in one particular way, that expression will not be protected since to confer copyright protection would monopolise the idea: *Kenrick & Co Ltd v Lawrence & Co (1890)*. So although copyright protection is broad, it is not without boundaries. At times, it is difficult to state with precision the extent of the creator's copyright.

Creators of copyright works now also enjoy the benefit of several moral rights included in the **CDPA 1988**. These are:

- the right to be identified as the author or director of a work (the paternity right) (ss 77–79);
- the right of the author or a director of a work to object to derogatory treatment of certain types of work (the integrity right) (ss 80–83);
- the right for everyone not to have a work falsely attributed to him (s 84);
- the commissioner's right of privacy in respect of a photograph or film made in private and domestic purposes (s 85).

By understanding the benefits of copyright protection an author can sell the copyright but retain the moral right to object if a work is distorted or mutilated.

A new moral right recently came into force in the UK, namely the artist's resale right. Resale royalties are the rights of visual artists to receive a percentage of the revenue from the resale of their works in the art market. Artists will be able to receive a royalty when their work is bought and sold, thereby profiting from the growing market value of the work. The **Resale Right Directive** came into force on 1 January 2006 for living artists and from 1 January 2012 for their heirs. The Directive sets out the standard royalty rate to be paid to an artist on resale of his or her work (that is after its first transfer by the artist). This means that when a living artist's work is re-sold on the UK art market for 1000 euros or more, s/he will be paid a royalty of up to 4 per cent of the sale price. The Resale Right is an optional provision of the **Berne Convention** (Art 14), where it also applies to writers' and composers' manuscripts and scores. It is envisaged that the new laws will greatly benefit struggling artists, without placing heavy administrative responsibilities on the art market. It is important to note, however, that the right does not apply to resales between individuals acting in their private capacity without the participation of an art market professional, nor to those acting in their private capacity selling to not-for-profit museums open to the public.

In summary, it is clear that the benefits of copyright and moral rights protection are substantial, enabling creators to earn a living from their work. It is widely held that strong intellectual property protection spurs creativity, which in turn opens new opportunities for businesses, governments and the general public.

Question 10

Critically analyse the concept of fair dealing under the **CDPA 1988**.

Answer plan

This is a straightforward essay question that requires a thorough discussion of the principles the courts use to assess the strength of a fair dealing defence.

- Sections 28–76 **CDPA 1988**;
- No definition of fair dealing: *Hubbard v Vosper (1972)*;
- *Hyde Park Residence Ltd v Yelland (2000)*;
- *Stilltoe v McGraw Hill Books (1983)*.

Answer

Copyright is only a partial monopoly: the law allows a number of exceptions whereby a copyright work may be lawfully copied without infringing the rights of the author. The wide range of permitted acts, exceptions and the fair dealing defences limit the copyright owner's rights. Fair dealing allows the copying or other use of a work which would otherwise infringe: (**CDPA 1988**, ss 28–76). Sections 28–76 of the **CDPA** provide a system of general and specific rights. A few examples of the most important of the 50 or so types of fair dealing include the use of copyright material for purposes of:

- research and private study (**CDPA 1988**, s 29);
- criticism or review (**CDPA 1988**, s 30(1));
- reporting current events (**CDPA 1988**, s 30(2));
- incidental inclusion (**CDPA 1988**, s 31).

However, the **CDPA 1988** does not define the term 'fair dealing'. According to Lord Denning in *Hubbard v Vosper (1972)*, 'fair dealing is impossible to define'. Nonetheless, case law suggests that a wide range of factors should be taken into consideration when determining whether the acts falls within the scope of fair dealing.

The relevant matters taken into consideration by the courts are whether the copying deprives the copyright owner of a sale that otherwise would take place, the size and proportion of the work copied and whether the infringer will obtain substantial financial gain from the infringement.

Anyone can make copies of a copyright work for the purpose of their own research or private study provided that it is within the scope of fair dealing (s 28 **CDPA 1988**). As fair dealing is not clearly defined, the only way to determine if the copy is within its scope is to consider the whole circumstances of the case.

In *Hubbard v Vosper (1972)* the defendant, who was a Scientologist for 14 years, wrote and published a highly critical book about Scientology, containing extracts from the plaintiff's book. The Court of Appeal held that whether the defendant could rely on the defence of fair dealing was a matter of degree and impression. Lord Denning provided further clarification and held that the relevant factors to be considered when determining fair dealing include the number and extent of extracts and the use made of the extracts. If the extracts were used as the basis of research, study, criticism, comment and review as per **CDPA** ss 29 and 30, this could amount to fair dealing.

However, if used to convey the same information in a competitive manner this would be unfair and would amount to infringement of copyright. In the *Independent Television Publication v Time Out Magazine* case, where the defendants attempted to rely on the defence of fair dealing for criticism and review, this failed because the purpose was to provide a television programme listing and had nothing to do with criticism or review. The same point was considered in *Pro Sieben Media AG v Carlton UK TV Ltd (1999)* where the defendants used a 30-second clip from a programme produced and owned by the claimant featuring a subject who had given an exclusive interview to the claimant. The defendant argued in the Court of Appeal that they were protected under s 30 by fair dealing for the purposes of news reporting, criticism and review. The Court of Appeal held that the degree to which the use of a protected work competed with exploitation of the copyright by the copyright owner was very important in assessing fair dealing.

The decision in *Pro Sieben* was later considered in *Newspaper Licensing Agency Ltd v Marks & Spencer plc (1999)*. The facts concerned the copyright in a typographical edition of a literary work. Lightman J established a three-stage test for raising a s 30(2) defence:

(1) reporting current events;

(2) fair dealing with copyright work – not an actual exploitation; and

(3) acknowledgment.

Another factor that should be considered is the status of the copied work – whether it is confidential or published. In *Hyde Park Residence Ltd v Yelland (2000)* a two-stage test was applied to determine whether the defence of fair dealing was available. First, it was necessary to ascertain the purpose of the act, for example if the purpose of such publication was within the ambit of reporting current events and whether the acts fell within the scope of fair dealing. Secondly, the work had not been previously made available to the public, which was an important indication that the dealing was not fair.

A financial motive behind making a copy must be considered when determining whether or not a copy falls within the fair dealing defence, as to allow another to financially benefit from someone else's work would be utterly contrary to the justification for copyright and Locke's Labour theory, where it is argued that the owner should benefit from the fruits of their work. In *Stilltoe v McGraw-Hill Books (1983)* the defendant published extracts of the claimant's books for sale to English literature students. The defence of fair dealing failed as the publication was for their own commercial gain and not for the benefit of the students, the only ones capable of raising a legitimate fair dealing defence.

In conclusion, fair dealing is important because the courts have often held that taking even a very small amount of work is sufficient for an infringement of copyright. The courts' findings will rely on key considerations such as the purpose of the use, the proportion of the use, its motive (if it was to compete with the original work it will amount to infringement) and the status of the other work as to whether it is confidential or published material.

Question 11

In 2006, Anne Smith, a graduate of the prestigious Royal College of Art, wins that year's £25,000 Jarwood Sculpture Prize with her work 'Tin' – a giant tin with the top left slightly ajar. Ms Smith says the work reflects her notion that 'beyond literal legibility and metaphorical ideas, sculptures should be ambivalent in their meaning and identity'. The winning 'Tin' sculpture will be sited in a park near Swindon. Judges praised its 'great intellectual depth and exceptional beauty' and said an aluminium sculpture would look 'outstanding' in the park.

Barry Barking, a journalist, writes an article in an arts magazine that is highly critical of Smith's sculpture. The article includes photographs of a series of four everyday tins and falsely claims that they are 'other works of genius by Anne Smith'. The sculpture is placed in the park, but when it is secured to the ground, the top of the giant tin closes and is no longer slightly ajar. Smith is devastated and claims that her work has been ruined. Meanwhile, Carol, a local Swindon potter, having seen the 'Tin' sculpture on display in the park, decides to recreate it in clay in a miniature version. She gives one of her clay 'Tin' sculptures to her new neighbour as a house-warming present. A buyer for Harrods sees it while visiting the neighbour's house and places an order for 100 more for the London store.

Advise the parties as to whether or not any of them have infringed intellectual property rights, and any remedies that may be available.

Answer plan

This is a difficult question that cannot be comprehensively answered with certainty in many respects.

- Does copyright subsist?
- Artistic copyright work (s 4 (2) **CDPA 1988**);
- Moral rights;
- Primary and secondary infringement;
- Defences and remedies.

Answer

In order to protect her work, a sculpture, Anne will have to show that copyright subsists in the work. Copyright comes into existence, or subsists, automatically when a qualifying person creates a work that is original and tangible. Section 1 of the

Copyright Designs and Patents Act 1988 provides that literary, dramatic, musical and artistic works be 'original'. An artistic work such as Anne's Tin sculpture must be original in the sense that it originates from her: *University of London Press v University Tutorial Press (1916)*. Expending skill, labour and judgement in creating the work is enough to deem the work to be original. Further, even though it looks like a commonplace tin, it will be protected as a sculpture because it has been made for the purpose of sculpture: *J&S Davis (Holdings) Ltd v Wright Health Group (1988)*. A sculpture is protected as an artistic work under s 4(2) irrespective of its artistic merit (s 4(1)(a) **CDPA 1988**). Therefore, it is clear that copyright will subsist in prize-winning sculpture, as it is likely to be original and not copied from another source: **CDPA 1988** s 1(1)(a).

As creator of the artistic work, Anne will be regarded as its author and as the owner of the copyright in it (s 9(1) **CDPA 1988**). Accordingly, Anne has the exclusive right to do certain restricted acts in relation to her copyright work during her lifetime, and her heirs will benefit for a further 70 years following her death. The restricted acts are set out in s 16(1) **CDPA 1988** and include copying, issuing copies to the public, renting or lending the work, for example. Anne can prevent a third party from carrying out any unauthorised activities concerning her sculpture.

Barry Barking has written an article in an arts magazine criticising Anne's sculpture. Does writing an article about Anne's sculpture infringe her copyright? This is unlikely here because Barry will be able to claim that his dealing with the sculpture is fair in that he is using the work for the purposes of criticism and review. This is a permitted act under s 30(1) **CDPA 1998**. Barry does not require Anne's permission to refer to her work in the magazine article. Indeed, Barry probably has copyright in his own article (a literary work within s 1(1)(a) **CDPA 1988**).

Article 27 of the Universal Declaration of Human Rights recognises that the creators of any scientific, literary or artistic production have both moral and 'material' rights, or 'economic interests', in their work which should be protected. Have any of Anne's moral rights been infringed?

Moral rights are personal rights conferred by s 94 **CDPA 1988** on the authors of primary copyright works and the directors of films. Moral rights are quite separate from the economic interests in the work. They are also distinct from the copyright in the work. Moral rights are concerned with protecting the personality and reputation of authors. An author's moral rights are protected as breaches of statutory duty, not, as copyright is, as a property right. The aim of moral rights is to protect an author's artistic reputation and integrity. Before the **CDPA 1988**, authors in the UK mainly had to rely on their common law rights in contract, defamation, passing off, injurious falsehood and breach of confidence to protect their reputation and integrity.

Has Barry infringed Anne's moral rights? By falsely attributing work to Anne by publishing pictures in his article and claiming that they were 'other works of genius by Anne Smith', Barry has infringed Anne's right against false attribution. Moral rights are separate from any economic interest in the work in question. They are concerned with protecting the personality and reputation of the author and are therefore protected as a breach of statutory duty and not as a property right. Anne has the right for the works in the photographs accompanying Barry's article not to be incorrectly attributed to her (ss 84–86). Here the false attribution is express by use of the caption. There is no requirement that Anne need have suffered any damage to assert the right: *Clark v Associated Newspapers (1998)*. Anne may wish to consider bringing an action against Barry for infringement of this moral right.

The Tin sculpture is placed in the park, but when it is secured to the ground, the top of the giant tin closes and it is no longer slightly ajar. It would appear that Anne's moral right of integrity may have been infringed. Past cases have involved the removal of site-specific artistic works. Sections 80–83 of the **CDPA 1998** provide that Anne can object to the derogatory treatment of her work if the work has been added to, altered or deleted (s 80(2)) in such a way as to amount to a distortion, mutilation or otherwise prejudicial treatment. In *Pasterfield v Denham (1998)* Overend J held that distortion or mutilation must have harmed the honour or reputation of an artist, and that a subjective sense of grievance did not suffice. This was later affirmed in *Confetti Records v Warner Music (2003)*. Here, as the Tin sculpture is a prize-winning sculpture, any change to its composition will be likely to harm Anne's honour or reputation.

Meanwhile, Carol has recreated the 'Tin' sculpture in a different material (clay) and in a smaller size and gives one to her neighbour as a gift. Only Anne, however, has the exclusive right to copy the work and issue copies to the public: s 16(1) **CDPA 1988**. Copying means 'reproducing the work in a material form'. Intention by the defendant is not relevant to finding infringement: Laddie J. in *Electronic Techniques v Critchley Components (1997)*. The facts show that there is a connection between the work and its alleged copy; and there is probably more than a passing resemblance to Anne's copyright sculpture. Changes to form, or dimension of a copyright work may also constitute reproduction (s 17(3) **CDPA 1988**). Accordingly, Carol has infringed Anne's copyright in the sculpture, although there is no *mala fides* and she has not profited from doing so. There is nothing to suggest that Carol could rely on a fair dealing defence. However, s 62 of the **CDPA 1988** concerns certain representations of artistic works on public display. A sculpture, for instance, if permanently situated in a public place open to the public, is not infringed by making a graphic work, photograph or broadcasting a visual image representing it. Would Carol's miniature sculpture fall into the category of graphic work and thus not infringe? In s 4 **CDPA 1988** 'graphic work' includes any painting, drawing, diagram, map, chart or plan, any engraving, etching, lithograph, woodcut or similar work. A sculpture is not included in the definition. Carol is not authorised by Anne to reproduce the 'Tin' sculpture and should not accept the order placed by the buyer for Harrods. In conclusion, Anne's best legal remedy, if she is interested in pursuing it, would be to apply for an order to have Carol deliver up all infringing copies of her work: s 99 **CDPA 1988**.

Question 12

Jessica is an experienced Human Resources Officer for the University of Trent and her employer has asked her to draft a completely new staff handbook. When she drafted this, she used a template that she had from her previous employer, the University of Rutland ('UoR') which was 100 pages long which she and two other UoR staff had drafted. She then made the following changes to the UoR template:

- Deleted 5 pages which were not relevant to Trent University.
- Included 5 new pages and added language required by statutes.
- Added 2 pages from other agreements, some of which she had authored and which were publicly available on the Internet to other UK universities.
- Created 3 new pages to cover complex new legal rights for employees over the age of 65 years.
- Edited all of the above for style and consistency.
- Made a large number of minor stylistic and grammatical revisions suggested by Mr Pickwick, the Head of Human Resources for Trent University.

The resulting Staff Handbook is about 105 pages long and is published on the University's intranet, accessible to all staff.

Several months later, Jessica's line manager Mr Pickwick calls her into his office for a meeting together with the University's in-house legal officer. Mr Pickwick informs Jessica that a letter has been received from her former employer claiming that the University of Trent has breached the copyright subsisting in the UoR Staff Handbook and must cease its use or agree to pay a licence fee.

Advise the University of Trent as to whether there is any basis for the claim of copyright infringement and any defences it may have.

Answer plan

This is a practical problem question concerning copyright infringement.

- Analyse whether copyright subsists in the UoR Staff Handbook as a literary work under s 3(1) **Copyright Designs and Patents Act 1988** ('CDPA 1988').
- Establish who owns copyright in the UoR Staff Handbook and the nature of the UoR's exclusive rights in its UoR Staff Handbook under s 16(1) **CDPA 1988**.
- Examine whether Jessica (and thereby her employer) has infringed any of the exclusive rights in the Staff Handbook.
- If so, consider any likely defences Trent University may have and any remedies available to UoR.

Answer

Copyright law in the the UK is governed by the **Copyright, Designs and Patents Act 1988** ('CDPA 1988') and in particular, Part I of the Act sets out the substantive copyright law. This means that the University of Rutland ('UoR') Staff Handbook will only be a copyright work if it meet the requirements of the **CDPA 1988**. The Act identifies three categories of works in which copyright subsists:

- original literary, dramatic, musical or artistic works;
- sound recordings, films or broadcasts;
- typographical arrangements of published editions.

The first issue is whether coypright subsists in the University of Rutland (UoR) Staff Handbook such that there is a copyright work capable of being infringed. A 'work' is not defined by the **CDPA 1988** except to say that a 'copyright work' means a work of any of those descriptions in which copyright subsists: s 1(2). Section 1(1)(a) **CDPA 1988** provides that copyright subsists in original literary works. Whether a work is a 'work' for copyright purposes is inseparable from whether it is 'original' since copyright will only subsist in an original work. The Act defines a 'literary work' as any work other than a dramatic or musical work that is written, spoken or sung: s 3(1). It appears that the UoR Staff Handbook will fall within the scope of the definition of 'literary work' and as such is *prima facie* copyright material for several reasons. The Handbook is original in the sense that it originates from the UoR's employee, Jessica (and perhaps other staff) and is the result of the authors' skill, labour and judgment: *Ladbroke (Football Ltd) v William Hill (Football Ltd) (1964)*. Further, case law establishes that this is not a qualitative standard, merely an indication that the work be recorded by means of letters or numbers: *University of London Ltd v University Tutorial Press Ltd (1916)* per Petersen J. The UoR Staff Handbook is fixed in writing as required by s 3(2) of the Act and also qualifies for protection under the heads of authorship or place of publication in ss 153–155 **CDPA 1988**. Copyright in the UoR Staff Handbook will last for the life of the author plus 70 years: s 12 **CDPA 1988**.

As it is established that copyright does subsist in the UoR Staff Handbook, the next issue is who is the copyright owner that can enforce the rights. We are told that when Jessica drafted the new University of Trent (UoT) Staff Handbook, she used a template that she had from her previous employer, the UoR, which was 100 pages long. Jessica is a former UoR employee. When a work is created by an employee in the course of employment, then copyright is automatically assigned to the employer by s 11(2) **CDPA 1988** except where agreed to the contrary. In *Beloff v Pressdram Ltd (1973)* the court cited with approval the dictum of Lord Denning that an employee is employed as part of the business and his work is an integral part of the business. So even though Jessica and two other UoR employees were the authors of the UoR Staff Handbook, copyright vests with the UoR as the employer and not with the former employee Jessica, unless her contract of employment with UoR provided otherwise, which is unlikely in this case. Accordingly, as copyright owner, only the UoR has the exclusive right to carry out the 'restricted acts' in relation to its staff handbook. These restricted rights include copying the work or a substantial part of it and publishing it: s 16(1), s 16(3)(a) **CDPA 1988**. Copying means 'reproducing the work in a material form'. If a third party has copied the UoR Staff Handbook, the UoR will have standing to sue in respect of copyright infringement.

Therefore the crux of the problem is whether copyright in the UoR Staff Handbook has been infringed by the UoT. There are two types of infringement. Primary infringement occurs when a person does, or authorises another to do, any of the restricted acts without the licence of the copyright owner: s 16(2). Secondary infringement is mainly concerned with dealings in infringing works of facilitating their production. In this case, the concern is primary infringement. Can UoR stop UoT using the copied portions of the UoR Staff Handbook without a licence? There are two key elements required in order to establish primary infringement. According to Denning LJ *Francis, Day and Hunter Ltd v Bron (1963)*, there must be:

(1) a causal connection between the copyright work and the alledgedly infringing work; and

(2) copying of a substantial part of the copyright work.

In other words, the court will consider if there is objective similarity between the two works and whether there is a causal connection between them.

As to the first element, for a work to be infringing, it must derive from the copyright work – it must have been copied by someone. Here, the causal connection is Jessica, the former UoR employee, who had access to the UoR Staff Handbook which she did indeed refer to as a template for the UoT Staff Handbook. The first element of the test for copying is satisfied.

Apart from a causal connection, in order to infringe, copying must be in relation to the work as a whole, or any substantial part of it: s 16(3)(a). The UoR's copyright will not be infringed unless a substantial part of its staff handbook has been used by UoT via its current employee Jessica. Whether the copying is substantial will be analysed on a qualitative rather than quantitative basis: *Ladbroke (Football Ltd) v William Hill (Football Ltd) (1964)* per Lord Pearce. It is a question of fact whether the degree of similarity is sufficient to warrant the inference that there is a causal connection between the two works.

Is there more than a passing resemblance to the UoR Staff Handbook? The court will consider firstly the value and secondly the amount of the material that UoT has repeated and how this has been used in the UoT Staff Handbook. Every case is decided on its individual merits. For example, in *Ludlow Music Inc. v Robbie Williams (2000)* it was held that one refrain from a song could amount to substantial copying. On the other hand, where a work is not copied in extracts, but slight modifications are made to the whole of it, the question is whether the alleged infringer has misappropriated a substantial part of the claimant's labour, skill and judgment: *Designers Guild Ltd v Russell Williams (Textiles) Ltd (No 2) (2001)*. In summary, a substantial degree of objective similarity, together with proof of access to the original work, is *prima facie* evidence of copying.

The court will assess whether the UoT has created a new literary document of its own by evaluating Jessica's and Mr Pickwick's skill, labour and judgment, and/or whether the the UoT Staff Handbook infringes that of the University of Rutland. On the facts, it would appear that there is some new material: 5 new pages which added language required by statutes; 2 new pages cut and pasted from other universities' staff handbooks which she found on the Internet (while potentially infringing, do not infringe the Rutland document); 3 new pages to cover complex new legal rights for employees over the age of 65 years; and minor stylistic and grammatical revisions. This means that approximately 8 percent of the materials have not been copied. Further, approximately 5 percent of the UoR material was deleted. So the issue is whether the remaining 87 percent of the Trent Staff Handbook was copied by Jessica from the UoR Staff Handbook.

On balance the second element of the test for copying is satisfied. If Jessica has not made any changes to the text of the UoR Staff Handbook it is highly likely that a court would find that the UoT Handbook substantially infringes the UoR Staff Handbook both qualitatively and quantitavely. Intention by the defendant is not relevant to finding infringement: *Electronic Techniques v Critchley Components (1997)*. The facts show that there is a connection between the work and its alleged copy, namely Jessica. The evidential burden will then shift to Trent University to show that it did not copy the UoR Staff Handbook. The permitted acts are set out in ss 28–76 of the **CDPA 1988**. However, there is nothing to suggest that the UoT could rely on a fair dealing defence as a staff handbook is not directly related to research, education, criticism or review.

If the copyright infringement action is successful, the UoT will be injuncted from publishing its staff handbook on its website and could be required to deliver up all infringing copies and/or pay damages to the UoR.

Question 13

James Buckingham is an accomplished modern lute player. In 1978, he wrote a composition for the song 'The Court', a piece for lute and voice that incorporated some elements of fifteenth-century court minstrel music. The song was recorded on his first album by his music publishing company, Medieval Times. Buckingham is the sole author of the musical composition and lyrics of the song 'Courtroom'. In 2006, the Beastie Guys, a rap and hip-hop group, used six seconds of music from Buckingham's 'Courtroom' in their song 'Beat the Court' without obtaining a licence from Buckingham. Buckingham seeks your advice as to copyright infringement.

Answer

The Beastie Guys have 'sampled' six seconds of Buckingham's copyrighted music and lyrics without permission. Sampling can be simply defined as the incorporation of pre-existing recordings into a new recording. It can be extended to include the incorporation of part or the whole of a 'tune' (a melody) and/or lyrics into another work. This is a common activity in music creation. To what extent is this practice legal? Does it infringe Buckingham's copyright? Copyright subsists in sound recordings, and in the music and lyrics to a song, pursuant to s 1(1) of the **Copyright Designs and Patents Act 1988**. Buckingham's right to his music in the composition 'The Court' arises from s 1(1) **CDPA 1988**, which states that copyright subsists in original musical works. Under the **CDPA 1988**, a song and its lyrics enjoy two separate copyrights: a copyright in the words and a separate copyright in the music or tune: *Redwood Music v B Feldman & Co Ltd (1979)*. Buckingham's lyrics will attract copyright protection as a literary work, namely words designed to be sung: s 1(1)(a) **CDPA 1988**. The musical composition will be protected as a musical work defined as 'a work of music, exclusive of any words or actions intended to be sung'.

The **CDPA** provides in s 16(1) that the owner of a work has a number of acts restricted to him or her, which are to:

(a) Copy the work.

(b) Issue copies of the work or lend or rent copies of the work to the public.

(c) Perform, show or play the work in public.

(d) Broadcast the work or include it in a cable programme.

(e) Make an adaptation of the work, and do any of the above in relation to such adaptation.

Therefore, any kind of sampling without the consent of the copyright owner will prima facie amount to infringement. To be clear, sampling without permission will usually infringe two copyrights – in the sound recording copyright (here this is owned by the music publishing company Medieval Times) and the copyright in the song itself (usually owned by the songwriter). In order for another party to carry out any of these activities, they must first gain consent from the original copyright owner or their agent. In the UK, collection societies such as the Performing Right Society and the Phonographic Performance Limited manage copyrights on behalf of copyright owners.

First, the UK legal test to determine infringement requires that a 'substantial' part of the original work must have been copied. Every case is decided on its individual merits. In *Hawkes & Sons v Paramount Film Services (1934)* it was held that use without permission of 20 seconds of a musical work, 'Colonel Bogey' (which lasted four minutes in total), infringed. The position in English law now seems to have reached the point that any 'recognisable' use would infringe. Accordingly, infringement will take place when, on hearing a bar of music, a listener can easily identify a similar sounding piece of music.

In *Lawson v Dundas (1985)* it was held that the four-note theme used as part of the Channel 4 signature tune was protected as a musical work. The 'substantial use' defence was again tested in *Produce Records Limited v BMG Entertainment International UK and Ireland Limited (1999)*. Produce Records owned the copyright in a sound recording, 'Higher and Higher', by the Farm. BMG manufactured and distributed the hit track 'Macarena' by the group Los Del Rio in the UK. This sampled a seven-and-a-half-second section of 'Higher and Higher'. No clearance had been obtained for the use of this sample and Produce Records brought proceedings for breach of copyright against BMG. BMG applied to strike out the proceedings on the basis that it was unarguable that the sample constituted a substantial part of 'Higher and Higher'. BMG argued that this was a question for the judge alone to decide when comparing the two recordings. Produce Records introduced expert evidence from a forensic musicologist on which parts of 'Higher and Higher' were more recognisable and memorable than others. Parker J rejected the strike-out application. He accepted that judges were not expert musicologists, and could be assisted by expert evidence as to whether it was or was not substantial, and also by the extrinsic factual evidence. In any event, having heard the two tracks, he thought that the Produce Records claim was plainly arguable, and that it should not be struck out. This decision reinforced the position that sampling sound recordings without the consent of the copyright owner is prima facie infringement of copyright if a substantial part of the original material is reproduced.

Currently, the owners of lyrics are in the same position. In 2002, it was held that even short samples of lyrics need copyright clearance. In *Ludlow Music Inc v Robbie Williams and others (2002)* Pumfrey J held that the singer Robbie Williams must pay damages to Loudon Wainwright III due to the similarity between lyrics in Williams' song, 'Jesus in a Camper Van', and Wainwright's earlier work.

In conclusion, Buckingham has a strong case to enforce his copyright against the Beastie Guys under s 16 **CDPA**. In addition, case law provides that even unauthorised use of just six seconds of music will amount to substantial copying. He will be entitled to several remedies including damages to compensate him for his loss of licensing fee or on a royalty basis. Alternatively, Buckingham may elect an account of the profits, whereby the Beastie Guys will have to give back a proportion of the profits they have made from their recording 'Beat the Court' as determined by the court.

Question 14

The Jenkins & Taplin advertising agency is engaged to create a non-broadcast media advertising campaign for the Merlandia Toy Company. The agency's photographer sets up a shoot at a privately owned stately home with extensive gardens. The photographer and his team pay their entrance fees to gain access to the property. A young female child model is artfully arranged in front of a sculpture of a dolphin, which is permanently on display in the grounds. The house is in the background.

As part of the Merlandia Toy Company's advertising campaign for the new mermaid doll, the photographs are published as part of an advertisement in a children's magazine. The following events occur:

1. the Arnott-Browns, the owners of the country house, claim that they did not give permission for it to be used as a background; and

2. Corey Dean, the sculptor who created the dolphin sculpture, wants to negotiate a licence fee and threatens to sue if a sum is not agreed.

Advise Jenkins & Taplin and the Merlandia Toy Company on liability.

Answer plan

This question concerns the commercial use of photographs of copyright works.

• Copyright in photographs and incidental inclusion;

• Artistic works s 4 **CDPA**;

• Public display of certain artistic works s 62 **CDPA**;

• Infringement and remedies.

Answer

Commercial use of photographs which feature copyright works can be problematic for a business such as the Merlandia Toy Company who use photographs in their advertising. Advertising photographs frequently feature an artistic work, such as a painting on a background wall. Here, the background in the photograph includes two forms of artistic work: (1) a country house, which in copyright terms is a work of architecture being a building; and (2) the dolphin sculpture. The Arnott-Browns and Mr Corey Dean will only be able to take action against the advertising agency and the toy company if their own copyright is enforceable.

Both the building and the sculpture are forms of artistic works that will enjoy copyright protection automatically where a qualifying person creates an original work that is original and tangible. Section 1 of the **Copyright Designs and Patents Act 1988** provides that literary, dramatic, musical and artistic works be 'original'. For copyright to subsist, the artistic works must be original in the sense that they originate from the creator: *University of London Press v University Tutorial Press (1916)*. Expending skill, labour and judgement in creating the work is enough to deem the work to be original.

First, it is clear that the dolphin sculpture is a traditional sculpture because it has been made for the purpose of sculpture: *J&S Davis (Holdings) Ltd v Wright Health Group (1988)*. A sculpture is protected as an artistic work under s 4(2) irrespective of its artistic merit (s 4(1)(a) **CDPA 1988**). Therefore, it is clear that copyright will subsist in the dolphin sculpture as it is likely to be original so long as the sculptor, Corey Dean has not copied from another source: **CDPA 1988** s 1(1)(a).

Secondly, copyright will subsist in a work of architecture being a building as an artistic work under s 4(1)(b) **CDPA 1988**. The architect's plans are protected as a graphic work and are not in issue here. However, s 4(1)(b) does not contain the rule that works in this group are protected, irrespective of their artistic quality. It is thought that it was not necessary to make such a provision in the Act, because a lack of artistic merit rarely arises where buildings are concerned. The question of artistic merit is more likely to arise in connection with modern art and sculpture.

As copyright prima facie subsists in both the building and the sculpture, including these works in a photograph for non-private use without permission from the copyright owner may constitute an unauthorised reproduction of the work: s 16(2) **CDPA 1988**. This could leave Jenkins & Taplin, the photographer and the Merlandia Toy Company liable to copyright enforcement proceedings.

Of course, even if a work does fall within the scope of copyright protection, no permission is required to photograph it if the term of copyright protection has already expired. In the UK, protection for an artistic work lasts for the lifetime of the artist plus 70 years after his death. It will be important to determine the date of subsistence of copyright in the stately home. If copyright in the building has expired, the Arnott-Browns will have no copyright to enforce.

In addition, whether or not permission is required also depends on how much of the work appears in the photograph. Usually, prior consent is needed to reproduce a substantial part of the work. But there are no general rules on this. Often, the quality of what is used may be more important than how much is used. Permission will be required if:

- a substantial part of the building (if it is still in copyright) or the dolphin sculpture has been used; or

- a small, but vital recognisable part of those works is used.

Fair dealing

Potentially, copyright laws can place significant restrictions on a photographer's choice of locations. But there are a number of important legal exceptions to copyright law that aim to strike a balance between, on the one hand, protecting the rights of the copyright owner and, on the other hand, the wider public interest. The permitted acts are set out in ss 28–76 of the **CDPA 1988**.

Incidental inclusion

The relevant permitted act in this case is found in s 31(1), which concerns incidental inclusion of copyright material. Section 31(1) provides that copyright in a work is not infringed by its incidental inclusion in an artistic work. An artistic work includes a photograph.

Artistic work on public display

Also, the parties may be able to rely on the exception to infringement in s 62 **CDPA** which provides that copyright in buildings and sculptures (among others), if permanently situated in a public place or in premises open to the public, is not infringed by taking a photograph. Accordingly, taking a photograph of something from a public place can be done lawfully as long as no privacy laws have been breached.

However, the stately home appears to be private property that is open to the public but only on payment of a fee. If it is not a public place, then the exception to infringement created by s 62 **CDPA** cannot be relied on. It is not clear if the home belongs to a scheme such as the UK National Trust or English Heritage. Properties in these schemes are private property and there are restrictions on the use of image subjects taken by photographers within the private land or property. If so, the photographer would need to seek permission to be on private property and will usually have to pay a fee for the privilege.

In conclusion, a number of fairly complex questions determine when permission from a copyright owner is required to include copyrighted material in a photograph intended for commercial use. Jenkins & Taplin's and the Merlandia Toy Company's strongest defence would be fair dealing/incidental inclusion, if indeed the subject matter in photographs confirm this. If the private stately home is the main subject of the photograph then the Arnott-Brown's permission will be required. Similarly, if a substantial part of the sculpture features in the photographs, a fee will need to be paid to the artist to secure permission to use the photograph commercially. In the future, the parties should familiarise themselves with potential copyright issues and it is good practice to require a warrant from the photographer that he has permission to use all the images depicted in the photograph.

Question 15

Richie Rich writes a monthly investment newsletter in which he includes a model investment portfolio ('the Rich Fund'). The front cover of the newsletter includes the title in logo form and the strap line 'Get rich with Rich!' The Rich Fund consists of 10–12 recommended stocks, which can and do change from month to month. In each issue of the newsletter, Richie includes the following information about the Rich Fund:

- the names of the recommended stocks;
- current price, 12-month high price and 12-month low price for each stock included in the portfolio, obtained from the live data provided by the London Stock Exchange; and
- analysis (narrative commentary) on each stock added to or dropped from the portfolio since the prior month's newsletter.

What elements, if any, of the Rich Fund newsletter are covered by copyright?

Answer plan

This question is concerned with determining which elements of a typical financial newsletter might attract copyright protection.

- Subsistence of copyright in a literary work;
- Idea/expression dichotomy;
- Copyright in the newsletter title, mastheads and straplines;
- Copyright in the arrangement of information in databases.

Answer

Copyright is a negative right that aims to provide protection to authors such as Richie Rich for their creations. Such creations are usually designated as 'works'. There is no statutory definition of 'work' in the **Copyright Designs and Patents Act 1988**, but case law suggests that its author must have expended a minimum level of effort. A similar principle is attached to the requirement of originality. The Rich Fund newsletter is typical of the genre of financial investment newsletters to which people subscribe in order to assist them to decide which shares or share funds are good investments. Many similar newsletters are published and Richie Rich will not have copyright in the idea for a financial newsletter. One of the fundamental concepts of copyright law is that copyright does not protect ideas, information or facts but instead protects the form in which those ideas, information or facts are expressed. This is known as the idea–expression dichotomy, which means that copyright will not be infringed when works based on the same ideas are independently created, provided the way in which those ideas have been expressed is not copied. The idea–expression distinction has been accepted and applied by the courts in the UK throughout the history of copyright, although not explicitly stated in the UK copyright legislation. What copyright protects is not the idea for the newsletter but 'the particular form of language by which the information which is to be conveyed is conveyed': *Donoghue v Allied Newspapers (1938)*. Therefore, the key issue to be assessed here is which specific elements of the material in the Rich Fund newsletter are of the kind that will attract copyright protection. Problems arise when there is nothing substantive enough to be protected or it is not 'original'.

Section 1(1) **CDPA 1988** provides that copyright will subsist in a literary work. A literary work is defined as any work, other than a dramatic or musical work, which is written, spoken or sung. As it is in writing, the Rich Fund newsletter will fall within this category of work. It would be wrong to think that the word 'literary' implies that an element of merit is required before a piece of writing can be treated as a copyright work. The case law establishes that this is not a qualitative standard, merely an indication that the work be recorded by means of letters or numbers. For example, in *University of London v University Tutorial Press (1916)* Petersen J explained that copyright existed in literary work 'expressed in print or writing, irrespective of the question whether the quality or style is high'. A commonplace work, such as a financial newsletter (or an exam paper, lottery coupon or a tide table) will usually attract copyright so long as the author has expended sufficient labour, skill and judgement in creating the work.

The title 'Rich Fund', masthead and strapline

Does copyright subsist in the newsletter's title, 'Rich Fund'? Titles and names have been refused copyright when they are not substantial enough to attract copyright in themselves. For example, no protection was given to the name of the song 'The Man Who Broke the Bank at Monte Carlo' in the *Francis Day and Hunter v Twentieth Century Fox (1940)* case. Nor was protection afforded to the 'WOMBLES' name in *The Wombles v Wombles Skips (1975)*. Therefore the title of the newsletter will not attract copyright protection. However, Richie Rich should be advised that if an unauthorised third party uses the 'Rich Fund' title, he could have an action for 'passing off' if the third party tries to persuade members of the public to buy another newsletter in the belief that they are choosing Richie Rich's newsletter.

Unfortunately, the strapline 'Get rich with Rich!' will be regarded as too trivial or small in terms of creative effort to attract copyright. In *Sinanide v La Maison Kosmeo (1928)* the advertising slogan 'Beauty is a social necessity, not a luxury' was held to be too slight a work to found allegations of infringement by the rival slogan 'A youthful appearance is a social necessity'. The slogan is potentially registrable as a trade mark nevertheless.

However, the masthead of the Rich Fund newsletter may attract copyright protection as a graphic artistic work under s 4(1)(a) **CDPA 1988**. In *IPC Magazines Ltd v MGN (1998)* the 'Woman' masthead was regarded as, at least arguably, a copyright work. In *IPC Media Ltd v Highbury-SPL Publishing Ltd (2004)* IPC unsuccessfully alleged that a rival magazine publisher, Highbury, had infringed its copyright in *Ideal Home* because Highbury had copied the 'look and feel' of *Ideal Home*. The allegations related to the front covers and certain internal sections in four of its issues and focused on the copyright in artistic works. Laddie J assessed the elements of a design for a magazine cover including the logo (the name of the magazine), the straplines (lines of text immediately above and below the logo), the hot-spot (so-called because, being just under the logo, it will be visible on racks of magazines for sale and would be important to attract buyers) but did not uphold IPC's claim of copyright infringement.

The names of the particular recommended stocks will not attract copyright as the courts will apply the *de minimis non curate lex* maxim. For example, a single word, EXXON, was refused copyright in *Exxon v Exxon Insurance (1981)* as it was held not to constitute an original literary work, the rationale being that it conveyed no information, provided no instruction and gave no pleasure. Further, the court noted that there was separate protection for names via the trade mark law. Indeed Richie Rich would be advised to confirm whether or not the names of stocks he mentions in his newsletter are already protected as trade marks belonging to others.

The stock price information obtained from the LSX

In his newsletter, Richie Rich reproduces the stock price information provided by the London Stock Exchange (LSX). He is not the creator of this information and as such cannot own or claim copyright in it. The LSX broadcasts all the activity of its markets live, in the form of data (information content) delivered by its LSX Infolect™ electronic database systems. A certain level of information is publicly available; however, access to higher levels of data is by licence only. Accordingly, the LSX will have copyright in its original database as a literary work under s 3(1)(d) **CDPA 1988** or via a *sui generis* database right which lasts for only 15 years. Copyright protects the arrangement of the data. The LSX will have expended labour, skill and judgement in creating the database involving substantial monetary, technical and manpower investment. Richie is able to lawfully extract and re-utilise insubstantial parts of the database for any purpose. Exceptions are also made for fair dealing and in particular reporting current events under s 30(2) **CDPA 1988**, provided that it is accompanied by sufficient acknowledgment. However, if he is reproducing substantial LSX data content, he will require a licence, otherwise he will be infringing the LSX's copyright. Typically, a provision of the licence is that the licensee agrees to credit the source of the information as being from the LSX.

Now we turn to the selection of the particular stocks to include in the Rich Fund newsletter. This would appear to involve the exercise of skill, judgement and experience and so will enjoy copyright protection: *Ladbroke (Football) v William Hill (1964)*. In this analogous case, the House of Lords held that coupons for football pools constituted original literary works. It was accepted that the 'vast amount of skill, judgement, experience and work' employed in building up the coupon constituted an original work. This was so, although the effort and skill had not gone into the production of the literary work itself, but into the commercial selection of bets to offer, providing a remedy against unfair competition. This principle applies, however commonplace the sources used.

The analysis and commentary

The analysis and commentary on each stock will certainly attract copyright protection as it is clear that the skill labour and judgement test is satisfied. Richie Rich will have no doubt exercised a sufficient degree of skill, use of knowledge, aptitude or ability, judgement or discernment in order to form his opinions by evaluating and comparing the different stocks. Copyright will subsist in this element of the newsletter, provided that the text originates from Rich and has not been copied from another source: *University of London Press v University Tutorial Press (1916)*.

Finally, for those elements of the newsletter which will enjoy copyright, the exclusive rights will last for 70 years after the author's death.

Question 16

A well-known and distinguished author, Priscilla Puritan, writes a serious and noble play about love conquering adversity in a small Canadian country town. Priscilla assigns her copyright in the play to UK television company, Channel Six. Channel Six rewrites the play and changes it into a vulgar farce starring the glamour model Jordana and her husband Pierre Antoine set in Nottingham and broadcasts it. Priscilla Puritan's name appears in publicity for the programme and in the credits as being associated with the writing of the play. Priscilla is livid and seeks advice as to her legal rights, whether these have been infringed and the nature of any cause of action she may have.

Answer plan

While the focus of this question is moral rights, students should not be penalised and indeed could be rewarded for discussing copyright law issues such as the fact that the play is a literary work and will attract copyright protection and/or the possibility of copyright infringement as a cause of action, so long as they do not neglect moral rights issues.

- Define and explain moral rights as the rights of authors which are independent of the economic rights under copyright law (Art 6 of the **Berne Copyright Convention**).
- The relevant moral rights in this problem are (1) the right to object to modification and derogatory treatment of the author's work [the 'integrity' right] (ss 80–83 **CDPA 1988**); and (2) the right to object to being falsely attributed as the author ss 77–79 **CDPA 1988**. Analyse each in turn with reference to the statute and relevant case law.

Answer

Prisicilla is the author and first copyright owner of a play in which copyright subsists as a literary work according to s 3(1) **CDPA 1988**. However, Priscilla has assigned (sold) her economic rights in the play to a UK television Company, Channel Six. She is appalled that Channel Six has rewritten the play transforming it into into a vulgar farce and that her name is associated with this tacky new version. Priscilla is clearly concerned about the integrity of her work as well as her reputation. Fortunately, the law does provide some rights that Priscilla can rely on to protect these qualities despite the fact that she has already assigned her economic rights in the play to Channel Six. The rights are known as moral rights. Since 1988, the UK **Copyright, Designs and Patents Act 1988** (CDPA 1988) has included the concept of protecting an author's personal integrity and reputation in relation to certain copyright works. Chapter IV of the Act is devoted specifically to the aim of protecting an author's artistic reputation and integrity. The concept of moral rights, that is rights relating to the author of a work, rather than the owner, were introduced to the UK fairly recently although the concept of moral rights is well-established in other European countries. An author of a copyright work, such as Priscilla, now enjoys the benefit of several moral rights which have been enshrined in the **CDPA 1988**. These are:

- the right to be identified as the author or director of a work (the paternity right) (ss 77–79);
- the right of the author or a director of a work to object to derogatory treatment of certain types of work (the integrity right (ss 80–83);
- the right for everyone not to have a work falsely attributed to him (s 84).

The legal foundation for the moral rights of attribution and integrity is Art 6*bis* of the **Berne Convention for the Protection of Literary and Artistic Works 1886** which originally recognised the concept of moral rights. Further, Article 27 of the **Universal Declaration of Human Rights** recognises that the creators of any scientific, literary or artistic production have both moral and 'material' rights, or 'economic interests' in their work which require protection.

In the UK, moral rights are personal rights conferred by s 94 **CDPA 1988** on the author of primary copyright works (such as a play) and the directors of films. They exist independently of the economic rights afforded by copyright and continue to exist even after the economic rights have been assigned. This means that even though Priscilla has assigned her economic rights in the copryight of her play, she will retain moral rights and can enforce them if they are breached. However, moral rights can be waived, or even fail for a lack of positive assertion on the part of the author so it will be crucial to confirm whether Priscilla asserted her moral rights as author of the play. Assuming she has done so, Priscilla will be able to rely on her moral rights. These rights are important as they give the author some control over her work in the future (even once the author no longer has any economic rights in the work) enabling her to control how it is used or modified in the future. The rights in ss 77, 80 and 85 **CDPA 1988** continue to subsist so long as copyright in the work subsists.

Breaches of an author's moral rights are protected as breaches of statutory duty and not as a property right. Priscilla's relevant moral rights on the facts are:

(1) the right to object to modification and derogatory treatment of the author's work [the 'integrity' right] (ss 80–83 **CDPA 1988**);

(2) the right to object to being falsely attributed as the author (s 84 **CDPA 1988**).

Turning first to the law surrounding Priscilla's right of integrity, ss 80–83 **CDPA 1988** concern the right of an author to object when their work is added to, altered or deleted (s 80(2)) in such a way as to amount to a distortion, mutilation or otherwise prejudicial treatment. Further, in *Pasterfield v Denham (1998)*, Overend J held that distortion or mutilation must be such to harm the honour or reputation of an artist and that a subjective sense of grievance did not suffice. Some evidence that there has been damage to an author's reputation is required according to *Confetti Records v Warner Music (2003)*. In that case, a 'garage' style music composer objected to the use of his single 'Burnin' by a rap group who added references to violence and drug use. Lewison J dismissed the case, in part, because no evidence of damage to the composer's reputation had been adduced. He held that s 80(2)(b) provided a two-part test:

(i) adaptation that amounted to distortion, mutilation, modification or other derogatory action; and

(ii) that this would be prejudicial to honour or reputation.

The right to object to derogatory treatment of the work extends to treatment which distorts or mutilates the work (s 80(2)(b)). It would appear on the authority of *Confetti Records v Warner (2003)* that Priscilla could successfully argue that Channel Six's adaption of her play fulfills the first element of the test as the original noble and serious qualities of the play have been undermined by the transformation into a vulgar farce set in Nottingham. In addition, farce is an entirely different literary genre than the original serious and noble tone of the play. However, in order to succeed, Priscilla will need to bring evidence as to how her honour and reputation have been prejudiced. This is more difficult and could require survey evidence. If this is necessary, it will be expensive for Priscilla to enforce her right of integrity in connection with her play.

As Priscilla's name appears in publicity and credits of the programme it may appear that her right to paternity has been respected. Section 77(2)(a) **CDPA 1988** specifically requires identification of the original author of an adaption as 'the author of the work, from which the adaptation was made'. However, Priscilla is concerned as being described as being 'involved' with the writing of the Channel Six adaptation when she had nothing to do with this. As such, it may be that including Priscilla's name as an author in connection with the Channel Six adaption is a false attribution: s 84 **CDPA 1988**.

Priscilla's moral rights could also be protected indirectly because the act complained of might involve a copyright infringement. For example, Priscilla may be able to successfully argue that Channel Six, without her permission, has made a 'parody' of her work. She might feel aggrieved because the parody contains a substantial part of the original work. However, only the copyright owner can take action for copyright infringement and Channel Six will not sue itself if Priscilla complains, so in this instance her only real avenue of redress is to rely on her moral rights.

CHAPTER 4

COMPUTER TECHNOLOGY AND COPYRIGHT LAW

A theme running through copyright law is that it is constantly adapting, whether in response to advances in technology or due to shifting perceptions regarding the extent of intellectual property protection. Computer technology developments with which copyright law has had to grapple include, but are not limited to:

- computer software programs;

- the circumvention of technological protection measures; and

- databases.

Computer programs have been protected by copyright in the United Kingdom since 1988, when the definition of 'literary work' in the **Copyright Designs and Patents Act 1988** was extended to include 'a computer program' and 'a database'.

An international consensus that computer programs should be protected by copyright emerged during the 1980s and was confirmed by Art 4 of the **TRIPS Agreement** and Art 4 of the 1996 **WIPO Copyright Treaty**.

Since computer programs and databases are protected under the **CDPA 1988** as literary works, the copyright owner can exercise all the exclusive rights attaching to literary works. In practice, the most valuable rights are those of reproduction and adaptation.

This chapter considers the nature of the legal protection afforded by the copyright law. The patentability of computer software is also problematic but is not covered in the text.

Question 17

Discuss the extent and effectiveness of the copyright law mechanisms that exist to protect computer software.

This is a broad question that requires the student to deal with a lot of material. In answering this question, it is important to examine the legislation, reported decisions relating to computer software, any specific regulations and any infringement issues that may apply.

- Original literary works (s 1(1) **CDPA 1988**);
- Section 3(1)(b) and (c) **CDPA 1988**;
- **Copyright (Computer Programs) Regulations 1992**;
- Infringement by literal copying and *Ibcos Computers v Barclays Mercantile High Finance (1994)*; *Cantor Fitzgerald International v Tradition (UK) Ltd (2000)*;
- Infringement by non-literal copying and *Navitaire Inc v Easyjet Airline Company (2004) and (2006)*;
- Defences under ss 50, 50A, 50B and 50BA **CDPA 1988**;
- Sections 17, 18 and 19 **CDPA 1988**.

Answer

It is now possible to say that computer software has been brought under the umbrella of copyright law relatively smoothly by way of a concerted effort on the part of the legislature and the courts to take the necessary steps to adapt copyright law to encompass this new form of expression. A piece of computer software comprises a program, which is a series of instructions expressed in code, intended to cause a particular result when used in computer hardware.

Computer programs are afforded copyright protection as a category of literary work and enjoy copyright protection under ss 1(1) and 3(1)(b) **CDPA 1988**. Also protected is preparatory design material for a computer program under s 3(1)(c). The **Copyright (Computer Programs) Regulations 1992** amended the **CDPA 1988** to apply to computer programs whenever created.

The normal copyright rules apply to computer programs. For example, in order to be an original literary work, the computer program must be the product of a substantial degree of skill, labour and judgement by the author: *University of London Press Ltd v University Tutorial Press Ltd (1916)*. However, the **CDPA 1988** does not define computer programs and this allows for law to adapt to evolving forms of computer software and/or technology. Case law suggests that for 'originality' to be found in a computer program, the court is particularly concerned with certain aspects including the algorithms or operational sequences and the structure or architecture of the program.

Copyright only protects expression and does not protect ideas. For example, the idea for a program to electronically manage a dental laboratory and the functions the program is to achieve are not protected by copyright: *Whelan Associated Inc v Jaslow Dental Laboratory Inc (1987)*. However, the code lines of the program, its algorithms, operational sequences, file structure and architecture may be protected by copyright once it is 'recorded in writing or otherwise' (s 3(2) **CDPA 1998**). This principle was explained in *Ibcos Computers v Barclays Mercantile High Finance (1994)* when Jacob J stated that 'UK copyright cannot protect the copyright of a mere general idea, but can protect the copyright in detailed ideas.' Fixation on a hard or floppy disk or hard-wired in a microprocessor in the form of micro code or micro programs would meet the fixation requirement under the Act. However, where there is only one way for a computer program to be expressed so as to achieve a particular technical result, this will not be protected by copyright: *Kenrick v Lawrence (1890)*, cited in *John Richardson Computers Ltd v Flanders and Chemtech Ltd (1993)*. This part of the program can be freely copied.

Section 11 of the **CDPA 1988** provides that the author of a work is the first owner in any copyright unless the author is an employee who creates the work in the course of employment.

Infringement: literal and non-literal copying

As with other literary works, a three-stage test for copyright infringement is applied:

(1) Does the work attract copyright protection?

(2) Has there been copying of the elements protected by copyright?

(3) Was the copying substantial?

The computer program must be assessed as a whole when considering whether copyright infringement has occurred. The **CDPA 1988** protects computer programs, not individual files or parts of a program. Similarly, it is a journal article as a literary work that is protected, not each individual sentence or paragraph. This is essential for the purpose of analysing cases in order to determine whether substantial copying has taken place. Separate programs can be combined into one program and this will be treated as a compilation. In *MS Associates v Power (1988)* the court identified two issues in relation to proving copying:

(1) the claimant has to prove that the defendant had access to the software program; and

(2) there are similarities between substantial parts of the programs.

The fact that two screen displays are similar is not proof of copyright – this is because the copyright protects the program itself, not the results obtained from it.

However, the legal protection for computer software raises two main concerns:

(a) literal copying defined as direct copying or duplication (for example games software, operating systems software and popular applications software);

(b) non-literal copying, usual of bespoke software for a business application (for example booking a holiday on the Internet) that is done by creating modified software to emulate the functions and operation carried out by the first software but in a different way.

It is (b) above that is the most troublesome for copyright protection law. The new software may have been created without access to the source code of the first software, but the first software has been relied on in order to gain an understanding of what it does and how it does it. This type of copying is known as non-literal or non-textual copying. It is possible to do this without infringing the copyright in the first computer software, by relying on some of the permitted acts that apply to computer software. However, it is also possible to indirectly infringe the first software's copyright if the infringer appropriates elements of the first computer program not explicitly contained in the first software.

In *Ibcos*, it was found that there were many instances of literal copying, for instance, common spelling mistakes; similar headings; redundant and unexplained bits of code which appeared in both programs; and that the allegedly infringing program contained a part of the original program in its source code while it did not actually use this part. Quantitative and qualitative issues were considered. It was held that substantial copying had occurred in relation to program structure, several individual parts of the computer program and in the file transfer programs.

However, more recently in *Navitaire Inc v EasyJet Airline Company (2006)* (a case involving non-literal copying) the court decided that in certain circumstances there would be no protection for the functionality of a piece of computer software against a new program that set out to emulate it. The facts were that Navitaire had licensed its software for a ticketless booking system to EasyJet since 1996. In 1999, EasyJet asked BulletProof to write a piece of software to perform essentially the same functions as the Navitaire software. The new software system was nearly identical in appearance and function to the Navitaire version. EasyJet was, therefore, no longer dependent on Navitaire for a software licence, upgrades and maintenance. EasyJet could also try to license the new system to third parties in direct competition with Navitaire. Navitaire sued EasyJet for copyright infringement based on:

• the substantial similarity between the 'look and feel' and overall functionality of the Navitaire software;

• the detailed copying of individual keyboard commands entered by the user to achieve particular results; and

• the copying of certain forms of results in the form of screen displays and reports, including icon designs so that the user interface looked the same.

Navitaire failed in its claim for non-literal copying. Curiously, the judge compared the software program to a pudding and explained that a chef who by trial and error manages to emulate the pudding does not infringe the copyright in the written version of the recipe. However, Navitaire did succeed with its claim that sufficient skill, labour and judgement had been used to create the Navitaire screen layout and icons and that these had been infringed (as an artistic work). In summary, EasyJet was held to have infringed Navitaire's copyright by reproducing a substantial part of the screen layout, regardless of the fact that the underlying source code was not found to have been copied. The practical effect of this decision was that EasyJet simply had to design new graphic interfaces to replace the infringing screens. The legal effect of the case indicates that the UK courts are currently unlikely to have sympathy for a claim by a software owner that the functional effects of their software have been copied where there has been no reproduction of the source code. It is the code that is protected by copyright, not the functioning of the software.

Currently, the UK position as regards the extent and effectiveness of copyright protection for computer software is that copyright protection should not be artificially extended where there is no question of the source code being copied.

Question 18

How does copyright law protect technological protection measures (TPMs) and has such protection adversely affected access to digital works?

Answer plan

This question needs to be answered in two parts. First, by establishing the current protection regime and then critically analysing the beneficial and detrimental aspects of the legal protection afforded to TPMs.

- **WIPO Copyright Treaty** and **WIPO Performers and Phonograms Treaty**;
- Part VII **CDPA 1988**; devices designed to circumvent copy-protection;
- TPMs and computer programs;
- Copyright infringement;
- *Sony Computer Entertainment Inc v Edmunds (2002)*;
- *Sony v Ball (2004)*;
- Defences and exceptions (s 296ZE **CDPA 1988**);
- Remedies.

Answer

With the introduction of legal protection for technological protection measures (TPMs), the WIPO Treaties create a unique new way of protecting copyright works as new digital and Internet-based uses emerge. A technological protection measure is a new development in the field of computer technology designed to reduce the ability to copy a work. The various forms of TPMs act as technological barriers to control access to a work. A common way of controlling access is encrypting or scrambling the content. The user will receive the data but must unlock or provide proof of authorisation by way of a password to make the information useable. Other types of TPMs include digital watermarking and digital fingerprinting which impair the quality of the copies made. Section 296(4) **CDPA 1988** defines copy-protection to include any device or means intended to prevent or restrict copyright of a work or to impair the quality of copies made.

As it stands, the use of TPMs is part of the exercise of the copyright owner's rights and is also important for consumers. According to the World Intellectual Property Organisation (WIPO), their use helps to deter piracy, encourage copyright owners to use new media such as the Internet and provide consumers with new ways of enjoying copyright works, but only if TPMs are meaningfully protected. The **WIPO Copyright Treaty (WCT)** and **WIPO Performances and Phonograms Treaty (WPPT)** require adequate protection and effective legal remedies against the circumvention of TPMs applied to protected works and phonograms (**WCT** Art 11 and **WPPT** Art 18).

If a copyright work such as a computer program includes a TPM and the TPM is unlawfully circumvented, this may result in civil liability or criminal prosecution. It is the copy-protection techniques designed to prevent or restrict unauthorised acts in relation to copyright works that are protected by copyright law. Circumvention devices, such as pirate decoders, also must be controlled if they are primarily designed or adapted to circumvent TPMs. The law does this by providing a range of remedies. There are civil remedies against:

- the act of circumvention itself (**CDPA 1988**, s 296(2));
- making and dealing in circumvention devices (**CDPA 1988**, s 296ZA(3)); and
- the provision of circumvention services (**CDPA 1988**, s 296ZD).

In order to get illicit devices out of circulation there are remedies that allow for their delivery up and seizure. There are also criminal sanctions against making and dealing in circumvention devices and the provision of circumvention services (**CDPA 1988**, s 296ZB).

Circumvention of technical devices relating to computer programs

Section 296 of the **CDPA 1988** deals with the circumvention of technical devices relating to computer programs separately from the circumvention of TPMs applied to other copyright works (**CDPA 1988**, ss 296ZA–ZF). The first important case in this complex area of copyright is *Sony Computer Entertainment Inc v Edmunds (2002),* which interpreted the unamended s 296. The facts of the case were that Sony produced PlayStation2 computer game consoles. CDs and DVDs made for use with the consoles carried authorisation codes. These elements of encrypted data also allowed Sony to prevent games bought from one area of distribution being used in a different region. The defendant imported a 'mod chip' (Messiah 2) which by-passed the authorisation process. The defendant argued that as the chips had legitimate uses, they had not been 'specifically designed or adapted to circumvent the form of copy-protection employed' as s 296 then provided. The court rejected this argument and it held that having other uses did not prevent a device being 'adapted to circumvent'.

The law was further developed in *Sony v Ball (2004),* which interpreted the new wording of s 296. This case was brought on the same facts, but against different resellers of the hardware. It was held that the mod chips continued to infringe Sony's copyright. Laddie J held that the 'sole intended purpose' of the Messiah 2 mod chip was to circumvent Sony's copy protection.

TPMs *and access to digital works*

There is debate as to whether TPMs will lead to excessive restrictions on access to works or even public domain materials. There are fears that TPMs have the effect of 'locking up knowledge'. Many library and documentation associations support the notion of free access to information, including digital information. Such organisations stress the importance of equality of access to the information and education in British society. For example, the novel *Pride and Prejudice* by Jane Austen is in the public domain and no longer protected by copyright. Copyright law would not prohibit free copying of this work, but a TPM would. The public domain is meant to be the global library of knowledge and with each year that passes, its catalogue increases as copyright expires and more works pass into the public domain. If TPM technology can be used to prevent access, there is a risk of perpetual monopoly rights leading to intellectual stagnation and reduced public education.

Consumers *and TPMs*

Other problems involving the use of TPMs are that they are said to reduce the functionality of copyright works, in that some forms of TPM prevent compact discs from being played on a computer. Access to digital works arises in connection with the distribution of free software, damage caused by TPMs to the overall security of a computer system, and reduced interoperability in computer systems – all of which affect consumers – are also being debated. Copyright owners employing the TPMs to protect their work from being copied still have a responsibility to properly label and use the TPMs sensibly.

Permitted acts and the s 296ZE mechanism

Section 296ZE **CDPA 1988** provides a remedy where a TPM prevents a permitted act. The section creates a mechanism for the Secretary of State to intervene where permitted acts appear to have been prejudiced. This mechanism relies on a person or personal representative of a class issuing a notice of complaint to the Secretary of State. The Secretary of State may then issue directions to the owner of the copyright work to permit access to the copyright work. However, this mechanism is an impractical method of obtaining access (which should be lawful in the first place) and it is unlikely to be used widely by the public.

Finally, the law has never granted copyright owners an absolute monopoly. The law attempts to strike a balance between granting a certain level of protection while at the same time providing a certain level of access and use. The law needs to protect the public against the use of TPMs which prevent lawful access to digital works.

Question 19

EasyTrain, a budget train company, acquired a licence to use a booking system from CisKoSystems, called 'BookIt'. EasyTrain used this for a while but eventually commissioned ComputersforIdiots, to write a similar new software booking system, called 'EnRoute'. It was important for ComputersforIdiots to produce software that created a program that looked as much like 'BookIt' as possible to assist customers with the transition. Also, existing information in the 'BookIt' database could be migrated to 'EnRoute'. Apart from one item of software called 'AllAboard', ComputersforIdiots did not have access to the 'BookIt' source code and did not decompile 'BookIt' to obtain the source code. What ComputersforIdiots did was to emulate the operation and functionality of the 'BookIt' software by carefully studying it in use to see how it behaved; what functions and operations it could perform; how it manipulated, stored and retrieved information; etc. This resulted in the 'EnRoute' program having a near identical screen layout and icons. CiskoSystems sued both EasyTrain and ComputersforIdiots for copyright infringement. Advise the parties.

Answer plan

This is a typical problem question involving non-literal copying of computer software. There appear to be two contentious issues: use of the 'AllAboard' part of CiskoSystems software, and use of the look, feel and business logic of the 'BookIt' program.

- Analysis of infringement by literal copying and *Ibcos Computers v Barclays Mercantile High Finance (1994)*; *Cantor Fitzgerald International v Tradition (UK) Ltd (2000)*;
- Analysis of infringement by non-literal copying and *Navitaire Inc v EasyJet Airline Company (2006)*;
- Defences.

Answer

The central issue is whether EasyTrain and its IT consulting firm, ComputersforIdiots, have infringed the copyright that CiskoSystems owns in its 'BookIt' software. Computer software is afforded copyright protection as a category of literary work and enjoys copyright protection under ss 1(1) and 3(1)(b) **CDPA 1988**. We will assume CiskoSystems has used a substantial degree of skill, labour and judgement in creating the 'BookIt' program and that it is an original work and not copied: *University of London Press Ltd v University Tutorial Press Ltd (1916)*.

The idea of a program to electronically manage a train fare booking system and the functions the program is to achieve are not protected by copyright law: *Whelan Associated Inc v Jaslow Dental Laboratory Inc (1987)*. Copyright law only protects the expression of the particular program including, for example, the code lines of the program, its algorithms, operational sequences, file structure and architecture once it is 'recorded in writing or otherwise' (s 3(2) **CDPA** 1998). This principle is contained in Jacob J's statement in *Ibcos Computers v Barclays Mercantile High Finance (1994)* where he explained that 'UK copyright cannot prevent the copying of a mere general idea, but can protect the copyright in detailed ideas.'

However, where there is only one way for a computer program to be expressed so as to achieve a particular technical result, this will not be protected by copyright: *Kenrick v Lawrence (1890)* cited in *John Richardson Computers Ltd v Flanders and Chemtech Ltd (1993)*. This part of the program can be freely copied.

ComputersforIdiots were tasked with producing software that had a similar look and feel to the 'BookIt' program. They had access to one piece of software, 'AllAboard', but not to the 'BookIt' source code, which was never decompiled. Decompilation is a technical process, like reverse engineering, whereby the object code is converted into a high-level language. For this to be feasible, the type and version of the high-level language must be known.

In *Ibcos Computers Ltd v Barclays Mercantile Highland Finance Ltd (1994)* Jacob J stated at p 296 that:

For infringement there must be copying. Whether there was or not is a question of fact. To prove copyright the plaintiff can normally do no more than point to bits of his work and the claimant's work which are the same and prove an opportunity of access to his work. If the resemblance is sufficiently great then the court will draw an inference of copyright. It may then be possible for the claimant to rebut the inference – to explain the similarities in some other way.

However, here the issue to be determined is more complex than mere literal copying. CiskoSystems are seeking copyright protection for the look, feel and functionality or business logic of the 'BookIt' software as against the new program 'EnRoute' that sets out to emulate it (non-literal or non-direct copying).

There can be no doubt that EasyTrain wanted the new EnRoute system, in respect of its appearance on a computer screen (user interface), to be substantially indistinguishable from the CiskoSystems software. It is also clear however, that ComputersforIdiots had no access to CiskoSystem's source code and that there had been no significant reverse-engineering of the CiskoSystem code. Accordingly there was no literal or direct copying of the CiskoSystem's code.

John Richardson Computers Ltd v Flanders (1992) was the first case in the UK to fully address the 'look and feel' of computer programs. The parties were both in the business of developing computer programs for use by pharmacists to produce labels for prescriptions and stock control. A literal comparison was not helpful as both programs had been written in different languages and bore no literal similarity. However, Ferris J found 17 objective similarities in the non-literal elements of the program.

CiskoSystems' strongest claim therefore lies in the substantial copying of its screen layout and icons. To the end user, the functions performed by both software systems looked identical on screen. In *Navitaire Inc v EasyJet Airline Company (2006)* non-literal copying of computer software was again in issue and the facts are very similar to the facts to hand. In *Navitaire* the form of screen displays and icons was held to constitute an artistic work protected by copyright, even though no source code had been copied: s 4(1)(a) **CDPA 1988**. The situation is analogous here and Ciskosystems is likely to be successful in its claim against both EasyTrain and ComputersforIdiots for copyright infringement of the EasyBook screen layout and icons.

However, this is not a satisfactory outcome for CiskoSystems because a substantial part of the value of the 'Easybook' program is unlikely to have been infringed. By studying and emulating the CiskoSystems 'BookIt' software, ComputersforIdiots have avoided the need to carry out systems analysis and to produce a function specification to create the 'EnRoute' program. It is arguable that this amounts to a degree of free riding on the skill, labour and judgment of CiskoSystems. Further, ComputersforIdiots will be able to easily redesign the EnRoute screen so that it no longer infringes the Easybook screen design.

However, according to the **Council Directive 91/250/EEC** of 14 May 1991 the law is clear that only the expression of a computer program is protected and that ideas and principles which underlie any element of a program, including those which underlie its interfaces, are not protected by copyright under this Directive. The UK case law in *Navitaire Inc v EasyJet Airline Company (2006)* applies this principle. Copyright protection of computer software clearly only covers the code which expresses a program and not the function of the software, nor its look and feel. This is a clear limitation on the legal protection afforded to computer programs.

Question 20

Discuss the decompilation right of computer programs and how it is enshrined in UK law.

Answer plan

This question requires an in-depth discussion of all aspects of the decompilation right and details of the legislative provisions that create it.

- **EU Software Directive (1991)**;
- **Copyright (Computer Programs) Regulations 1992**;
- Exception to copyright infringement;
- Background to the introduction of the decompilation right;
- What is permitted under the decompilation right?

Answer

Decompilation is a technical process, like reverse engineering, whereby the object code is converted into a high-level language. It is common practice in the software industry to reverse-engineer a computer program by converting the object code into source code. This enables the programmer to discover how the program works, and this knowledge can be used to make a new program. Usually, the aim is for the new program to be compatible with the first program – this is called decompilation for interoperability. Article 6 of the **EU Software Directive** introduced this practice as a defence against copying. Article 6 provides that decompilation is allowed where 'reproduction of the code and translation of its form are indispensable to obtain the information necessary to achieve the interoperability of an independently created computer program with other programs'.

Accordingly, the law only allows the reverse analysis decompilaton technique to be used for the purpose of achieving interoperability.

This defence, or the 'decompilation right' as it is now known, was implemented in s 50B of the the **Copyright Designs and Patents Act 1988 (CDPA 1988)** under the heading 'Computer programs: lawful users' via the **Copyright (Computer Programs) Regulations 1992 (CCPR)**.

The decompilation right in s 50B permits a lawful user of a copy of a computer program expressed in a low level language:

(a) to convert it into a version expression in a higher level language (s 50B(1)(a) **CDPA 1988**); or

(b) incidentally, in the course of converting the program, to copy it (s 50B(1)(b) **CDPA 1988**),

subject to certain conditions. The aim of the decompilation is usually to obtain interface details. For example, X may develop a new accounting software to facilitate its transactions with Bank Y. X will need to know the details of the Bank Y's various computer operating systems so that it can work in the computer's operating environment. X's new accounting program must be compatible with existing programs. This would be a lawful exercise of X's decompilation right to information concerning interfaces so that interoperability can be achieved.

According to s 50B **CDPA 1988**, the conditions that must exist for decompilation right to be exercised are: (1) that it is necessary to decompile the program to obtain the required information to create an independent program which can be operated with the program decompiled or with another program ('the permitted objective') (s 50D(2)(a) **CPDA 1988**); and (2) the information so obtained is not used for any purpose other than the permitted objective (s 50D(2)(b) **CDPA 1988**).

The decompilaton right does NOT exist:

(a) if the potential decompiler has ready access to the information needed to obtain interoperability (**CDPA 1988**, s 50D(3)(a)). For example, if the interfaces are expressed in the user manual or are available from the owner of the program on request;

(b) if the information obtained is communicated to third parties when this is not necessary to achieve interoperability (**CDPA 1988**, s 50D(3)(c));

(c) when the information obtained is used to create a computer program that is similar in its expression (**CDPA 1988**, s 50D(3)(d)).

The decompilation defence can only apply to a 'lawful user'. This is a person who has the right to use the computer program and who has obtained this right under a licence or otherwise. Licensees and their employees are clearly lawful users. It seems logical that independent consultants and all persons who need to use and eventually copy the program if they are to exercise their lawful duties (for example receivers, auditors, solicitors executing a search order). Also included are people who obtained a copy of the computer program through rental or loan. If the decompilation right is restricted by any term or condition in a licence agreement, the particular term or condition is void.

The **Copyright and Related Rights Regulations 2003** added s 50BA to **CDPA 1988,** which provides:

(1) It is not an infringement of copyright for a lawful user of a copy of a computer program to observe, study or test the function of the program in order to determine the ideas and principles which underlie any element of the program if he does so while performing any of the acts of loading, displaying, running, transmitting or storing the program which he is entitled to do.

(2) Where an act is permitted under this s, it is irrelevant whether or not there exists any term or condition in an agreement which purports to prohibit or restrict the act.

The defence of fair dealing for the purpose of non-commercial research or private study may also be relied on in defence of decompiling a program (s 29 **CDPA 1988**).

The permitted acts made possible under decompilation right must neither unreasonably prejudice the legitimate interests of the copyright owner in the first program, nor seriously harm the normal exploitation of the first program: Art 6(3) **EU Software Directive**.

The advantage of the decompilation right for the public is that it makes it possible for competitors to gain access to the technical details of an operating program, should the owner not make that information available. This in turn enhances competition enabling independent software producers to develop new software that can operate with existing software, creating more software options for the consumer. There would appear to be adequate restrictions built into the **CDPA 1988** to deal with any unlawful exercise of the right.

Question 21

Intellectual property legislation has traditionally balanced monopoly protection with user access to the protected property. The *sui generis* database right introduced by the **Database and Information Society Directive** led to fears of monopoly powers over raw data and information and erosion of the traditional balance. Is this a reasonable assessment? Discuss.

Answer

The *sui generis* database right was created because copyright was not able to protect non-original databases, which are nevertheless valuable and involve much work to create. Some form of protection was necessary to protect the work that had been invested in making the database. According to the **Copyright and Rights in Databases Regulations 1997**, reg 13(1), the new database right exists if there has been a substantial investment in obtaining, verifying, or presenting the contents of the database. This regulation creates an enforceable property right.

There are many different types of database, both electronic and non-electronic, which benefit from this protection. For example: lists of clients and their addresses, product and price lists or indeed anything that can be stored in a computer's memory, provided it is expressed in a digital form. Databases using computer programs typically have indexes, format and layout files. Many databases such as the UK Patent Office's GB esp@cenet patent database are now available online. One notable exception however, is that the database right does not apply to music compilations on CD-ROM.

The database right is similar to copyright in that a database does not need to be registered. The right subsists automatically as soon as the material that can be protected exists in a recorded form. However, the term of protection under database right is much shorter than under copyright. The database right lasts for 15 years from making but, if published during this time, then the term is 15 years from publication: reg 17, **Copyright and Rights in Databases Regulations 1997**.

The fact that a database may also be protected by copyright law does not affect the subsistence of the database right. The definition of 'database' is the same for both copyright and database right law.

Infringing acts

Where a database contains individual works of copyright, they will remain protected by copyright law. However, if a person takes more than one work, he will not only infringe the individual copyrights in those works, but may also infringe the copyright in the database as a whole and/or the database right. The repeated and systematic extraction of insubstantial parts may infringe the database right (even if the copyright in the database is not infringed).

Infringing acts are defined in reg 16 as the extraction or re-utilisation of all or a substantial part of the contents of the database without the consent of the owner. Regulation 12 defines these key terms, which are summarised below:

- 'extraction' means the permanent or temporary transfer of those contents to another medium by any means or in any form;
- 're-utilisation' means making those contents available to the public by any means; and
- 'substantial', in relation to any investment, extraction or re-utilisation, means substantial in terms of quantity, quality or a combination of both.

The first database right case to arise before an English court was *The British Horseracing Board Ltd and Ors v William Hill Organisation Ltd (2001)*. One of the main criticisms of the *sui generis* database right was that it enabled publicly available information to be protected, as the UK decision in this case appeared to confirm. The wider public issue, was that the contents of the BHB database were widely published and in the public domain, so that the finding of infringement was alarming.

The case concerned information related to horseracing that was originally contained in the BHB database, for example racehorse owners, racing colours, trainers and jockeys. BHB spent upward of £4 million per year to obtain and manage the data. Authorised third parties were licensed by BHB to use the data. Identical data subsequently emerged on the William Hill Organisation's (WHO) Internet betting service website. BHB claimed that most of the information came from its database, and WHO's use was unlicensed as they had received it indirectly from a licensed user, Satellite Information Services. BHB claimed its database right had been infringed, first, by the extraction or re-utilisation of a substantial part of the database, under Art 7(1) of the Directive, and secondly, by the repeated and systematic extraction of insubstantial parts of the contents of the database, under Art 7(5). Laddie J found in favour of BHB. WHO appealed to the Court of Appeal which requested a preliminary opinion from the European Court of Justice.

As a result of its consideration of the meaning of the terms 'investment', 'extraction and re-utilisation', 'substantial and insubstantial part' and the phrase 'repeated and systematic extraction and re-utilisation', the European Court of Justice (*Case C–203/02* 9 November 2004, unreported) imposed a substantial restriction on the potential for the subsistence of the database right, which contradicts the reason it was introduced in the first place, namely to protect the investment in making a database not otherwise able to be protected by copyright law. The Court of Appeal had to apply the ECJ's interpretation of the terms to the facts of the case: *The British Horseracing Board and Ors v William Hill Organisation (2005), CA*. The Court of Appeal held that, to the extent that the BHB database was an official list of identified names of runners and riders, it was not subject to the database right because the BHB, as governing body, was the only organisation who could produce such a list. To be protected, the database had to consist of a collection of existing independent materials. Accordingly, WHO's use did not infringe because there was no right in the database.

There is no question that substantial investment went into creating the BHB database, yet BHB failed in its claim for protection under the database right.

More recently, in *Fixtures Marketing Ltd v OPAP (2004)* the courts considered the definition of a database. It was held that it was irrelevant whether a database contains materials created by the database maker himself, or taken from other sources, nor was the fact that a database contained sporting information significant. What was important was to interpret the definition within the context of its purpose as defined in the Directive. Accordingly, protection was designed to encourage development of systems for storing and processing information. A database should therefore consist of a collection of independent materials, separable from one another without their informative value being affected. It is for this reason that a collection of audiovisual, cinematographic, literary or musical works does not fall within the definition. The requirement that the database contents be systematically arranged and individually accessible then presupposes a 'fixed base' and technical or other means to allow retrieval of independent items. The court expressed the view that football league fixture lists fell within this definition.

Although, the database right has been demonstrated to have achieved very little in terms of economic benefits for their owners, the wide scope of the database right means that concerns about the protection over a database's contents (which amounts to monopolising information) continue to exist unchanged.

CHAPTER 5

REGISTERED DESIGN AND DESIGN RIGHT

Designs play a vital role in marketing and consumer choice. Considerable resources and expense go into creating design features that provide a competitive edge in the marketplace. Many products are neither inventive nor constitute copyright works, but are marketed with features that have an artistic, aesthetic value. It is these features, either of appearance or arrangement of a commercially exploited article, which are the subject of design protection. One can therefore say that legal protection for design falls between patents and copyright. Examples of products which fall into the design sphere include jewellery, textiles, white goods, sunglasses, cars, aircraft, etc.

Traditionally, design rights have been regarded as the least important intellectual property right after copyright, patents and trade marks. However, this perception is changing. First, commercial designs are gaining considerable economic importance in the marketplace. Secondly, as a result of the implementation of new design laws, the level of legal protection afforded to designs has increased. Finally, the owners of registered design and design rights appear to be more active in enforcing their rights through the courts.

UK design law legislation is now over 200 years old. Currently, designs are protected via a combination of a system of:

- registered designs under the **Registered Designs Act 1949** (as amended); and
- the unregistered 'design right', a residual role for copyright.

Both forms of protection are governed by the **Copyright Designs and Patents Act 1988**. Community design law will not be covered separately as the principles are similar.

Question 22

The concepts of 'originality' and 'commonplace' have caused considerable difficulty in interpretation and application. It is not surprising that these two concepts have taken up a considerable amount of court time in providing guidance as to their meaning and ambit.

Discuss with reference to relevant legislation and case law.

Answer plan

This question requires a knowledge of the relevant case law to set out how two key terms of design right created by s 213 **Copyright Designs and Patents Act 1988** have been interpreted by the courts.

- Subsistence of the design right under s 213 **CDPA 1988**;
- Discussion of the terms 'original' and 'commonplace';
- *Farmer's Build Limited v Carrier Bulk Materials Handling Ltd (1999)*;
- *Baby Dan AS v Brevi SR (1999)*;
- *Dyson Ltd v Qualtex (UK) Ltd (2004)*;
- *Ocular Sciences Ltd v Aspect Vision Care Ltd (1997)*.

Answer

The **Paris Convention** and the **TRIPS Agreement** require their signatories to provide protection for industrial design, but only in general terms. In the UK, designs are protected through the system of registered designs under the **Registered Designs Act 1949** (as amended) (**RDA 1949**) and via the design right under s 213 **CDPA 1988**, with a residual role for copyright.

The historical basis for the UK's design regime began with copyright as an important source of protection; however, copyright was abused in the design field in relation to non-aesthetic designs in the motor vehicle industry: *British Leyland v Armstrong (1986)*. This led to the reform of the registered design regime in the 1980s and the introduction in 1989 of the new unregistered design right in ss 213–264 (Part III) **CDPA 1988**. The new unregistered design right protects functional designs (designs lacking eye appeal) and aesthetic designs. It was intended that the introduction of the new design right would prevent copyright protection being used in connection with industrial products in an anti-competitive way. Functional, industrial designs would no longer be protected by copyright except in very limited circumstances. 'Artistic' industrial designs could still qualify for copyright protection, but if used 'industrially', the term of protection was reduced to 25 years.

The unregistered design right is defined in s 213(1) **CDPA 1988** simply as '. . . a property right which subsists in accordance with this Part in an original design'. In particular, according to s 213(2) **CDPA 1988**, a design right will subsist in any aspect of the shape or configuration (internal or external) of the whole or part of an article, that is original. The term 'original' means original in the sense that it is not 'commonplace' in the design field in question at the time of creation: s 213(4) **CDPA 1988**. However, uncertainties arise in relation to the requirements under s 213(4) **CDPA 1988**.

The originality requirement

Originality is most likely to be an issue where the claimant's design is based on an earlier design. Alternatively, the originality in the later design relates to improvements or variations to the earlier design(s). The case law provides some insight into the courts' approach to assessing originality. *Farmer's Build Limited v Carrier Bulk Materials Handling Ltd (1999)* and *Baby Dan AS v Brevi SR (1999)* are cases where the designs in question were improvements over their own earlier designs.

In relation to the originality requirement in *Farmer's Build* it was held that a design has to be original in the sense that it is the independent work of the designer. This is akin to the requirement of originality in UK copyright law. The court set out a restrictive approach to the concept of 'commonplace', but nevertheless confirmed that it is not a test of novelty.

David Young QC (sitting as deputy judge) in *Baby Dan AS v Brevi SR (1999)* reached the conclusion that if the features giving originality represent a small change from earlier designs, the scope for infringement of any design right subsisting is likely to be narrow.

In *Dyson Ltd v Qualtex (UK) Ltd (2004)* the defendants admitted copying but sought to prove that some of Dyson's designs were not original becaue they were based on earlier Dyson designs and therefore a new design right did not subsist. Justice Mann determined that if a later design is created using skill and effort and is an interpretation of an earlier design on which it is based, it is likely to be an original design in which UK design right can subsist. He qualified this by stating that a design is unlikely to be original where the skill and effort really is in reproducing, in the 'tracing' sense of copyright, the previous design and making minor modifications which are not visually significant.

Design must not be 'commonplace'

A design which is original in the 'copyright sense' as referred to above, may nevertheless still lack originality for UK design right purposes if the design is commonplace: s 213(4) **CDPA 1988**. However, there is no legal definition of 'commonplace'. Its meaning is imprecise, vague and ambiguous.

It is important to remember that an original design may only be an 'aspect' of the whole of an article or part of an article. It is that particular aspect which must be assessed for originality and whether or not it is 'commonplace'. If the aspect is commonplace, then no UK design right will subsist.

Farmer's Build (1999) is the leading authority as to the meaning of 'commonplace'.

Mummery LJ stated that the concept 'commonplace' in s 213(4) **CDPA 1988** should be construed narrowly rather than broadly. He reasoned that many designs of functional articles that fall within the definition of a 'design' are likely to be 'commonplace' if that term is construed broadly in the sense of 'well known'. In his judgment, Mummery LJ quoted from the Parliamentary debate on the Bill that introduced the design right and noted that it was Parliament's intention to avoid giving design right to 'mundane, routine designs of the kind which are common currency in the particular field in question'.

Other relevant case law enables us to further clarify the meaning of 'not commonplace'. For example, in *Ocular Sciences Ltd v Aspect Vision Care Ltd (1997)* Laddie J stated that 'the flavour of the word [commonplace] is along the lines . . . any design which is trite, trivial, common-or-garden, hackneyed or of the type which would excite no peculiar attention in those in the relevant art is likely to be commonplace . . .'. In *Dyson Ltd v Qualtex* it was held that the term 'commonplace' did not depend on marketing in the UK. The court explained that the design must be commonplace in the UK in the sense that UK designers in the field would have to be aware of the design to an extent sufficient to make it commonplace if the statutory exemption is to operate.

When carrying out a practical analysis in the *Farmer's Build (1999)* case to determine whether or not the particular design of an article was commonplace, Mummery LJ adopted the following approach. The first step is to determine if the design is taken from or copied from an earlier article. Step two involves a comparison of the claimant's design with the designs of other contemporaneous articles in the same field (including any infringing article) in an objective manner in light of all the evidence in order to confirm any similarities. Has the claimant's design been copied from any other design in the design field? If it has not been copied, then the claimant's design is original. Step three is to consider if the claimant's design is 'commonplace'. This comparative exercise is one of fact and degree. It is common sense that the closer the similarity of the design features, the more likely it is that the design is commonplace and therefore not original. If aspects of the claimant's design are only to be found in the defendant's design (and not vice versa), the court may rule that the claimant's design is original.

In conclusion, design owners who want to enforce their UK design right are advised to highlight the aspects of their designs which are unique or seen only in few other designs by reference to evidence of the design field in question. Designs that are commonplace, so well-known, ordinary or routine will not acquire design right.

Question 23

The British fashion house Emerald Eyes has a highly respected 'creative' team that spent six months producing its range of 'Glitter' leather shoes. In particular, its

4-inch heel 'Emeraldina' shoes (which retail at over £1000) have been phenomenally successful and there is a long waiting list. All the shoes are made by hand using the finest calf leather in Emerald Eye's atelier in London. Each pair takes a skilled shoemaker over 30 hours to make. Green coloured Swarovski crystals are glued to the shoe leather in a diamond pattern on the toes of each shoe.

On 5 January 2006, Emerald Eyes discovered that the UK supermarket TEES-COO was carrying a pair of very similar shoes which sell for £35 a pair. The TEESCOO shoes have received substantial press in the tabloids and are the latest 'must have' bargain among fashionistas. Cheaper plastic crystal shapes are glued in a diamond pattern on the toes of the shoes. Emerald Eyes is enraged, but realises that only successful products are copied. Emerald Eyes' board of directors wishes to issue proceedings against TEESCOO over the alleged copying of its 'Emeraldina' shoes.

Unfortunately, Emerald Eyes did not register any intellectual property rights in the Emeraldina shoes so they are uncertain whether they have a cause of action against TEESCOO.

Advise Emerald Eyes as to any rights they may have against TEESCOO, what remedies have been successful in court, or any other advice you can offer that is relevant to Emerald Eyes' predicament.

Answer plan

Problem questions on designs often focus on registrability and infringement.

This problem requires a practical problem-solving approach to assessing the merits of Emerald Eyes' right to stop TEESCOO from copying, together with a consideration of any remedies that will be available.

- Subsistence of a unregistered design right in the Emeraldina shoes: s 213 **CDPA 1988**;
- Infringement of the design right;
- Surface decoration: s 213(c)(2) **CDPA 1988**;
- *Lambretta Clothing Co Ltd v Teddy Smith (UK) Ltd (2005)*.

Answer

Even though Emerald Eyes has not registered the Emerald Eyes shoe design, it may nevertheless be able to rely on the unregistered design right to stop TEESCOO from infringing the design. Section 213(2) **CDPA 1988** defines a 'design' as any aspect of the shape or configuration (internal or external) of the whole or part of an article. To qualify for protection the Emerald Eyes shoe design must have been recorded in a design document(s) dated after 1 August 1989 and be original, not be subject to exclusion and qualify for protection under s 213(5) **CDPA 1988**. To fulfil the requirement for originality, three requirements must be met:

- the design must not be commonplace in the field of design in question (s 213(4));
- it must originate with the designer (here the creative team collectively); and
- it must not have been copied.

It the above requirements are fulfilled, an unregistered design right will subsist automatically in the Emerald Eyes shoe design. The analysis as to whether or not design right subsists in the shoe design is a complex exercise. First, it involves an understanding of the definition of design. Secondly, one must assess the many possible combinations of features of the whole design which could each constitute the design, and in each of which design right may subsist. In respect of the possible designs, an assessment will need to be made as to the originality and, in particular, whether or not any of the designs are commonplace. UK design right can, therefore, potentially subsist in a number of possible designs, being a combination of the aspects of the shape and configuration of an article created by the 'creative team' using skill and effort, and which are not commonplace. Once this has been ascertained, one must assess whether the design right is excluded by reference to the statutory exclusions.

Statutory exclusions and surface decoration

Design right does not subsist in a method or principle of construction: s 213(3)(a) **CDPA 1988**. A design is excluded if it is a 'must fit' or 'must match' feature of shape or configuration (s 213(3)(b)(i) and (ii) **CDPA 1988**, respectively). Nor will design right subsist in surface decoration: s 213(3)(c) **CDPA 1988**. The Swarovski crystals applied in a diamond pattern on the toe of the Emeraldina shoes are clearly a form of three-dimensional surface decoration which is excluded from design right protection under s 213(3)(c) **CDPA 1988**. In *Mark Wilkinson Furniture v Woodcraft Designs (1998)* Parker J held that 'cock beading' was surface decoration, and excluded from protection. More recently, the Court of Appeal in *Lambretta Clothing Co Ltd v Teddy Smith (UK) Ltd (2004)* decided that the pattern of colours applied to a garment was surface decoration.

Given that the Emeraldina shoe design is said to have been produced by a highly regarded 'creative' team that spent six months working on the design, in the absence of further details, we will assume that the remaining aspects of the design will qualify for design right protection. However, it would be helpful if Emerald Eyes could produce a design document that is dated to assist it to prove that it was the first creator of the design. What is protected is the shoe design itself and not the substrate on which it is recorded, or to which it is first applied. Emerald Eye's design right will subsist for 15 years from the date on which the design is recorded or an article is made to the design.

Who owns the design right?

The next issue to consider is who owns the design right and as such, who has enforcement rights. A design right is a property right owned by the person who is the designer: s 215 **CDPA 1988**. Here a 'creative team' developed the Emeraldina design. They are probably all employees of Emerald Eyes so it will own the design by virtue of the express or implied terms of the employees' contracts of employment. However, if any of the members of the creative team are consultants or contractors, or the shoe design was commissioned, Emerald Eyes should ensure that the designers have assigned their rights to Emerald Eyes in return for good consideration.

Assuming that Emerald Eyes owns the design right in the shoe design, as the owner Emerald Eyes has certain rights to prevent unauthorised activities. Under s 226(1) **CDPA 1988**, Emerald Eyes has the exclusive right of reproducing the Emeraldina shoe design by making articles to that design for commercial purposes. 'Commercial purposes' are defined by s 263(3) as things done with respect to the article to be sold or hired in the course of business. Here TEESCOO is selling similar shoes to the Emeraldina design for £35 a pair and this is a purely commercial venture. If it is established that the Emeraldina design has been copied, this will amount to primary infringement, as it is done without a licence. However, if TEESCOOS is not making the infringing copies but dealing in infringing articles by selling them in a retail store, it will be guilty of secondary infringement where it knows or has reason to believe that the shoes infringe the Emeraldina design (s 227(1)).

Has TEESCOO copied the Emeraldina shoe design?

It is a requirement that copying is established before infringement can be proved. It is not true, as Emerald Eyes' Board of Directors has suggested, that 'what is worth copying is worth protecting', according to Laddie J's decision in *BBC Worldwide Ltd v Pally Screen Ltd (1998)* (the 'Teletubbies' case). The court must decide whether TEESCOO's allegedly infringing article is made exactly or substantially to the Emeraldina design.

Section 226 **CDPA 1988** requires a claimant to establish copyright or copying of a substantial part. Infringement is judged in terms of the entirety of the article, not just by confiding attention to the corresponding parts. On this basis, Emerald Eyes should be advised that it has a prima facie cause of action against TEESCOO for design right infringement under the **CDPA 1988**.

In the alternative, an action may lie in passing off if Emerald Eyes can prove that goodwill attaches to its Emeraldina shoe design. It is possible for shapes and colours to be protected by way of passing off: *Reckitt and Colman v Borden Inc (1990)*; *William Edge & Sons Ltd v William Nichols & Sons Ltd (1911)*. However, an action in passing off is unpredictable and it will be necessary to show that Emerald Eyes has goodwill in the appearance of the goods. If the goods are extremely distinctive and well-known, as is suggested on the facts, a claim may succeed.

Remedies

It would be practical to advise Emerald Eyes to consider settling the dispute by requesting TEESCOO to enter into a mutually beneficial licensing agreement. This would enable Emerald Eyes to profit from the past and future sales of its Emeraldina shoe design. However, if a licensing agreement is unlikely, then Emerald Eyes has a range of avenues open to it in terms of remedies. It should first apply for an interim injunction requiring TEESCOOS to immediately refrain from selling infringing copies of the shoes: s 229(2) **CDPA 1988**. Once the action has been heard, if judgment is in favour of Emerald Eyes it has the option of either an award of damages or an account of profits in respect of the design right infringement under s 229 (2) **CDPA 1988**. Where the rightholder has a choice of damages or account of profits, s/he should make an informed choice: *Island Records Ltd v Tring International plc (1995)*. Emerald Eyes could also apply for an order requiring TEESCOOS to deliver up any remaining infringing copies in its possession (s 230 **CDPA 1988**) or an order for disposal (s 231 **CDPA 1988**)

In terms of advice for the future, Emerald Eyes should consider implementing a policy to actively consider whether it is commercially sensible to register its designs under the **Registered Designs Act 1949** or continue to rely on the design right in s 213 **CDPA 1988**. Under s 1(3) of the **Registered Designs Act 1949** a product is defined to include a handicraft item; as the shoes are made by hand, the relevant aspects of the design could be registered and enjoy protection for a period of 25 years instead of just 15 years under design right.

Question 24

Critically analyse the key changes to the UK law of registered designs following the reforms to the regime in 2001 and 2006.

Answer plan

The essay question anticipates a discussion of the pros and cons of the reforms to design law.

- 2001 reforms implementing the **Directive on the Legal Protection of Designs (Directive 98/71/EC)**;
- Wider scope of designs that are protected;
- 12-month grace period introduced;
- New infringement provisions;

- Stricter novelty requirement.
- Regulatory Reform (Registered Designs) Order 2006.

Answer

The **Registered Designs Act 1949 (RDA 1949)** has been substantially amended since it was first passed, although the basic rationale for the system remains the same. The fact that British designers have traditionally been less likely to register and protect their designs compared to designers in other EU countries such as France and Germany and the recent theme of deregulation and harmonisation among EU member states on the legal protection of designs has prompted a review of the whole UK registered design system. Accordingly, the idea behind the more recent reforms is to make it easier to protect new designs and encourage innovation in the design field.

The 2001 Reforms

The first raft of reforms occurred in 2001 in order to implement the **Directive on the Legal Protection of Designs (Directive 98/71/EC)**. The aim of the Directive is to harmonise the laws of EU member states and to lead to further Community design harmonisation.

Registered design owners have benefited from the 2001 reforms in several respects. First, there has been an increase in the type of things that are registrable under the **Registered Designs Act 1949 (RDA 1949)**. For example, graphic symbols are now registrable (s 1(3) **RDA 1949**), although earlier trade marks cannot be registered as designs. Secondly, a 12-month grace period was introduced by s 1B(6)(d) **RDA 1949**. Thirdly, the provisions relating to infringement have been amended to the advantage of the design owner. Fourthly, the UK Patent Office has confirmed that it will continue its previous practice of not examining applications with reference to prior art. This makes registration a very streamlined process. The fact that these changes and practices directly benefit the owners of registered designs has had a positive effect on the attractiveness of registered design protection since 2001. As a consequence, the registered design system is increasingly being relied on by enterprises to protect the intellectual property in their designs.

Novelty

However, a more stringent definition of novelty has been introduced which demonstrates that the 2001 reforms have implemented stricter registration requirements. In particular, s 1B of the **RDA 1949** provides that 'a design is new if no identical design or those differing only in immaterial details has been made available to the public before the relevant date' of the application for the registered design.

The first aspect of the definition of novelty should be relatively easy to apply in practice in that it should not be difficult to judge whether design application is identical or not to previously disclosed designs. However, a more difficult question will be to assess the extent of any 'immaterial details' and whether, in a particular case, design differences are enough to make a design whose validity is being challenged sufficiently different and therefore not identical to any prior art designs.

Further, the novelty rule amounts to a qualified form of worldwide novelty (s 1(B)(5) and (6)). A design is novel where, at the application date, it could not have been known to commercial persons in the European Economic Area, specialising in the relevant design field. This is subject to a 12-month grace period (s 1B(6)(d) **RDA 1949**).

The 2006 Reforms

An additional wave of new rules were introduced on 1 October 2006, when the UK designs registration system changed with the coming into force of the **Regulatory Reform (Registered Designs) Order 2006**, the **Registered Designs Rules 2006** and **the Registered Designs (Fees) Rules 2006**.

The key change is that the examination process will be simplified with the cessation of novelty examination and the examine will not compare a design with the prior art. This means that there will be no examination of new applications on the grounds of novelty and individual character. This will bring the UK system into line with the system used for the registration of Community-wide designs.

Applicants for registered designs are now able to use a new multiple application form which will be quicker and cheaper than making single applications. This change will remove the administrative burden and costs on those who need to apply to register a number of new designs at the same time.

There will be no ability to withhold some classes registered designs from public inspection. In the past some classes of designs were registered but unavailable for public inspection for a period of two or three years. Instead, the new rules allow all applicants to delay the publication of and registration of their design for up to 12 months if they so wish. The purpose of the 12-month grace period is to enable official publication of the registered design to coincide with the product launch and reduce the risk that the design will be copied before it is marketed by the designer.

The final significant change to the registered design regime is that there is a new consequence for not filing – a counterstatement has been introduced, namely that the registrar may treat the registered design owner as not opposing the application. The counterstatement must state which allegations are denied or admitted, and which allegations the registered proprietor requires the applicant to prove.

In conclusion, the changes to the UK registered design regime over the past five years have, on the whole, made registering and protecting new designs less complicated. This should increase the number of registered design applications sought by British designers, further supporting innovation in the design field.

Question 25

Compare and contrast the protection afforded by the design right under the **Copyright Designs and Patents Act 1988** with the protection provided to designs registered under the **Registered Designs Act 1949**.

Answer

Designers have to make a commercial decision as to whether to (1) register a design and achieve monopoly protection or (2) rely on their automatic 'design right', which will enable them only to prevent others from copying.

Duration of protection

A design may be registered under the **Registered Designs Act 1949 (RDA 1949)** and enjoy monopoly protection for a period of 25 years from the application date. Alternatively, a design right will arise automatically, provided the relevant requirements under s 213 **CDPA 1988** are met. No registration is required and consequently, this is the cheaper and easiest option. However, a design right is not a monopoly right but an exclusive right to prevent copying. The design right only provides 15 years of protection from the end of the calendar year first recorded in a design document or first made, or, if design is made available for sale or hire within five years of the above starting point, 10 years' protection from the end of the calendar year that first occurred. A licence of right is available for the last five years of protection to enable third parties to use the design with authorisation. It is clear that the design right is a lesser right than a registered design, but it is a very practical and economical option for designers.

Nature of the protection

However, the registered design and the design right do not protect exactly the same things. The registered design protects the overall appearance of the design, excluding features dictated by technical function. On the other hand, the design right only protects three-dimensional aspects of design, excluding surface ornamentation. The design right protects both functional and aesthetic aspects of the design.

83

Originality requirement

There are also differences in the way in which 'originality' is assessed. A registered design must be new (that is not identical to any existing design) and the design must also have individual character. A design protected by the automatic design right must also be original in the sense that it is not copied from an existing design and further, it must not be commonplace.

Enforcement

Whereas, with the design right, the owner must prove that the design was directly copied in order to enforce their rights, the clear benefit of owning a registered design is that when dealing with infringers, there is no need to prove the design was directly copied in order to enforce rights. Further, the design right owner must also keep documentary records to prove the date on which the design right was created. This burdern can outweight the cost of registering a design, provided that the design meets the criteria for registration.

Costs

The cost to register a design is reasonable, but whatever the cost it will always be more that the automatic design right, which does not cost anything at all.

Protection abroad

A key consideration is that the owner of a registered design in the UK can extend protection for the particular design to certain foreign countries, mostly members of the Commonwealth. Reciprocal protection for a design reliant on the design right is only available in a limited number of territories.

The owner of a commercially valuable design must carefully assess whether relying on the design right under the **CDPA 1988** provides a sufficient degree of protection. If not, then the best path is to apply to register the design. Design registration gives the design owner a monopoly on their product design and is additional to any design right or copyright protection that may exist automatically in the design. The registered design owner will then be in a position to grant others permission (licence) to use their design.

CHAPTER 6

PATENTS

The patent law system recognises that innovation and technological developments, both crucial tools for a country's financial and social wealth, cannot be motivated solely by market competition. The basic requirements for a patent to be registered in the UK are that it:

- be novel (new);
- possess an inventive step (non-obviousness);
- be capable of industrial application;
- not be excluded for being 'unpatentable' subject-matter.

If an application does not satisfy these conditions, a patent will not be granted by the UK Patent Office.

Patents are territorial rights and to date there is no such thing as an 'international patent'. However, administrative procedures for filing patents in multiple international jurisdictions have been streamlined and there are moves to attempt to harmonise the patent system at a European Union level.

A new **Patents Act 2004** has been passed which amends the **Patents Act 1977** in certain respects. Further, the Gower's Report on Intellectual Property was released in 2006 which confirms that the current UK system is generally 'fit for purpose', although the report contains many recommendations for improvement.

Patent law covers a large volume of fascinating material and it is hoped that the selection of questions and answers that follow map on to the topics contained in the undergraduate patent law syllabus.

Question 26

Frank Fysch, a keen fisherman and inventor (in his spare time) from the East Midlands, consults you regarding his latest invention, a new type of reel release mechanism to be used with a standard fishing rod.

Frank sold his rights to a previous invention to an international company for a flat fee of £20,000 but feels he didn't get as much as he could have for it because he sold after having produced a working prototype. The company has since gone on to sell thousands and made substantial profits from his earlier invention.

This time around, Frank, who feels he has established his reputation as an inventor in the field, wishes to apply for a patent in the UK and offer it to several companies to bid on. In doing this, he hopes to achieve a higher up-front fee for licensing his invention, as well as future royalties.

Advise Frank as to the patentability of his reel release mechanism and the steps involved in the patenting process.

Answer plan

This is a very practical problem requiring the student to be broadly familiar with the key aspects of the UK's patent law system and a fundamental aspect of the US patent law system.

- Patentability of the fishing reel mechanism (a mechanical device) and the four conditions for filing a patent set out in s 1(1) **Patents Act 1977 (PA 1977)**;
- The patent application routes;
- The concept of absolute novelty and confidentiality prior to patent application;
- The novelty test and the state of the art;
- Inventive step s 3 **PA 1977** and the *Windsurfer* test (*Windsurfing International Inc v Tabur Marine (1985)*);
- The procedural process for filing a patent application.

Answer

Frank Fysch can apply for a patent to protect his new rod release mechanism (a mechanical device) if certain legal requirements are met. Under the **Patents Act 1977** there is no definition of an invention. However, certain requirements must be met for a UK patent to be granted. The requirements for obtaining a grant of a UK patent are now applicable in most of the important countries in the world due to the effects of various international conventions, especially the **Patent Co-operation Treaty (PCT) 1970**. The exception is the United States.

In order to determine *who* is entitled to a patent it is necessary to institute a reference in time which will establish precedence by one inventor over another in case two or more inventors create the same invention. The two traditional references in time presently applicable in different jurisdictions are:

(i) the date of filing, in the so-called 'first-to-file system' as used in the UK; and

(ii) the date in which an invention is first reduced to practice, in the so-called 'first-to-invent system' used in the US.

Each system is said to have its own advantages in that the former provides certainty of ownership, whereas the latter ensures that the true inventor is rewarded with monopoly rights.

As a patent is a territorial right, Frank should apply for protection in both the UK and the US. He has two options: (1) file separate national applications with each of the UK and US patent offices respectively; or (2) as both countries are signatories to the **Patent Cooperation Treaty 1970**, he could opt for this route, which offers an international patent filing system to expedite the application process for registering patents in PCT member states. The second option is particularly attractive if Frank later wishes to file in any further countries. For the purpose of this answer we will focus on a UK national filing through the UK Patent Office.

Frank's UK patent application must comply with certain administrative formalities as well as meeting the requirements for a patentable invention. There are four key legal, rather than administrative, requirements to be satisfied to conclude that a patentable invention exists in the new rod reel mechanism and before Frank will be granted a UK patent. The invention must:

(1) be novel: s 2 **PA** 1977;

(2) involve an inventive step: s 3 **PA** 1977. In other words, the invention must be a technical advance over existing technological understanding ('the state of the art') which is not obvious;

(3) be capable of industrial application: s 4 **PA** 1977;

(4) not be excluded by law from being patented: s 1(3) **PA** 1977 (for example not a method of treating the human and animal body; not a plant or animal variety, nor be contrary to public policy or morality).

These legal requirements cannot be understood without first being aware of three other fundamental concepts in patent law. These are the concepts of:

(1) the priority date of the patent;

(2) prior art; and

(3) the person skilled in the art, sometimes referred to as the 'man skilled in the art' or 'the skilled man'.

A knowledge of these concepts is necessary to understand the process by which patents are granted and to appreciate how a patent might be attacked as being invalid. The classic defence to a patent infringement claim is to show that the patent is invalid.

The priority date of the patent application is the date on which it is tested against the 'state of the art': s 5(1) **PA 1977**. This is normally the filing date of the application (unless an earlier date is claimed in the UK Patent Office, European Patent Office, or Paris Convention country).

The prior art or state of the art is defined in s 2(2) **PA 1977** as comprising all matter made available to the public before the priority date of the invention. This includes all knowledge anywhere in the world on the subject matter of the invention. Novelty-destroying prior art could include information that is part of common general knowledge, information disclosed by an earlier user of the invention, information disclosed in a single copy of a published document or by oral communication. Frank must ensure that he keeps the new reel mechanism absolutely confidential until he files a patent application. Only then will he be able to freely disclose his invention to the international companies and others (unless the companies agree to sign strongly drafted non-disclosure agreements).

Inventive step is a very different question to that of novelty and involves a qualitative assessment of the invention by reference to the 'skilled man'. The new reel mechanism should not be obvious to a person skilled in the art, having regard to all matters forming part of the state of the art at the priority date of the patent: s 3 **PA 1977**. In deciding whether Frank's invention is obvious, the test in *Windsurfing International Inc v Tabur Marine (1985)* as modified by *PLG Research Ltd v Ardon International Ltd (1995)* can be applied:

(1) Identify the inventive step or concept.

(2) At the priority date, what was the state of the art relevant to that step?

(3) Identify the differences between the invention and the state of the art.

(4) Do the differences constitute steps which would have been obvious to the skilled man, or is there a degree of inventiveness?

In applying the *Windsurfer* test the scope of the state of the art is narrower for inventive step than it is for novelty (s 3 **PA 1977**) because earlier patent applications do not form part of the state of the art.

Finally, Frank's application must be capable of industrial application: s 4(1) **PA 1977**. This should not be a problem because the new reel mechanism clearly produces some tangible and physical consequence. In *Chiron v Murex Diagnostics (1996)* Morritt LJ at 178 stated that 'the section requires that the invention can be made or used "in any kind of industry" so as to be "capable" or "susceptible of industrial application" '. The connotation is that of trade or manufacture in its widest sense and whether or not for profit.

Assuming that Frank's invention meets the four legal requirements, he should feel confident about filing his application with the UK Patent Office. The procedural steps will involve the following:

1. Completing the Patent Form 1/77. The patent application must contain a

specification containing a description of the invention, as well as a claim for the patent and any drawing referred to in the description or the claim as well as an abstract.

2. Filing (s 5(1) **PA** 1977).

3. Preliminary examination and limited search (s 17 **PA** 1977) within 12 months from filing date. The application is referred to a patent examiner for a preliminary examination and search to ensure that the application complies with the Acts requirements.

4. Publication (s 16(1) **PA** 1977) by Patent Office in the Official Journal (Patents) allowing public inspection of the claims. Publication of the patent application can give rise to third-party objections to the grant of the patent.

5. Substantial examination and search within six months after publication, requested by applicant.

6. Grant – comptroller must publish notice in the Official Journal of Patents; Certificate issued to the applicant.

7. Monopoly lasting 20 years for patent proprietor.

Question 27

Discuss the key advantages and disadvantages of patenting an invention under the **Patents Act** 1977.

Answer plan

This question encourages the student to carry out an objective evaluation of the advantages and disadvantages of patenting, drawing on all aspects of the patent law system, but using only relevant material. Never start an essay with the phrase, 'In this essay I am going to . . .'. The marker knows what you need to do. The sooner your writing focuses on the question, the more marks you will attract. One of the most common and useful beginnings to a patent law essay is to start with an explanation of what a patent does.

- Compile a list of advantages and discuss them in a logical order.

- Similarly, compile a list of disadvantages and discuss them in a logical order.

- Concluding remarks.

Answer

Patents protect new, industrially applicable inventions and give the inventor or proprietor (the 'patentee') a legally recognised monopoly to work the invention for a period of up to 20 years. There are both advantages and disadvantages to patent protection, as the procedure for obtaining a granted patent is costly, lengthy and complex. It is important to consider the pros and cons before either publishing the invention or applying for the patent.

Advantages of patent protection

The key advantage of filing a patent is that a patent monopoly is granted for a firm duration of 20 years and can prevent unauthorised third parties from using the invention during that period. While under monopoly protection, the **Patent Act 1977** provides that only the patentee is lawfully allowed to commercially exploit the invention through manufacturing and licensing. The scope of that right in any particular case is determined by the claims in the patent specification. This usually includes reverse-engineering, since a valid patent protects the ideas and information in the way described in the patent's claims and using such information obtained via reverse-engineering in the ways described in the patent claims will infringe the patent. The patentee is even protected against someone who subsequently creates the same invention entirely through his or her own efforts.

Other advantages of obtaining a granted patent include:

(1) The fact that the patentee has the ability to file for protection in other jurisdictions using the original priority date.

(2) Once the patent application is filed, the information contained in it can be freely disclosed without loss of proprietary rights.

(3) The subject-matter susceptible to patent protection has expanded.

(4) A patent is a form of property that can be licensed to generate royalties and future income.

(5) Once granted, the patent owner can sue for patent infringement dating back to the priority date.

(6) There is no legal requirement to file for a patent and an inventor could decide to keep the invention secret.

(7) The decision to file a patent application is not irrevocable, it may be withdrawn at any time before publication by the Patent Office.

Disadvantages of patenting

On the other hand, the key disadvantage of filing a patent is that the patentee, in return for patent protection, must consent to publication of the details of the new invention. This means that third parties can 'invent around' or improve on the invention. Other significant disadvantages include:

(1) The costs and length of time to secure a patent which on average, takes over three years.

(2) The fact that the patent provides a mere 20-year monopoly, after which anyone may exploit the invention.

(3) Patent protection is territorial and will only cover the UK, although patents may, if certain requirements are met, be filed in other countries for an additional cost via the **European Patent Convention (EPC)** and **Patent Cooperation Treaty (PCT)** routes. The patent application may need to be translated if filed in other jurisdictions, further adding to the costs involved. If the **EPC** or **PCT** route is used, the patent application will still need to undergo a national phase in each designated country.

(4) Given the importance of the claims determining the scope of the patent monopoly, a patent specification should be prepared by a patent attorney or a person familiar with the state of the art of the invention and the patent process, again increasing the cost of the patent process.

(5) Disclosures by others can ruin novelty. Nothing can be done if someone else engaged in similar research makes the invention public before a patentee applies for a patent.

(6) Even once the patent has been granted, opposition proceedings may be started. This means that the patent can be challenged and possibly revoked.

(7) The patentee must pay ever higher fees to continue to renew the patent until the 20-year monopoly has expired.

(8) Although not required for legal protection, the patented invention should be marked with the granted patent number as a deterrent for potential infringers.

(9) Unless the patent owner reserves its rights, once a patent product has been sold, the purchaser has an implied right to sell that product to anyone in the world, who in turn has the same right. This can cause problems for patentees who want to control commercial export and import of their products.

In conclusion, while there are certainly several disadvantages to the patent law system, the UK Patent Office reports steadily increasing levels of patent application activity. Indeed, patent activity is mushrooming across virtually every sector of the UK economy as patentees seek to gain a proprietary market advantage, an exclusive hold over a new technology. Registered patent rights have also seen a boom in revenues derived from patent licensing and have served as a hidden motive behind a number of the biggest corporate mergers in the last decade. It is not just the UK economy that is affected by these trends, patent activity is on the rise worldwide, spurred in part by the World Trade Organisation's **Agreement on Trade-Related Aspects of Intellectual Property Rights (TRIPS)**. Concerns have been raised about the recent trends in patent activity – the patenting of biotechnological inventions, business methods and databases – and that these may actually stifle academic freedom, scientific inquiry and technological innovation. However, there is little doubt, as evidenced by dozens of studies by economists and most recently Gower's *Review of Intellectual Property*, published in December 2006, that the patent system is, on balance, an effective instrument for fostering innovation and technology diffusion.

Question 28

Are patents necessary as incentives for the development of new inventions, for example, in relation to medical methods?

Answer plan

Although this question appears to focus on patents and the exclusion of medical methods from patentability as well as novel new uses, the underlying theme the student will need to ensure is covered relates to the 'reward for innovation' theory.

- Discuss the requirements for patentability, and the medical method exclusion in s 4A **Patents Act 1977**.
- Explain the methods of treatment, for example surgery, therapy and diagnosis.
- Consider the types of medical methods that are not excluded from patentability.
- First and second medical use.
- 'Reward for innovation' theory.

Answer

Patents are monopoly rights. However, there is a widely held view that patent protection or patent monopolies are inappropriate for the medical field and in particular for medical methods. Consequently, some areas of medical invention such as methods of treatment, surgery, therapy and diagnosis have been removed from patentability. Indeed, Art 2(3) of the *Agreement on Trade Related Aspects of Intellectual Property 1994 (TRIPS)* allows members to exclude from patentability methods of medical treatment on humans and animals. The *European Patent Convention 2000 (EPC)* incorporates the exclusion of medical methods in Art 53 on public policy grounds. These medical methods are now excluded from patentability under s 4A of the **Patents Act 1977** (recently amended by the *Patents Act 2004*), which states:

(1) A patent shall not be granted for the invention of –
   (a) a method of treatment of the human or animal body by surgery or therapy; or
   (b) a method of diagnosis practised on the human or animal body.

The exclusion of methods of treatment and diagnosis reflects the concern to ensure that such methods can be freely disseminated by the medical profession in the public interest: *Schering and Wyeth's Application (1985)*.

In *Shell/Blood Flow (1993)* 'treatment' was defined as any non-insignificant intentional physical or psychic intervention performed directly or indirectly by one human being on another using means of medical science. In the same case, 'surgery' was defined as 'medicine concerned with the healing of disease, accidental injury or bodily defects by operating on the living body. This includes both conservative (non-invasive) procedures and operative (invasive) procedures using instruments.

The decision in *Unilever (Davis's) Application (1983)* confirmed that both pre-ventative and curative treatments fell within the meaning of 'therapy' and are therefore excluded.

However, a method of contraception, for example, was allowed in *Schering's Application (1971)*, as contraception did not amount to the treatment of disease. A method of treatment for lice infestation was held to be patentable in *Stafford-Miller's Application (1984)*, because it was regarded as a treatment for lice rather than a treatment for a disease. In contrast, a method of abortion was refused a patent in *Upjohn's Application (1976)*.

The exclusion is only for methods of treatment; the **Patents Act 1997** does not exclude:

• medical device claims for medical hardware provided they meet the usual criteria of novelty, inventive step and industrial applicability;
• substance claims, for example for pharmaceuticals; or
• claims for medical uses for known substances (this was a special concession with regard to novelty and was the result of lobbying by the drug industry).

This shows that although there are some restrictions on the patentability of medical methods in the public interest, the **Patents Act 1977** nevertheless allows for a wide degree of patentability. In the recent past, where doubts arose as to the patentability of an invention involving a method of treatment, claims were made in the form of a 'Swiss' claim, developed in the Swiss Patent Office. The Swiss claim extends to second medical uses of known medical substances and covers the method for making a known substance for a new use. Swiss claims were controversial, because it was argued that novelty in the invention is lacking, but nevertheless, they are applied in the UK.

Now however, as a result of reforms contained in the **Patents Act 2004**, s 4A **PA 1977** is amended to provide:

(1) Subs (1) above does not apply to an invention consisting of a substance or composition for use in any such method.

(2) In the case of an invention consisting of a substance or composition for use in any such method, the fact that the substance or composition forms part of the state of the art shall not prevent the invention from being taken to be new if the use of the substance or composition in any such method does not form part of the state of the art.

(3) In the case of an invention consisting of a substance or composition for a specific use in any such method, the fact that the substance or composition forms part of the state of the art shall not prevent the invention from being taken to be new if that specific use does not form part of the state of the art.

Methods of medical treatment nonetheless involve substantial work, financial investment and time to develop and turn into something practical and successful. Without the incentive of a patent monopoly, people may not do that work or spend the time and money developing medical methods of treatment. One could argue that the courts' role is not to uphold any claim to a monopoly for an idea which requires investment and risk to bring to market, only for those ideas which are new, non-obvious and enabled as required by the **Patent Act 1977**.

The medical industry is predicted to continue its impressive growth as the population enjoys greater longevity and innovation stimulates demand for new medical treatments. Patents are critical to investment in such innovation, especially where lead-times to market are long. The medical field of patents has its own set of exclusions from patentability for reasons of policy and ethics. But it is clear that the boundaries of patentability in relation to medical methods will continue to be tested and the extent of patentable subject matter is likely to continue to expand.

Question 29

Do morality and public policy have a role to play in the patent system? Critically discuss with reference, in particular, to biotechnological inventions and the relevant UK and EU jurisprudence and legislation.

Answer plan

This is an essay question that could potentially be answered in a wide range of ways and the topic can generate very strong views. Nevertheless, students should be wary of writing an answer with 'too much opinion, and not enough law'. It is difficult to be prescriptive as to how one might approach an analysis of the European Patent Office jurisprudence on the issues of morality and public policy, as so much depends on the individual's opinion. However, the main emphasis should be on analysis of the jurisprudence on morality and public policy. For a complete answer, discuss aspects of the following:

- s 1(3) **Patent Act 1977**;
- biotechnological inventions and the development of patent law;
- *Harvard/OncoMouse* litigation and the utilitarian balancing exercise;
- Art 53(a) of the **European Patent Convention**;
- Sched A2 **Patent Act 1977**.

Answer

Section 1(3) of the **Patents Act 1977 (PA 1977)** provides that where the commercial exploitation of an invention is contrary to public policy or morality, the invention is unpatentable, so morality clearly has *some* role to play in the patent system. There is little modern UK jurisprudence given that the circumstances in which the commercial exploitation of an invention would be contrary to public policy or morality are extremely rare. However, the decision of the European Patent Office (EPO) in *Harvard/OncoMouse (1991)* involved a consideration of a biotechnological genetic engineering invention and the issue of patentability. The science of biotechnology concerns living organisms, such as enzymes, proteins and plasmids. As scientists have developed new processes to modify the genetic composition of living organisms, the field has grown in importance because such inventions may directly affect mankind's future existence, particularly in relation to medicine, food, agriculture, energy and protection of the environment.

Why protect biotechnological inventions?

As in other fields of technology, there is a need for legal protection in respect of biotechnological inventions because they are nevertheless the creations of the human mind just as much as are other inventions. Biotechnology inventions are generally the result of substantial research, inventive effort and investment in sophisticated laboratories. Typically, enterprises engaged in research only make investments if legal protection is available for the results of their research. As with other inventions and industries, the need for investment in research and development efforts creates an obvious need for the protection of biotech inventions. This need is not only in the interest of inventors and their employers, but also in the public interest of promoting technological progress.

The patenting of biotechnology innovations has been accompanied by controversy, as has the use of some of these new innovations. Policy makers of all countries, however, have been careful to avoid extending patent rights to things as they exist in nature or to natural phenomena. A new plant species discovered in the wild, for instance, cannot be patented and neither can laws of nature.

The line between discovery and invention can be difficult to draw, but it is clear that a 'mere' discovery must be developed and applied in some way before it constitutes an invention. Therefore, finding a naturally-occurring compound in the human body would be considered to be a discovery, but processes used to isolate or purify such a compound or a synthetic version of the naturally occurring compound would be inventions.

Inventions contrary to public policy or morality

Examples of subject matter contrary to public morality or policy in s 1(3) **PA 1977** include obscene matter and possibly inventions which involve criminal acts. However, s 1(4) **PA 1977** provides that just because an invention is illegal it is not sufficient cause to deem the invention to be contrary to public policy or morality.

The famous decision of the EPO in *Harvard/Onco-Mouse (1991)* developed the law and established that morality and public policy should be assessed using a 'utilitarian' balancing exercise. Harvard University had made an application for a genetically engineered live mouse (or other non-human mammal) which had an increased susceptibility to cancer for use in cancer research. A patent had been granted in the US; however, in the European Patent Office (EPO) it was first refused. After the University appealed, the European Board of Appeal sent the application back to the EPO Examining Division. They provided instructions on the application of the provisions at issue including Art 53(a) of the **European Patent Convention** (the counterpart of s 1(3) **PA 1977**) and the patent was eventually granted. The Board of Appeal set out the 'approach' to be taken when conducting a 'utilitarian' balancing exercise. This involved the EPO weighing up the suffering of the onco-mouse and the possible environmental risks posed by the genetically modified mouse against other factors, such as the usefulness of the invention as an aid to cancer research to humans. The EPO determined that the patenting of the onco-mouse was not immoral. However, the prohibition in s 1(3) **PA 1977** on patenting inventions which are generally offensive still remains, and would be appropriate to control unwelcome animal experimentation.

Patents Act 1977 Sched A2 implements EU Biotech Directive 98/44/EC

Because of the specific legal and scientific concerns regarding public policy and morality relating to genetic engineering, **PA 1977** Sched A2 provides clear guidance on biotechnological inventions that are contrary to **PA 1977** s 1(3). This Directive, in effect, harmonises EPO jurisprudence to the moral and public policy concerns in relation to biotechnological inventions.

(i)   **PA 1977** Sched A2 para 3(b) provides that human cloning processes are not patentable inventions. The formation and development of the human body and mere discoveries of elements of the human body (this includes gene sequences) are not patentable inventions. However, where a technical process is used to isolate or produce elements (including genes) from the human body, this may be patentable (**PA 1977** Sched A 3(a)).

(ii) **PA 1977** Sched A2 para 3(c) provides that processes for modifying human germ line genetic identity, that is genetic changes that can be passed to the next generation, are not patentable inventions.

(iii) **PA 1977** Sched A2 para 3(e) specifically provides that genetic engineering of animals which is likely to cause the animal to suffer without a substantial medical benefit either to man or animals, does not constitute a patent invention.

(iv) Animal and plant varieties or essentially macrobiological processes (**PA 1977** Sched A2 para 3(f)).

PA 1977 Sched A provides that although biological products and processes are not, per se, unpatentable, certain biological subject matter cannot constitute patentable inventions.

In *Harvard College v Canada (Commissioner of Patents) (2002)* where the *Oncomouse* litigation saga continued, the Supreme Court of Canada ruled that the Oncomouse was not patentable, despite the many patents for it then held in the US, Japan, Australia and the European states. The majority, in a 5:4 split decision, held that patenting of higher life forms was a matter for Parliament and not the courts. Subsequently, the Technical Board of Appeal has further restricted the European patent to 'transgenic mice'.

In each country, the laws on patentability of biotechnological inventions need to be consulted to learn the availability of patent protection and its scope. The convergence of this new technology with legal and regulatory systems makes biotechnology an evolving and dynamic component of IP law.

Question 30

Explain the principles of law used by the courts to determine the scope of a patent claim.

Answer plan

This question requires a detailed discussion of the relevant case law that has developed the current legal principles used to determine the scope of a patent claim. The answer should focus on the leading cases, especially the decisions of the House of Lords on the subject.

- Art 69 of the **European Patent Convention (EPC)** given effect in UK law by s 125 of the **Patents Act 1977**;
- *Catnic Components Ltd v Hill & Smith Ltd (1982) HL*;
- *Kirin-Amgen Inc and others v Hoechst Marion Roussel Ltd and others (2004) HL*;
- *Mayne Pharma Pty Ltd v Pharmacia Italia SpA (2005) CA*.

Answer

Determining what a patent means and covers is of central importance in terms of the patent monopoly granted. Two recent judgments from the House of Lords and the Court of Appeal have clarified how the issue of determining the scope of a patent claim should be approached.

It is vital that the scope of the monopoly conferred by a patent can be clearly determined. The patentee needs to know how far the patent's monopoly extends. Third parties have a legitimate interest in knowing as clearly as possible where the boundaries are, so they can both avoid infringement and compete legitimately at that point.

Deciding the scope of the patent's claims is fundamental to determining whether the patent is valid, and whether it is infringed. If a particular element in a claim has a wide meaning then it will be easier to show that the patent is invalid because something already known or obvious falls within it, and how broad the claim is will determine whether the infringer is caught or not. The patentee needs to be able to make it clear that they lay no claim to prior art or insufficiently enabled products or processes which would invalidate the patent. As a consequence, deciding the true extent of the protection afforded by a patent is often the most significant issue in patent litigation.

How is the scope of a patent determined?

There is a combination of statute and judge-made rules of legal construction. The most important provision is Art 69 of the **European Patent Convention (EPC)**, which is given effect in United Kingdom law by s 125 of the **Patents Act 1977**, which provides that the extent of the protection conferred by a European patent or a European patent application shall be determined by the terms of the claims. Nevertheless, the description and drawings shall be used to interpret the claims.

In the House of Lords case of *Kirin-Amgen Inc and others v Hoechst Marion Roussel Ltd and others (2004)*, Lord Hoffmann (giving the judgment of the Court) set out the key factors that should guide the approach to determining construction of a patent:

- The author of a patent specification is using language to make a communication for a practical purpose. A rule of construction which gives their language a meaning different from the way it would have been understood by the people to whom it was actually addressed is liable to defeat their intentions.

He specifically approved the well-known passage in Lord Diplock's speech in *Catnic Components Ltd v Hill & Smith Ltd (1982)*:

A patent specification should be given a purposive construction rather than a purely literal one derived from applying to it the kind of meticulous verbal analysis in which lawyers are too often tempted by their training to indulge.

- Construction is not concerned with what the author meant to say. There is no window into the mind of the patentee. Construction is objective in the sense that it is concerned with what a reasonable person (in patent matters, the notional addressee) to whom the utterance was addressed would have understood the author to be using the words to mean.

- The meaning of words is a matter of convention, governed by rules, which can be found in dictionaries and grammars. What the author would have been understood to mean by using those words is not simply a matter of rules. It is highly sensitive to the context of and background to the particular utterance. It depends not only upon the words the author has chosen but also upon the identity of the audience they are taken to have been addressing and the knowledge and assumptions which one attributes to that audience.

- In the case of a patent specification, the notional addressee is a person skilled in the art. That person comes to a reading of the specification with common general knowledge of the art. That person reads the specification on the assumption that its purpose is both to describe and to demarcate an invention – a practical idea which the patentee has had for a new product or process – and not to be a textbook in mathematics or chemistry or a shopping list of chemicals or hardware. It is this insight which lies at the heart of 'purposive construction' as set out in *Catnic*.

- 'Purposive construction' does not mean that one is extending or going beyond the definition of the technical matter for which the patentee seeks protection in the claims. The question is always what the person skilled in the art would have understood the patentee to be using the language of the claim to mean. And for this purpose, the language the patentee has chosen is usually of critical importance.

- The patent specification is a unilateral document in words of the patentee's own choosing, usually chosen upon skilled advice. But it must be recognised that the patentee is trying to describe something which is new and of which there may be no generally accepted definition. The skilled person will therefore understand that the patentee must in some respect have departed from conventional use of language.

- One has to adopt a principle of construction which actually gives effect to what the person skilled in the art would have understood the patentee to be claiming.

- Lord Hoffmann expressly rejected the American principle of the 'doctrine of equivalents', which allows the patentee to extend their monopoly beyond the claims (the leading US case is *Graver Tank & Manufacturing Co Inc v Linde Air Products Company (1950)*).

- Lord Hoffmann approved the English approach to deciding whether equivalents fall within the scope of the claims ('the Protocol questions' set out by the Court of Appeal in *Wheatly v Drillsafe Ltd (2001)*), although he recognised that there were some limitations to them. But, whereas the principle of purposive construction is the bedrock of patent construction, and is universally applicable, the Protocol questions are only guidelines (not legal rules), and are more useful in some cases than in others.

As a result, in determining the extent of protection of a patent there is only one compulsory question, namely that set by Art 69 and its Protocol: what would a person skilled in the art have understood the patentee to have used the language of the claim to mean? As Lord Hoffmann stated, everything else, including the Protocol questions, is only guidance to a judge trying to answer that question. You cannot sensibly do anything until you have construed the claims. Even if you do follow the Protocol questions, they simply provide a formal justification for a conclusion which may have already been reached on other grounds.

Person skilled in the art and common general knowledge

Proper consideration and determination of who the skilled addressee of the patent is (the so-called person skilled in the art) and what the common general knowledge was at the relevant date are critical to determining the scope of the patent claims. The court will consider issues such as the meanings of technical terms, what is old and what is new in the specification, what the state of the art was at the relevant date. In addition, the state of the art is also normally the subject of searches for publications and/or prior uses.

Other legal principles of patent construction

There are a number of patent-specific rules of construction which will remain unaltered by the House of Lords' judgment in *Kirin-Amgen*. For example, patents often refer to specific proportions or ranges (for example a mixture of 70 per cent to 80 per cent of chemical one and 20 per cent to 30 per cent of chemical two). The question arises as to whether these limits are to be treated as absolute, or whether some deviation is to be permitted with the result that any deviation outside the stated range may still amount to an infringement. Such ranges are normally interpreted strictly, which will continue to be the case following *Kirin-Amgen* (as they are a form of claim limitation voluntarily chosen by the patentee). In *Auchinloss v Agricultural and Veterinary Supplies (1997)* the judge held:

> ... [W]here the patentee has defined an integer of his claim in terms of a range with specified numerical limits at each end, his purpose must be taken to have been to claim thus far and no further. His reason may not be apparent, but it may exist all the same, for instance it may be buried in the prior art.

Other recent developments

In the Court of Appeal case of *Mayne Pharma Pty Ltd v Pharmacia Italia SpA (2005)*, Jacob LJ further developed the principles of construction set out by Lord Hoffmann in *Kirin-Amgen Inc (2004)*. These are summarised below as follows:

(a) Art 69 states that the extent of protection is determined by the terms of the claims. It goes on to say that the description and drawings shall be used to interpret the claims. In short the claims are to be construed in context.

(b) It follows that the claims are to be construed purposively – the inventor's purpose being ascertained from the description and drawings.

(c) The claims must not be construed as if they stood alone – the drawings and description only being used to resolve any ambiguity. Purpose is vital to the construction of claims.

(d) Nonetheless, purpose is the overriding concern. The court is concerned with the meaning of the language used.

(e) If the patentee has included what is obviously a deliberate limitation in his claims, it must have a meaning. One cannot disregard obviously intentional elements.

(f) Where a patentee has used a word or phrase which might have a particular meaning (narrow or wide), it does not necessarily have that meaning in context.

(g) There is no general 'doctrine of equivalents' as used in US patent law.

(h) However, a purposive construction can lead to the conclusion that a technically trivial or minor difference between an element of a claim and the corresponding element of the alleged infringement nonetheless falls within the meaning of the element when read purposively. This is not because there is a doctrine of equivalents: it is because that is the fair way to read the claim in context.

Conclusion

Mayne Pharma and *Kirin-Amgen Inc* are landmark cases that provide helpful guidance to determine how patent claims should be construed. The UK legal position has been further clarified and UK patentees should be confident that they can approach the commercial exploitation and defence and/or enforcement of their patents with greater certainty and precision than before. Conversely, this judicial guidance will also assist competitors to identify imprecision and uncertainty in the meaning of patents.

Question 31

The newly promoted Research and Development Director of a scientific research company consults you regarding six projects currently afoot. He needs to allocate limited financial resources and wants to fund only those projects capable of being protected by and exploited by patents. Advise on the patentability of each of the following projects:

(a) a new type of non-invasive laser heart by-pass surgery;

(b) the discovery of the technique of DNA cloning which allows genes to be trans-planted between different biological species;

(c) the leukemia-fighting drug 6-mercaptopurine;

(d) a stem cell line to treat autism which results in the test mice developing autism;

(e) an improved microphone for use in a foetal monitor to hear a foetal heartbeat;

(f) a new variety of rose plant called Princess Consort Camilla.

Answer plan

In terms of structure of the answer it is important to briefly introduce the task at hand and the law, followed by a detailed consideration of each project clearly logically discussed in alphabetical order (a)–(f) concluding with a thoughtfully reasoned ranking of the projects based on your earlier analysis.

- Introduce the **Patents Act 1977** ('PA 77') criteria for patentability.
- Note that s 1(2) **PA 77** sets out a list of things which are not considered to be inventions and s 1(3) excludes inventions contrary to public policy.
- Put the analysis of the projects into context eg purpose of the analysis.
- Analyse each project (a)–(f) in turn and reach a conclusion on whether the invention is patentable.

Answer

A patent is a legal document that grants a potentially economically valuable limited twenty-year monopoly to make, use and sell the patented invention. In return the patentee must publish the practically useful technical information concerning the invention to the public. The patent law system in the United Kingdom is governed by the **Patents Act 1997** and **Patents Act 2004**. The system is justified on the basis that the monopoly granted provides incentive for new inventions. The basic requirements for a patent to be registered in the UK are set out in s 1 of the **Patents Act 1977** ('PA 77'). In essence, for an invention to be patentable, it must:

(1)   be novel: s 2

(2)   involve an inventive step: s 3

(3)   be capable of industrial application: s 4, and

(4)   not be excluded by law from being patented: s 1(3).

A range of factors need to be taken into account when evaluating whether to patent an invention. The issue of concern is the extent to which the various projects involve subject matter that is patentable. This is sometimes controversial because patent law must determine whether to grant property rights in a new technological invention which may raise complex cultural, political and social questions.

There are several ways that subject matter that is potentially patentable under the **PA 1977** is regulated. First, to be patentable an invention must be capable of 'industrial application': s 1(1)(c). Secondly, s 4A(1) provides that a patent shall not be granted for methods of medical and veterinary treatment. Thirdly, s 1(2) provides a non-exhaustive list of things which are not regarded by law to be inventions (eg a discovery, scientific theory or mathematical method). Fourthly, Schedule A2 paragraph 3(f) states that a patent shall not be granted for 'any variety of animal or plant or any essentially biological process for the production of animals or plants, not being a microbiological process or the product of such a process'. Finally, accordingly to s 1(3) patents will not be granted for immoral invention or inventions contrary to public policy.

The patentability analysis that follows will assist the Research and Development Director determine which projects are likely to result in granted patents that can be subsequently successfully economically exploited by the company.

Project analysis

(a) A new type of non-invasive laser heart by-pass surgery

The issue is whether this non-invasive (non-scalpel) form of surgery is excluded under s 4A(1)(a) **PA 77**. This section provides that a patent shall not be granted for an invention of a method of treatment of the human body by surgery. In *Shell/Blood*

Flow (1993) EPOR 320 the word 'surgery' was judicially considered and defined as medicine concerned with the healing of disease, accidental injury or bodily defects operating on the living body. 'Surgery' was held to include both conservative (non-invasive) and operative (invasive) procedures using instruments. The non-invasive laser heart by-pass surgery fits within the definition and therefore is non patentable subject matter. However, the R&D Director should be advised that the laser hardware may be patentable if it meets the requirements of s 1(1) **PA 77** as it is not excluded by s 4A. For example, the method by which the laser controls power and/or accuracy may be new and involve an inventive step.

(b) The discovery of the technique of DNA cloning which allows genes to be transplanted between different biological species

Prima facie, a 'discovery' is not patentable 'as such' according to s 1(2) **PA 77**. However, if a mere discovery may be further developed and applied in some way it may constitute a patentable invention. In other words, the method of demonstrating the discovery or transforming it into a product may make the discovery patentable. In *Chiron (1996)* FSR 153 Morrit LJ held that biological material isolated from its natural environment or produced by means of a technical process may be the subject of an invention even it if previously occurred in nature. The use of the word 'technique' in the description of the project suggests a degree of development. However, biotechnological inventions are caught by the public policy and morality exception in s 1(3) **PA 77**. Nevertheless, Schedule A2 **PA 77** provides additional guidance in paragraphs 3(b)–(c) which state that the 'technique' must not be excluded on the grounds of public policy or morality. Human cloning *per se* is not patentable: Rule 23d, Art 53 EPC, however, the decision in *Leland Stanford Modified Animal (2002)* EP 2, confirms that controversial technology itself is not a bar to patenting. Accordingly, a carefully worded set of patent claims detailing the specific enabling technique may be patentable. Note also that the creation of inter-species embryos is foreseen in the new **Human Fertilization and Embryology Act 2008.**

(c) The leukemia-fighting drug 6-mercaptopurine

Administering a drug *per se* is not the same as a method of treatment: *John Wyeth & Bros Ltd's Application (1985)* RPC 545. Accordingly, a drug to treat leukaemia is potentially patentable and not excluded subject matter under s 4A which provides that the exclusion shall not extend to 'an invention consisting of a substance or composition used in any such method'. Indeed, there are strong arguments in favour of patenting drugs to reward pharmaceutical companies for their up front research and development costs. However, a patent search would reveal that 6-mercaptopurine first synthesised in 1951, was patented, is in the public domain, forms part of the state of the art and is therefore not patentable, unless the project has resulted in a *new use* for an existing drug which may be patentable. The patentability of a new use of an existing drug is covered by s 1 in the **Patents Act 2004**.

(d) A stem cell line to treat autism which results in the test mice developing autism

This project concerns a biotechnological invention. Advances in stem cell technology raise issues about the patentability of stem cells and processes involving these cells. Uncertainty about what can be patented in this field arises due to s 1(3) **PA 77**, as amended to implement EU Biotech Directive 98/44/EC, which excludes inventions that are contrary to public policy or morality. However, Schedule A2(3)(e) PA 77 confirms that subject to a human medical benefit, inventions can be patentable even though animals may suffer. A case in point is *Harvard/Onco Mouse* series of case law beginning in 1990 in which a patent was granted to Harvard University by the EPO following a 'balancing exercise'. This determined that the usefulness of the method for genetically engineering mice causing them to develop life-threatening cancer to further cancer research in humans, outweighed the mice' suffering. By analogy, it is likely a patent would be granted for this project as autism is a condition that is currently incurable in humans, subject to s 1(1) **PA 77**.

(e) An improved microphone for use in a foetal monitor to hear a foetal heartbeat

The microphone is a medical mechanical device which is *prima facie* patentable provided it meets all the criteria it is novel, has an inventive step (non-obvious to a person skilled in the art) and is industrially applicable (s 1 **PA 77**). Even minor improvements to existing technology may be patentable. If the 'improvement' represents a development to the foetal heart monitoring process (eg by providing additional information relating to the foetus) not previously known then it is potentially patentable.

(f) A new variety of rose plant called Princess Consort Camilla

Plant varieties are not patentable under **PA 77** as they are subject to a parallel *sui generis* regime which covers plant breeders' rights. Monopoly rights in new plant varieties are enshrined in the **Plant Varieties Act 1997** ('PVA 97') which grants monopoly protection in a plant variety that is distinct, uniform, stable and new for a period of 15 years: ss 4–7 and Sch 2 **PVA 97**. Monopoly rights for the rose variety should be pursued under this regime. Note however, that under s 3(2) of the **Plant Breeders' Rights (Naming and Fees) Regulations 2006**, a name will be rejected if it is 'misleading'. This extends to names containing the name of a natural person, so as to convey a false impression concerning the identity of the applicant, the person responsible for the maintenance of the variety. The R&D Director should be advised to seek the permission of Her Royal Highness before proceeding with this name.

Question 32

Patent law confers employee inventors with a statutory right to claim compensation for an invention owned by the employer for which a patent has been granted. Critically analyse the effectiveness of the statutory employee inventor compensation scheme in light of the recent House of Lords decision in *James Duncan Kelly, Kwok Wai Chiu v GE Healthcare Ltd (2009) EWHC 181* which concerned such a claim.

Answer plan

The topic of law reform regularly arises in exams, so a student should ensure that they are familiar with the changes to the patent law system as a result of new patent legislation.

- Introduce the statutory inventor employee compensation scheme in ss 39–41 **Patents Act 1977.**
- Briefly summarise the facts of *Kelly and Chiu v GE Healthcare Ltd (2009).*
- Explain the new four step approach for determining *whether a patent is of outstanding benefit to an employer.*
- Consider the rationale for the introduction of s 10 **Patents Act 2004.**

Answer

The conventional justification for the existence of the patent law system is to give inventors and investors an incentive, namely a twenty-year monopoly to make, use and sell an invention in return for disseminating technical information to the public. A statutory compensation scheme for employee inventors was introduced in the UK in 1978 via ss 39–41 **Patents Act 1977** (PA 1977). In essence, the general rule under s 39 **PA 1977** is that an employee's patent will belong to the employer provided it was made in the course of normal duties or was reasonably expected to result form the carrying out of his duties: s 39(1)(a).

Section 40 **PA 1977** allows the employee to claim compensation in certain limited circumstances if s/he is able to successfully argue that the patent in question provided an 'outstanding benefit' to the organisation (or in the second case that the benefit to the employee is inadequate in relation to benefit derived by the employer from the patent). Thus under the **PA 1977** compensation could not be awarded unless it was shown that the benefits in question result from the invention having been patented, rather than merely from the intrinsic merits of the invention itself: *Memco-Med Ltd's Patent (1992)*. In practice s 40 **PA 1977** has been very difficult to rely on as it is generally felt that the bar is set too high. An employee inventor could secure compensation only if it was proved that the employer had derived 'outstanding benefit' from the patent (not the invention itself) having regard to the size and nature of the employer's undertaking: s 40(1)(b). This was a very high hurdle to overcome. Only three cases were brought by employee inventors under this scheme and none of them were successful (*GEC Avionics Ltd's Patent {1992} RPC 107*; *British Steel Plc's Patent {1992} RPC 117*; *Memco-Med' Ltd's Patent {1992} RPC 403*). There is no previously reported case of a successfully contested employee inventor compensation award under the Act.

Kelly and Chiu v. GE Healthcare Limited {2009} EWHC 181 (Pat)

In early 2009 in a ground-breaking ruling in the Patent Court, Mr Justice Floyd made the first ever court award of compensation under the **PA 1977** to employee co-inventors. Sizeable sums of £1m and £500,000 were awarded to the co-inventor research scientists Drs Duncan Kelly and Kwok Wai Chiu respectively for their work in creating a diagnostic tool for detecting heart defects whilst employed by Amersham International Plc (now GE Healthcare Limited). This was the first case in which it had been possible for claimants to prove that the patent to which they had contributed was of 'outstanding benefit' to the employer.

Briefly, the case involved GE Healthcare (formerly Amersham International), a multinational corporation with expertise in medical imaging and information technologies. The company is a US$17 billion segment of the American General Electric Company and the first GE business to be headquartered outside the United States. In the 1980s, GE Healthcare employed Dr Duncan Kelly and Dr Ray Chiu as research scientists, both of whom were crucial to the investigation and development of the first synthesis of the P53 compound. This compound was the basis for a radioactive imaging agent, trade marked MYOVIEW, patented in the 1980s which proved to be a great commercial success for GE Healthcare. Launched in the UK and Japan in 1994, followed by the US in 1996, the product was very profitable. With R&D costs of £2.4m, first year sales of MYOVIEW were £4.47m and in the third year were in excess of £20m. Total sales were in excess of £1.3 billion up to 2007. The precise profit figures were not published in the judgment, but were provided to the court as confidential information. In contrast, on retirement Dr Kelly was earning £71,500 per annum plus benefits with the company and Dr Chiu had left the company after two years employment having earned not more than £15,000 per annum.

The law

Drs Kelly and Chiu claimed under sections 40 and 41 of the **PA 1977** for a share of the benefit derived by their employer from the MYOVIEW patent. Section 41(4) lists factors which determine the fair share to be awarded to the employee inventor. The court should take into account: (a) the nature of the employee's duties, his remuneration and the other advantages derived from the employment or derived from the invention; (b) the effort and skill which the employee has devoted to making the invention; (c) the effort and skill of any other person devoted to jointly making the invention as well as advice and other assistance contributed by any other employee who is not a joint inventor; and (d) the employer's contribution to the making, developing and working of the invention by his provision of advice, facilities or otherwise. Section 41(5) deals with the issue of awarding a fair share of compensation to joint employee inventors.

The difficulty is that while the statute lists the factors which determine the fair share to be awarded to the employee inventor, there had been no judicial guidance as to their interpretation. It is clear however, that the UK inventor must be wholly or mainly employed in the UK, or if they have no main place of employment, be employed by an employer within its UK operations.

Applying the law

In the instant case, two issues arose to be decided by the court: (1) how to determine the required scale of outstanding benefit to an employer that would merit an award of compensation to an inventor; and (2) the level of compensation the employee inventor should be awarded. The decision in *Kelly and Chiu* provides much needed guidance as to how these key issues should be determined.

Mr Justice Floyd, a Patents Court judge appointed to the High Court in 2007, firstly confirmed that Drs Kelly and Chui were indeed co-inventors of the Myoview patents. He then turned to consider the key contested question of whether the patents were of outstanding benefit for their employer. In doing so, he developed a four step approach. This involved asking firstly whether the patent was a cause of some benefit. If yes, then secondly it was appropriate to consider how much of the total benefit could be attributed to the patent. This is a complex issue involving apportioning benefit from multiple causes. Thirdly, one must determine whether the benefit was 'outstanding'. Floyd J remarked that the concept of 'outstanding benefit' means more than significant and 'out of the ordinary' or 'something special'. The benefit has to be greater than one would normally expect to arise from the employees' work. Finally, by reason of statute, it has to be just to make the award. On this question, Mr Justice Floyd stated that the court would be in a position to recognise situations in which it would be unjust to make an award, as and when they arose.

The judge then turned to the amount of the compensation. The Court was presented with evidence that the total sales of Myoview between 2002 and 2007 amounted to some £1 billion. However, Mr Justice Floyd recognised the difficulties in quantifying the value of the benefit to the employer. He assessed what he considered to be the 'absolute rock bottom figure for the benefit from the patents' to the employer as £50 million. He then considered the nature of the employees' duties, remuneration and other advantages from the employment and concluded that Dr

Kelly and Dr Chui were entitled to a 2 per cent (£1,000,000) and 1 per cent (£500,000) share respectively of the benefit derived by the employer from their invention. On this basis, the judge resolved that these figures represented a fair and just reward to the employees.

This is certainly a new development and it is unclear whether this decision could lead to a number of employees claiming compensation for their inventions from their employers. It is clear, however, that a high threshold of 'outstanding benefit' remains.

Section 10 PA 2004 Compensation of employees for certain inventions

In order to further the policy of rewarding employee inventors, the **Patents Act 2004** (PA 2004) amends **PA 1977** in several respects including compensation for employees of certain inventions.

Section 10 **PA 2004** ('Compensation of employees for certain inventions') is an attempt to lower the high threshold by stating that the benefit to the employer should be assessed not only by reference to the patent itself, but also against the invention from which the patent arises. The commercial implications of s 10 means employees will have a right to claim compensation if their employer gains a benefit from either the invention, the patent or both. In the event, s 10 **PA 2004** is a token gesture as far as employee-inventors are concerned and some commentators have suggested that the outstanding benefit principle should have been repealed altogether.

Although, as before, compensation may be awarded only in respect of inventions which have been patented, it will no longer be necessary to show that the benefit in question flows from the patent itself (as opposed to the invention). Such benefits flowing from the patent will continue to be taken into account; however, if the invention has been beneficial for other reasons, those benefits may now also be taken into consideration. What constitutes an outstanding benefit will continue to depend on such factors as the size and nature of the relevant undertaking, which may be the whole or a division of the employer's business. Section 10(3) to (5) **PA 2004** make consequential changes to s 41, which lays down how the amount of compensation awarded under s 40 is to be assessed. Sub-section (6) makes consequential changes to s 43.

Sub-section (7) ensures that, for the purposes of assessing benefits under s 40(1) or (2), and for the purpose of calculating the amount of compensation under s 41, those benefits which arise after the relevant patent has ceased to have effect (whether by expiry, surrender or revocation) cannot be taken into account.

Sub-section (8) is a transitional provision which ensures that the amended provisions do not apply to existing patents, nor to a patent for which an application is made before the amendments come into force.

Section 10(2) was introduced in order to further the policy objective of the employee compensation scheme, introducing the element of 'invention' as well as the patent.

Concluding remarks

The legislative amendments introduced in the **PA 2004** were designed to make it easier to obtain such compensation by allowing for compensation whether either the patent or the invention, or both, are of outstanding benefit to the employer. This is thought to be a lower barrier that employee inventors need to overcome. Cases are now beginning to trickle in before the courts. Nevertheless, the landmark decision in *Kelly and Chiu v GE Healthcare (2009)* HL will hearten employee inventors across the UK as it clarifies when inventors will be able to share in the benefits of a patent granted to their employers.

Question 33

Does the patenting of biological material conflict with traditional justifications for patent law, and in particular John Locke's (1632–1704) Labour theory?

Answer plan

A good answer will critically assess whether the traditional philosophical rationales justifying the grant of patent monopolies are still relevant when considering modern dilemmas over the patentability of certain biological material.

- **Patent Regulations 2000** inserting s 76A and Sched A2 which implement the **EU Biotechnology Directive**;
- The Human Genome Project;
- Locke's Labour theory.

Answer

The principal purposes of a patent law system are to recompense invention, encourage disclosure of inventions, thus stimulating further advancements, and protect ideas in the public domain. In return for a limited monopoly, the traditional justifications for the patent law regime rely on the concept of reward for labour (the 'Labour theory') and the disclosure of useful inventions in the public interest, among others. However, these traditional justifications for the legal protection of intellectual property rights often conflict with modern moral and ethical considerations, especially in connection with biotechnological inventions. Biotechnology is the development of commercial products from biological processes.

The UK patent law regime is regulated by the **Patents Act 1977**. Under the Act, inventions are patentable if they meet the criteria set out in s 1(1) of the **Patents Act 1977**. However, s 1(3) of the Act excludes the patenting of inventions contrary to public policy and morality. This provision has become increasingly important in the context of patenting biological inventions. Further, the Act was amended by the **Patent Regulations 2000** inserting s 76A and Sched A2 which implement the **EU Biotechnology Directive**. Biotechnological inventions are now defined in s 130 of the Act as 'products or processes containing biological material, that is, material containing genetic information and capable of being reproduced in a biological system'.

Does the patenting of biological material conflict with John Locke's (1632–1704) 'Labour theory' which was conceived several centuries ago? It is well known that Locke identified labour as the original and just foundation of property. In brief, Locke's was a labour theory of property. Locke viewed private property ownership as legitimate and he argued that the labourer should be rewarded for his efforts. But, he stated that the reward for labour was conditional, so that 'there must remain objects of similar qualities in sufficient quantities to supply others'. In other words, Locke was concerned to grant some form of reward, so long as that reward was not detrimental to the public interest.

In relation to biotechnological inventions, the conditional aspect of Locke's labour theory is reflected in the arguments propounded by some scientists in relation to the Human Genome Protect ('HGP'). The HGP identifies all the human genes and determines the sequence of base pairs for the entire human genome, storing information in databases for further advancements in biotechnology. Succinctly, the genome is the 'complete set of genetic information of an organism'. On the one hand, the raw sequence of the human genome is a natural manifestation of nature, not made by the human hand. On the other hand, the other format consists of the cloned or isolated and purified partial DNA fragments. The DNA fragments must be excised from the natural context of the human genome, isolated, purified and cloned before scientists can study them. Since the sequenced gene fragments do not exist in their natural state and are therefore 'not nature's handiwork', they are patentable subject matter.

However, certain scientists argue that instead of allowing human genes, tissues and organs to become privately owned commercial property controlled by business for a twenty-year term, the intellectual property law community should work towards creating a global treaty to jointly administer data concerning the human genome and the gene pool for other plants and animals on behalf of future generations. In line with Lock's Labour theory, the community should ensure that sufficient genetic information is available for use by others.

More recently, modern legal academic Professor Michael Pendleton has argued against promoting private interests because in his view progress has been made only by re-combining pre-existing knowledge. Pendleton's theory provides that 'no one own an idea . . . all ideas lie within the public domain'.

The creation of a global treaty to jointly administer data concerning the human genome and the gene pool for other plants and animals on behalf of future generations could be said to be a combination of Locke's Labour theory (don't take more than you need) and Pendleton's theory that an invention cannot be attributable to an individual or small group of people. Elaborating further on Locke's Labour theory and in line with Pendleton's theory, Nozick asserts that the labourer should be entitled only to the 'value added', not to the total value of the resulting product. Further, it is not only the object and the labour added that have value, but the thoughts and ideas of those who came before (affirming Pendleton).

The counter-argument is that a patent monopoly is the key means of rewarding research-based industries, such as the biotechnological and pharmaceutical industries, enabling them to recoup their massive research and development invest during the patent term where they have the exclusive right to exploit their invention. It is estimated that it takes on average more than ten years to create a useful biotechnological product or process and to market it. Patents protect against competition at the vulnerable early stages of development and converts a risky investment into a saleable commodity. In particular, the patent system protects a patentee's invention from prospective infringers by preventing others from copying, making, using, offering for sale, or selling another's work without consent. However, most prospective gene patentees seek patent rights on genetic sequences, which lack intrinsic marketability or definite utility. Should DNA sequences be protected by patents? Is there a need to put an end to the international rush to patent DNA fragment sequences with no known function? Clearly, however, genetic research contributes to the development of many of today's breakthrough pharmaceuticals and diagnostic tests.

Nevertheless, some scientists object to patents over biological material because of the effect on research in that permission needs to be obtained, licence fees paid in order to use the information. Indeed, one of the strongest arguments opposing DNA sequence patenting is the assertion that such patenting hinders innovation rather than promoting it and so holders of DNA sequence patents have the capability to deprive researchers and physicians of any use of that sequence for diagnosis, treatment, or development of disease treatments. It is argued that scientific integrity is being compromised by commercialism and the giving of property rights over 'nature' and further that patent monopolies are being used as a device to monopolise industries and restricting the flow of ideas. In the scientific community, knowledge is usually developed in a cooperative manner through the open disclosure of new knowledge and peer testing of that knowledge. Accordingly, the growing trend towards the commercialisation of research has led to the practice of promoting secrecy and hindering the exchange of information amongst researchers in biotechnology. It is true that information-sharing between laboratories seems to be inhibited by patents and licensing. In other words, until researchers acquire patent rights, publication of research findings may be delayed and the commercialisation of genetic research diminishes the collaborative efforts in scientific research.

Certainly, there are criticisms of the current system of granting patents for bio-technological inventions. However, historically, there is a long tradition in granting patents for purified natural products such as that granted to Louis Pasteur (1822–95) for yeast 'free from organic germs of disease'. In *Parke-Davis & Co v H.K. Mulford & Co (1911)* it was held that purified human adrenaline was patentable because, through purification, it became 'for every practical purpose a new thing commercially and therapeutically'. Some hold the view that as gene sequences already exist naturally and are discovered rather than invented, they should not be patentable. How can the genetic codes which stimulate and codify the make-up of every living cell and organism be bought and sold? This view is supported by the Bio-Industry Association, the trade industry representing the UK biotechnology industries.

In addition, many people believe that it is morally and ethically wrong to treat life, and thus biological material, as commercial property. DNA sequence patenting has been attacked on religious grounds based on the notion that genetic manipulation is the same as 'playing God', and that the fruits of such work should not be rewarded with patent control.

On the other hand, the patent system significantly benefits society by expediting the discovery of new medications, technologies and non-infringing improvements, while decreasing consumer costs through the development of non-infringing substitutes. Further, the patent law principles may already provide the means to adapt to biotechnological inventions. For example, as the process of isolating gene sequences becomes more commonplace, it will inevitably become harder to show an inventive step which is a legal pre-requisite to the grant of a patent. It is also interesting to contrast the case of biological material with that of chemical elements in the period table. Such elements were largely non-obvious when first isolated and purified, and very useful, but they were not held to be patentable because they were discoveries of nature, despite the human ingenuity involved in isolating them. In conclusion, there is need to find a viable compromise that protects knowledge in the public domain and encourages further biotech research.

CHAPTER 7

REGISTERED TRADE MARKS

A trade mark is a sign used in relation to goods or services so as to indicate a connection in the course of trade between the goods or services and some person having a right to use the mark.

A system for registered trade marks was developed in the nineteenth century and the legal regime is now enshrined in the **Trade Marks Act 1994 (TMA 1994)**. The **TMA 1994** implements **Council Directive 89/104/EEC**, makes provision for the Community Trade Mark (**Council Regulation (EC) 40/94**) which creates a single trade mark right extending throughout the European Union and gives effect to the Madrid Protocol for the Registration of Marks Internationally.

The key advantage of registering a trade mark is the mark is afforded greater legal protection and there is no need to prove elements of passing off and reputation in the mark. The trade mark registration system protects any sign that is capable of being represented graphically: s 1(1) **TMA 1994** and currently there is a wide range of marks that are capable of registration including conventional marks such as pictoral marks such as letters, words, pictures or drawings and unconventional trade marks including signs such as slogans; three-dimensional (3-D) signs (shapes); colours; sensory signs, for example auditory (sound signs); gustatory (taste signs, olfactory (scent) signs and gestures; action signs; and incredibly, holograms.

The legal purpose of a trade mark is to prevent others from using the mark and benefiting from the goodwill attached to the mark. A trade mark constitutes personal property and a monopoly over a registered trade mark can be renewed by the proprietor indefintely.

Question 34

Imagine you are a Trade Mark Examiner employed by the UK Patent Office's Trade Marks Registry. You have received the following applications to register trade marks. Examine the applications and set out the grounds of any objections you may have to the registration of the proposed marks.

(a) TM Application 1: 7 DAYS A WEEK, by a taxi service.

(b) TM Application 2: OLYMPIC, for shaving products for men.

(c) TM Application 3: The colour RED, for a telecommunications company.

(d) TM Application 4: The scent of a NUTMEG, by a furniture manufacturer, to be applied to furniture.

(e) TM Application 5: 'Catch a wrinkle in time', for a cosmetics preparation.

(f) TM Application 6: BACARDI, for a company that produces vodka.

Answer plan

This question should be answered in order that is (a)–(f). The best approach to this type of question is to answer each part in turn, clearly identifying the separate parts of the answer. Unless you are told otherwise, it is reasonable for you to assume that each subsection carries equal marks. This means you may want to allocate equal time to each part.

- Absolute grounds of refusal in the **Trade Marks Act 1994 (TMA 1994)**;
- Relative grounds of refusal **TMA 1994**;
- Protected emblems and Olympic symbols, **London Olympic Games and Paralympic Games Act 2006**;
- Colour marks;
- Scent marks.

Answer

A trade mark is a sign used in the course of trade to indicate the source of goods or services and distinguishes them from the goods or services of other traders: s 1 **TMA 1994**. Any sign that distinguishes will meet this requirement, according to the decision in *AD2000 Trade Mark (1996)*. A trade mark is primarily a badge of origin, and it is used so that customers can recognise the product of a particular trader. As a result, trade marks are valuable commercial property and the choice of an appropriate mark requires care and effort. It is not compulsory to register a trade mark, but since registration provides considerable legal advantages it is highly desirable. However, not all marks are capable of being registered as trade marks. The substantive law of trade marks is contained in the **Trade Marks Act 1994 (TMA 1994)** which implements the **Trade Marks Directive (Directive 89/104/EEC)**. A trade mark application is examined to determine if it complies with the Act and whether there are grounds for rejecting it. Objections to the registration of a mark may be raised either by the Trade Marks Registry during examination or by third parties during opposition proceedings. The grounds for refusing registration are divided into two categories:

- *absolute grounds* for refusal (**TMA 1994** ss 3 and 4) which are concerned with objections based on the mark itself; and
- *relative grounds* for refusal (**TMA 1994**, s 5); these are concerned with conflict with third-party rights.

(a) TM Application 1: 7 DAYS A WEEK, by a taxi service

Many trades advertise that their goods or service are provided seven days a week.

The mark breaches s 3(1)(c) **TMA 1994,** which prohibits the registration of a mark which consists exclusively of the 'time of rendering the services' and therefore is exclusively descriptive. However, a mark falling into this category could still be registrable if it has become distinctive in use, but this appears unlikely here.

The mark is also possibly in breach of s 3(1)(d) **TMA 1994** because it could be considered to be customary in the current language.

Both reasons are 'absolute grounds' for refusal.

(b) TM Application 2: OLYMPIC (word mark), for a company's men's shaving products

This mark is in breach of s 4(5) **TMA 1994** as a specially protected emblem. In the United Kingdom special laws have been passed to give extra protection to some of the Olympic Games' marks. The proposed mark also breaches s 3(1)(a) of the **Olympic Symbol etc (Protection) Act 1995 (OSPA)** because the word 'Olympic' is a protected word under that Act. The **OSPA** protects the Olympic and Paralympic symbols, mottos and various words. Added protection is provided by the new **London Olympic Games and Paralympic Games Act 2006**. This prevents the creation of an unauthorised association between people, goods or services and London 2012.

(c) TM Application 3: The colour RED for a telecommunications company

In the UK, the concept of a sign or trade mark is very wide and includes non-conventional trade marks such as a single shade of colour or a colour combination. The decision in *Phillips v Remington (1998)* provides that anything that conveys information can be regarded as a sign. Section 1(1) **TMA 1994** states that the sign must be capable of being represented graphically. This can be done by citing the Pantone colour identification system number in the trade mark application: *Libertel (2003)*.

(d) TM Application 4: The scent of a NUTMEG – by a furniture manufacturer to be applied to furniture

A 'scent mark' or 'olfactory mark' is regarded as a non-conventional mark which is more difficult to register because of the difficulty of representing the scent graphically, as required by s 1(1) **TMA 1994**. A sign must be represented in such a way that a third party is able to determine and understand what the sign is. In the case of *Ralf Sieckmann (2002)*, the ECJ constructed a test which provides that the graphic representation must be:

(i)   clear;

(ii) precise;

(iii) self-contained;

(iv) easily accessible and intelligible;

(v)   durable; and

(vi) objective.

Before the decision in *Sieckmann* some scents had been registered as trade marks using written descriptions of scents, which had previously been regarded to meet the graphic representation requirements of s 1(1) **TMA 1994**.

Following the decision in *Sieckmann,* verbal descriptions, chemical formulae and a sample were all rejected as being insufficient to graphically represent a scent. As a result, it is highly unlikely that olfactory signs will be registrable as trade marks in the foreseeable future.

(e) TM Application 5: 'Catch a wrinkle in time', for a cosmetic preparation

Slogans are registrable as trade marks provided that they have the capacity to individualise the goods or services of one undertaking provided they are not comprised of signs or indications which directly describe the goods or services or their essential characteristics, and are not devoid of distinctive character for any other reason.

In *Nestle SA's Trade Mark Application (Have a Break) (2003)*, the High Court ruled that registration of these words would not be granted as a trade mark because the phrase was not distinctive. However, the slogan 'Catch a wrinkle in time' probably is distinctive because it is fanciful and therefore is likely to be registrable. In *'Das Prinzip der Bequemlichkeit' {'The Principle of Comfort'} C–64/02 P*, the ECJ stated that slogans serving a promotional function which is not obviously secondary to any trade mark meaning will be objectionable because average consumers are not in the habit of making assumptions about the origin of products on the basis of such slogans. Further, it is clear that the slogan is not descriptive of the product and therefore is in breach of s 3(1)(c) **TMA 1994**.

(f) TM Application 6: BACARDI, for a company that produces vodka

It is well known that the mark BACARDI is associated with the alcoholic rum drink. Here, there is likely to be an objection to registration of the mark in connection with spirit that is vodka-based on the relative ground of refusal contained in s 5(2)(a) **TMA 1994**. Section 5(2)(a) provides that a trade mark shall not be registered if it is identical with an earlier trade mark and is to be registered for goods or services similar to those for which the earlier trade mark is protected. Vodka and rum are similar goods as they are both spirits (alcoholic drinks). Although the products have very different producers, it is common to find them being bought and sold by the same merchants and customers, and sold through the same outlets.

Question 35

Should colours or scents be protected by trade mark law? What problems may arise in protecting them? Critically analyse the relevant legislation and case law.

Answer plan

This question requires the student to consider unconventional signs at the cutting edge of trade mark law. The essay should focus equally on colour marks and scent marks and the key European Court of Justice decision in order to attract the maximum award of marks.

- Colour or scent marks as an unconventional sign or badge of origin;
- *Libertel Group BV v Benelu-Merkenbureau (2004)*;
- Section 1(1) **TMA 1994** and the PANTONE colour identification system;
- Colour depletion theory and the shade confusion theory;
- *Ralf Sieckmann (2002) ECJ*.

Answer

A trade mark is a 'sign' or 'badge of origin' that is used to identify certain goods and services as those produced or provided by a specific person or enterprise. A trade mark helps to distinguish those branded goods and services from similar ones provided by another trader. Trade marks fall into two categories, namely conventional and unconventional trade marks. Conventional trade marks include pictoral marks such as letters, words, pictures or drawings The range of non-conventional trade marks include signs such as slogans, three-dimensional (3-D) signs (shapes), colours, sensory signs (for example auditory sound signs; gustatory taste signs, olfactory scent signs) and gestures, action signs and even holograms.

Is a colour or a scent capable of acting as a sign or a badge of origin as required by s 1(1) **TMA 1994**? There is no statutory definition as to what is meant by the term sign and there are very few restrictions placed on what may be registered as a trade mark. In *Wrigley/Light Green (1999)* the notion of a 'sign' was interpreted as being a very broad, open and general term encompassing all conceivable types of marks. Accordingly, the concept of a 'sign' in current UK trade mark law is very broad.

Section 1(1) **TMA 1994** provides that to be registrable, a trade mark must be a sign capable of graphical representation. Additionally, the mark must be distinctive, not be descriptive, nor be excluded under the **TMA 1994**.

Does trade mark law currently protect colour or scent signs? The answer to this question depends on whether the unconventional marks are capable of graphical representation. In the past there have been difficulties with graphically representing unconventional marks such as colours and scents. However, while there is now a solution for graphically reprsenting colour marks, the same cannot be said for scent marks.

Colour marks

While not specifically mentioned in s 1(1) **TMA 1994**, it is clear that colours are prima facie registrable where they are used as a trade mark. The main problem will be showing the mark is distinctive. In the leading case on colour marks, *Libertel Group BV v Benelux-Merkenbureau (2004)* Libertel was refused registration for the single colour orange (depicted without any reference to a colour code) by the Benelux Trade Mark office. The ECJ was asked whether a single colour could be distinctive. The ECJ held that it must decide as a preliminary matter whether a single colour could constitute a trade mark. The ECJ stated that that colour cannot be presumed per se to constitute a sign (without more), since it is normally merely a property of things. However, depending on the context, a colour may constitute a sign. A specific shade of colour can be registered, either as a single colour, or as a colour combination. Some examples of colour marks include colours applied to:

- pharmaceuticals (*Smith Kline and French's Trade Mark (1975)*);
- stripes on toothpaste (*Unilever's Application(1984)*);
- single colours (such as orange for 'technical and business consultancy services in the area of plant cultivation, in particular the seed sector': *KWS Saat AG v OHIM (2002)*).

Applications usually include a colour specimen, but these are not sufficiently durable according to *Libertel (2004),* and the graphic representation of a colour now requires the designation of the colour using an internationally recognised colour identificaton system, for example PANTONE. In assessing the potential distinctiveness of a given colour as a trade mark, regard must be had to the general interest in not unduly restricting the availability of colours for other traders in the same field. However, this leads us to the policy arguments against the registration of colours as trade marks. In this regard, there are two particulary interesting theories to explore: the colour depletion theory and the shade confusion theory.

Colour depletion theory

This theory advocates that by registering one colour as a trade mark, the choice of colours left to other manufacturers will then be more limited. The more colours are trade marked in one area of trade, the fewer the colours will be available for other manufacturers, and the list of available colours will therefore run out. Granting trade mark protection for colours is thought by some to be unfair and anti-competitive. Whilst the virtually unlimited combination of letters ensures that word marks do not hinder competition, the same is not true in relation to colours. It is argued that the limited quantity of colours, and the need for one type of colour as opposed to another in a given area of trade contributes to a state of unfair competition. This contention has been respected very strictly in the Netherlands, where the Benelux Trade Mark Office refused to register the single colour orange as a trade mark on the grounds that, *inter alia*, the colour orange played an important role as a national colour: *Libertel (2004)*.

Shade confusion theory

This essence of this theory is that colours cannot function as trade marks because colours and their different shades can easily lead to confusion. This is a valid point not merely for infringement procedures but also when consumers are choosing goods prior to purchase. Using only slightly different shades of one colour as trade marks is likely to create confusion in the mind of consumers. Such potential for confusion allows us to infer that colours scarcely help consumers to identify the manufacturer of the goods on which the shade of the colour is applied, thereby failing to serve the prime purpose of trade marks as a sign capable of distinguishing enterprises or as a badge of origin.

Scent marks

Scent or olfactory marks also encounter practical difficulties carving out a monopoly and they are unlikely to be registrable in the foreseeable future. The leading case is *Sieckmann (2003)*, where an application for a Community Trade Mark (CTM) described the structural formula of a pure chemical for a particular scent and stated that samples of the scent might be obtained from local laboratories. The scent was also described verbally as 'balsamically fruity with a slight hint of cinnamon'. The German Patent Office rejected the application. On appeal, the German Patents Court considered that scents could, from an abstract point of view, constitute an appropriate means of distinguishing the products of one enterprise from that of another, but it expressed doubts as to whether an olfactory mark was capable of being graphically represented. It referred the question to the European Court of Justice (ECJ). The ECJ was asked to decide whether the requirement for graphical representation could be satisfied by a chemical formula, a description, a deposit, or a combination of these elements.

The ECJ rejected 'verbal description', 'chemical formulae', or a sample as being insufficient to graphically represent a scent. It held that none of these methods of representation would suffice and a combination of these options would be even less likely to do so. According to the Court, for a sign to be registrable under Art 2 of the Directive, it must have a distinctive character and be capable of being represented graphically in a clear and precise form that is understandable to the majority of manufacturers and consumers. The Court did not consider it possible to represent a scent with sufficient clarity and precision so that it was understandable to all.

Before the decision in *Sieckmann*, scent marks were registrable but the current position is that registration of scent marks seems unlikely until an agreed system of graphic representation exists. This will be difficult because although a scent is unique, the molecules of a scent must have actual contact with the potential consumer. The further away the consumer is from the scented product, the more difficult this will be. This problem is even more complex when factoring in any environmental conditions affecting the scent. Temperature, the level of humidity and wind conditions can change the strength of a scent. These factors can make the scent more difficult for the nose to detect as well as potentially altering the chemical composition of the scent, making it a different one than originally existed. A scent will also be altered when other scents interact with it. Due to its gaseous nature, a scent is very easily modified by the existence of nearby smells. That said, virtually every single individual's perception of a scent is different depending on the surrounding environment, the distance between the human body and the scent, whether the person experiences sinusitis, etc.

Question 36

L'Oceane plc is a producer and marketer of luxury perfumes. The company was established in the mid-19th century and had traded in the UK for over a century. It is the proprietor of well-known UK registered trade marks, some in the form of word marks alone, and others being word and figurative marks including a representation of a wave-shaped bottle and packaging for its best-selling 'Vagues de Desire' (waves of desire) perfume. L'Oceane invested in expensive advertising for its 'Vagues de Desire' perfume across several media, employing a famous and beautiful actress as the 'spokesmodel' for its campaign.

Another firm, Bella Ltd had produced and marketed imitations of fine fragrances since 1990. Bella Ltd offered for sale a range of fragrance products at one third the price, some of whose bottles and packaging were generally similar to those of products of L'Oceane plc. However, the similarity was unlikely to mislead professionals. Even the public could clearly identify that Bella's products were 'knocked off' and were inferior products to those of L'Oceane plc. Bella Ltd provided their retailers with lists which compared the scent of their 'knock off' product with that of the L'Oceane product which was being imitated, in each case identified by reference to the word mark by which the L'Oceane product was known.

L'Oceane plc is vigilant in protecting its brand and wishes to bring trade mark infringement proceedings again Bella Ltd. What is the likelihood of success of such an action? Advise L'Oceane.

Answer plan

This fact scenario is based on the common situation where one firm 'knocks off' or imitates the brand of another as was the case in the recent decision in *L'Oréal SA and others v Bellure NV and others (2009)* WLR (D) 203. The answer to this problem question therefore requires a detailed knowledge of trade mark infringement law, comparative advertising law and the facts and judgment of the *L'Oreal SA v Bellure* case which concerns s 10(6) **Trade Marks Act 1994** ('TMA 1994').

- Introduce the law and function of trade marks.
- Consider whether the facts here point to actual trade mark infringement (consider *Arsenal Football Club plc v Reed (2001)*). If not, what can L'Oceane plc do to protect its mark?
- The key issue to be tackled is whether 'knock off' imitation perfumes which clearly are not trade marked goods, but were marketed in a way that 'winked at' L'Oceane's famous perfume brands, have infringed L'Oceane's registered trade marks.
- Introduce the law relating to comparative advertising and how it may be relevant to the facts in issue.
- Evaluate whether Bella Ltd's marketing actions are protected as a permissible form of comparative advertising.

Answer

In the UK, trade mark law is governed by the **Trade Marks Act 1994** (TMA 1994) and is essentially territorial, meaning that a UK registered trade mark is only protected in the UK. Section 1(1) of the **TMA 1994** defines a trade mark as 'any sign capable of being represented graphically which is capable of distinguishing goods or services of one undertaking from those of other undertakings'. We are told that L'Oceane has registered trade marks so we can assume that these marks meet the criteria of the Act.

Trade marks can be very valuable in that they have a number of functions to play in modern business. The traditional view is that a registered trade mark, such as L'Oceane's word marks and pictorial marks, function as an indicator of origin of the goods so that consumers reliably recognise the 'Vagues de Desir' branded perfume as originating from L'Oceane and not from some other enterprise such as Bella. This trade mark protection benefits the public as a guarantee of quality and also benefits L'Oceane in the marketplace by distinguishing its products from those of its competitors. This 'indicator of origin' function was confirmed by the European Court of Justice (ECJ) in several cases including *Arsenal Football Club plc v Reed (No. 2) (2003)*. However, registered trade marks also play another important function in terms of their publicity value in that they create brand attractiveness and reputation. For example, a distinctive mark may not identify only origin, but also quality, reputation and renown of the producer particularly through the investment.

The **TMA 1994** implements the **Trade Marks Directive 89/204** so the final word on interpreting the terms of the Act lies with the European Court of Justice (ECJ) to ensure a uniform approach across the European Union. There has been significant debate in trade mark law circles over the extent to which the **TM Directive**, implemented into the UK **TMA 1994**, intended to give protection to the publicity value of registered trade marks, independently from their function as indicators of origin. Indeed, some European countries, such as the Benelux countries, already recognise this second function of registered trade marks. The language of the **TM Directive** is ambiguous. On the one hand, some argue that interpreting the **TMA 1994** to grant protection over this secondary function is simply common sense given modern advertising and brand attractiveness. On the other hand, would granting such protection give too much power to wealthy established brand owners such as L'Oceane to dominate aspects of language and shape to the detriment of healthy competition?

Is this a case of Bella infringing L'Oceane's trade marks? The owner of a registered trade mark has exclusive rights in the trade mark which are infringed by its use in the UK without consent: s 9 **TMA 1994**. The four main grounds for infringement are set out in s 10(1)–(3). They are the same as the relative grounds for refusal of registration (s 5(1)–(3)). To infringe, the sign must be used in the course of trade: s 103. Bella Ltd provided their retailers with lists which compared the scent of their 'knock off' product with that of the L'Oceane product which was being imitated, in each case identified by reference to the word mark by which the L'Oceane product was known. Bella used L'Oceane's marks on identifical products. Is this an infringement under s 10(1)(a) **TMA 1994** (s 5(1)(a) RMA Directive)? We know that both professionals and the public can identify that Bella's products were 'knocked off' and were inferior products to those of L'Oceane plc, in other words that the products did not originate from L'Oceane. Does providing such a list amount to infringing trade mark use? Bella will argue that providing a comparison list is non-trade used as the word marks referred to in the list is not used in a 'trade mark sense', that is as an indicator of origin. There is a trilogy of cases that deal with these issues.

First, the question as to whether trade mark use is required to find infringement was referred to the ECJ by the High Court in *Arsenal Football Club plc v Reed (2001)*. The ECJ held that the rights of a trade mark owner to prevent a third party from using his mark extended to any situation where such use was liable to affect its essential function as a guarantor of origin. Use in the course of trade is use which 'takes place in the context of commercial activity with a view to economic advantage and not as a private matter'.

The next case to consider the meaning of 'infringing use' was the ECJ's decision in *Adam Opel AG v Autec AG (2007)*. Opel manufactured the Opel Astra car and was the registered owner of the OPEL mark for motor vehicles and toys. The defendant, Autec, manufactured scale model cars and used the Opel mark on the radiator grille of a scale model of the Opel Astra. Opel brought an action for trade mark infringement. In its defence, Autec argued that its use of the Opel mark was not 'trade mark use' as the public would know that Autec's scale model car products which carried the registered trade mark did not come from Opel, the car maker. The ECJ again confirmed the principle established in *Arsenal v Reed (2003)* namely that infringing use of a registered trade mark is use which affects the essential functions of a mark, in particular its use as a badge of origin. It concluded that as the average toy car consumer would not assume that the Opel mark on the Autec scale model car was a badge of origin, but rather an indication that this was indeed a scale model of an Opel car, then the origin function of the Opel mark as registered for toys, would not be affected and was therefore not infringing use.

Any use of a registered trade mark that damages the origin function of the mark will be infringing whether or not it is trade mark use. On the facts here, there is no damage to the origin function of the mark. Neither professionals nor consumers believe that Bella's products originate from L'Oceane. Everyone is aware that Bella's products are inferior 'knock offs'. There is nevertheless a market for less expensive 'knock off' perfumes. The key issue here is whether Bella takes unfair advantage of the reputation in L'Oceane's marks when producing its 'knock off' imitation perfumes and whether this amounts to infringing use.

Most recently, in the third of the 'trade mark trilogy' of cases on important trade mark questions which were referred to the ECJ by the Court of Appeal, the question of what constitutes infringing use of a trade mark was considered in *L'Oreal v Bellure (2007)*. This is clearly a case on point and has distinct similarities to the facts and legal issues arising involving L'Oceane plc and Bella Ltd. In *L'Oreal v Bellure*, the claimant, L'Oreal, argued that the use of its trade marks in Bellure's comparison list was infringing trade mark use. Bellure argued that their use of L'Oreal's marks was purely descriptive and not infringing trade mark use. L'Oreal responded that Bellure's use of their marks went beyond purely 'descriptive' use and took unfair advantage of L'Oreal's reputation, reputation or brand attractiveness being a second function of a trade mark distinct from an indicator of origin function. However, Lord Justice Jacob noted that while Bellure's use of the L'Oreal's marks did in fact assist the sales of their 'knock-off' perfumes, such use did not affect L'Oreal's image or the essential indicator of origin function of L'Oreal's registered trade marks, nor did it adversely impact on L'Oreal's sales. He stated, 'No one is deceived. No one thinks any less of the original brands.'

Jacob LJ referred the following question to the ECJ to determine:

Where a trader, in an advertisement for his own goods and services, uses a registered trade mark owned by a competitor for the purpose of comparing the characteristics (and in particular smell) of the goods marketed by him with the characteristics (and in particular the smell) of the goods marketed by the competitor under the mark in such a way that it does not cause confusion or otherwise jeopardise the essential function of the trade mark as an indicator or origin, is that infringing?

In other words, could there be unfair advantage without (a) confusion or (b) detriment to the earlier mark?

In its judgment issued on 18 June 2009, the ECJ found in favour of L'Oreal and responded that article 5(2) of **TM Directive 89/104** must be interpreted as meaning that the taking of unfair advantage of the distinctive character or the repute of a mark, within the meaning of that provision, does not require that there be a likelihood of confusion or a likelihood of detriment to the distinctive character or the repute of the mark or, more generally, to its proprietor. The advantage arising from the use by a third party of a sign similar to a mark with a reputation is an advantage taken unfairly by that third party of the distinctive character or the repute of that mark where that party seeks by that use to ride on the coat-tails of the mark with a reputation in order to benefit from the power of attraction, the reputation and the prestige of that mark and to exploit, without paying any financial compensation, the marketing effort expended by the proprietor of the mark in order to create and maintain the mark's image.

How can unfair advantage be proved? The ECJ stated that in order to determine whether the use of a sign takes unfair advantage of the distinctive character or the repute of the mark, it is necessary to undertake a global assessment, taking into account all factors relevant to the circumstances of the case, which include:

- the strength of the mark's reputation and the degree of distinctive character of the mark;
- the degree of similarity between the marks at issue and the nature and degree of proximity of the goods or services concerned.

As regards the strength of the reputation and the degree of distinctive character of the mark, the Court has already held that the stronger that mark's distinctive character and reputation are, the easier it will be to accept that detriment has been caused to it. It is also clear from the case-law that the more immediately and strongly the mark is brought to mind by the sign, the greater the likelihood that the current or future use of the sign is taking, or will take, unfair advantage of the distinctive character or the repute of the mark or is, or will be, detrimental to them.

On the facts, Bellure had created a link, they had done so for commercial advantage and with the intention of creating an association with L'Oreal. This amounted to taking unfair advantage of L'Oreal marks. This means that the extent of exclusivity offered by a registered trade mark goes beyond a mark's essential function as an indicator of origin and is broader than how the English Courts have traditionally interpreted trade mark use. The ECJ has confirmed that the indicator of origin function is not the only relevant function for infringement purposes. Trade mark owners can prevent 'free riding' even when there is no loss of any sort suffered by the brand, if it can be shown that there is no due cause for the mark to be used. For example, use of a slogan such as, 'the De Beers of mineral water' would be prohibited and actionable by De Beers, the diamond firm, even if there is no loss or damage. Therefore, presenting a product as a replica or imitation will be a trade mark infringement. Applying this decision, L'Oceane is now likely to be successful should it bring an action for trade mark infringement against Bella for using its marks without authority or payment of compensation. L'Oceane should insist Bella pay a licence fee for use of its marks to compensate L'Oceane for its marketing efforts expended in order to create and maintain the mark's image.

Question 37

Is the law that relates to the use of registered trade marks in comparative advertising fair?

Answer plan

This is an essay question designed to elicit a discusion of recent developments in the law of comparative advertising which is closely linked to the law of registered trade marks.

- Define and explain the term 'comparative advertising'.
- Discuss how the **TMA 1994** allows for comparative advertising by virtue of section 10(6).
- Introduce the **Control of Misleading Advertising (Amendment) Regulations 2000**.
- Undertake a critical analysis of the line of case law including: *Card v Advanta (1996)*, *Vodafone v Orange (1997)*, *Cable & Wireless plc v British Telecommunications plc (1998)*, *British Airways plc v Ryanair Ltd (2001)*, *O2 Ltd v Hutchinson 3G UK Ltd (2006)*, *L'Oreal v Bellure (2007)* and *Intel Corporation Inc v CPM United Kingdom Ltd (2008)*.
- Reach a conclusion as to whether, in your view, the law relating to the use of registered trade marks in comparative advertising is fair.

Answer

Comparative advertising or 'knocking copy' is advertising which identifies a competitor. It can be direct or indirect, positive or negative. This type of advertising, particularly when it identifies a competitor or a competitor's goods or services by referring to a registered trade mark, is of particular concern to trade mark owners because their competitors normally seek to make unfavourable comparisons with their own goods or services, or to take advantage of being associated with the market leader's brand.

In the UK in recent years there has been a distinct rise in comparative advertising and a corresponding increase in the legislative and regulatory provides and litigation in the courts. Under the **Trade Marks Act 1994** (TMA 1994), only the proprietor or registered user of a trade mark is entitled to reproduce it. However, comparative advertising in all media will often reproduce a competitor's trade mark. Section 10(6) of the **TMA 1994** provides that 'nothing in the preceding section (s 10(1)–(3) on infringement) shall be construed as preventing the use of a registered trade mark by any person for the purpose of identifying the goods or services as those of the proprietor or licensee'. This is qualified to prohibit detrimental use of the mark. The Act states, ' . . . but any such use otherwise than in accordance with honest business practices in industrial and commerical matters shall be treated as infringing the registered trade mark if the use without due cause takes unfair advantage of, or is detrimental to, the distinctive character of the mark'.

The key piece of legislation that covers comparative advertising is the **Control of Misleading Advertising (Amendment) Regulations 2000** which implemented **Directive 97/55EC on Comparative Advertising**. The effect of this Directive was to harmonise EU law so that both indirect and direct comparative advertising are allowed in all EU member states, subject to certain conditions.

Is the law that relates to the use of registered trade marks in comparative advertising fair? In order to answer this question, it is necessary to consider the relevant case law. Several cases have been decided which have interpreted the meaning and scope of section 10(6) **TMA**. In three early cases, *Barclay Card v Advanta (1996)*, *Vodafone v Orange (1997)* and *Cable & Wireless plc v British Telecommunications plc (1998)* the claimants all failed to persuade the court that their trade marks had been infringed by comparative advertising. These cases would seem to indicate that trade mark owners would have a difficult time in stopping comparative advertising which made reference to their registered trade marks as it was difficult to prove that the competitor had taken 'unfair advantage'. These three cases also indicated that the UK courts had adopted a fairly permissive approach to comparative advertising.

The next important case to clarify the law on comparative advertising was *British Airways plc v Ryanair Ltd (2001)* in which Jacob J confirmed the interpretation of s 10(6) **TMA** 1994 which had emerged in the earlier cases. In particular, British Airways alleged that the price comparisons and the destinations referred to by Ryanair in its comparative advertising were misleading and that this meant Ryanair's advertisement was 'not in accordance with honest practice in industrial and commercial matters' to use the language of s 10(6) of the Act. In his judgment, Justice Jacob established several important principles. First, that the primary objective of s 10(6) is to permit comparative advertising and that so long as the use of the competitor's mark is honest, there is nothing wrong in telling the public of the relative merits of competing goods or services, using the registered mark to identify them. The test for honesty is objective based on whether a reasonable reader would say that the advertisement is not honest, given the full facts. Honesty is to be guaged against what is reasonably expected by the relevant public of an advertisement concerning the particular goods or services in issue and that the public are aware of advertising puffs. The court will not make a minute 'word for word' analysis of the content of the advertisment, but will take a more broad-brush approach in recognition of the way that the majority of people would consider an advertisement. The advertisement should be read as a whole, so that, for example constitutent parts of a mailshot would be read together. Justice Jacob found in favour of Ryanair holding that its comparative advertisements were substantially true, and even if they might be offensive this did not amount to infringement of British Airway's trade marks.

The **Trade Marks Directive 89/104/EC (TMD)** provides that under certain conditions a trade mark owner is entitled to prevent third parties from using a sign that is identical or similar to its own trade mark, including use in advertising. In contrast, the **Comparative Advertising Directive (CAD) (97/55/EC)** permits the use of a rival's trade mark in comparative advertising provided that the advertisement fulfills certain conditions set out in Article 3a of that Directive. Examples of these conditions include that a comparative advertisement must not be misleading, that it must not discredit or denigrate a trade mark, and that it must not take unfair advantage of a trade mark.

In order to confirm the law relating to comparative advertising, the UK courts sought clarification from the European Court of Justice (ECJ) on the interpretation of the two directives. In the first case, *02 Holdings Ltd & anor v Hutchison 3G UK Ltd (2008)*, the ECJ handed down its judgment on 12 June 2008, commenting on the inter-relationship between the two directives. In *Intel Corporation Inc v CPM United Kingdom Ltd (2008)*, Advocate General (AG) Sharpston gave her Opinion on the definition of 'unfair advantage', a concept contained in both the **TMD** and **CAD**. A third case, *L'Oréal SA & ors v Bellure (2007)* concerned comparative advertising lists. Below we will consider the effect these three cases could have on brand owners seeking to prevent their registered trade marks from being used in comparative advertisements.

02 v Hutchison (2008) (the 'Bubbles Case') concerns O2's UK trade mark registrations for static pictures of bubbles used to advertise its mobile phone services. O2 was upset by how a rival mobile phone service provider, Hutchison 3G, used images of bubbles in water when comparing its charges with those of O2 in its television advertising campaign. The bubbles used in Hutchison 3G's advertisement were similar to O2's registered bubbles trade mark.

Although the price comparison in the disputed advertisement was correct and did not mislead customers into believing that there was a trade connection between O2 and Hutchison 3G, O2 sued for trade mark infringement on the ground that the bubbles in Hutchison 3G's advertising were not necessary to make the price comparison between the two services. The High Court dismissed the claim and O2 appealed to the Court of Appeal. Lord Justice Jacob of the Court of Appeal referred questions to the ECJ to clarify whether:

- the use of a competitor's trade mark in a comparative advertisement in such a way that it does not cause confusion or otherwise jeopardise the essential function of the trade mark as an indication of origin amounts to use within Article 5 TMD; and

- the use of a competitor's registered trade mark in a comparative advertisement has to be 'indispensable' to comply with the conditions in the CAD, and if so, the criteria by which indispensability is to be judged.

Mengozzi AG handed down his Opinion on these questions on 31 January 2008. In summary, he concluded that the CAD provides an exhaustive code in relation to comparative advertising. However, if any of the conditions were not met, the sanction would be an action for breach of that directive by the relevant competition authority in the relevant member state. In Mengozzi's view, use of a registered trade mark for comparative advertising purposes does not fall within the ambit of the trade mark infringement provisions in the **TMD**, and a trade mark proprietor does not have a right of action to prevent the use of its mark.

If the ECJ had followed this Opinion, the case would have had major implications for trade mark owners in the UK, since it would have deprived them of the remedy of commencing trade mark infringement proceedings in comparative advertising cases. Instead, they would have been confined to relying on the laws applying the **CAD**, which in the UK are enforced by the Office of Fair Trading and other bodies with very limited enforcement powers.

Fortunately for trade mark owners, the ECJ did not follow all of Mengozzi AG's recommendations, and declined to answer all the Court of Appeal's questions. The ECJ ruled that a registered trade mark owner is not entitled to prevent a third party's use of a sign identical with, or similar to, its own mark, if used in a comparative advertisement satisfying all the conditions laid down in Article 3a **CAD**. The court noted that when a comparative advertisement includes a sign likely to cause confusion on the part of the public, which includes the likelihood of association between the sign and the mark, that advertisement would not satisfy one of the conditions laid down in Article 3a **CAD**. In this scenario, it would then be for the courts to consider whether there was trade mark infringement. The effect of this judgment on the law relating to comparative advertising is that the court will firstly consider whether all the requirements of the **CAD** are met and, if not, only then will the court consider whether the registered trade mark has been infringed. The issue of whether the use of a competitor's mark in comparative advertising must be 'indispensable' to comply with the conditions set out in Article 3a **CAD** remains unresolved as the Court refused to rule on this point. The next step is for the Court of Appeal to apply the ECJ's ruling to the facts. Given that O2 itself has admitted that the bubble imagery in Hutchison's advertising was not misleading, it is likely that the Court of Appeal will conclude that the advertisement complies with all the conditions under the **CAD**, so that no trade mark infringement issues arise and O2's claim will fail.

Next we turn to the *Intel v CPM (2008)* case and the concept of unfair advantage. As mentioned above, one of the requirements for compliance with the **CAD** is that the advertisement must not take unfair advantage of the reputation of a trade mark, trade name or other distinguishing marks of a competitor or of the designation of origin of competing products. The concept of 'unfair advantage' is also contained in the **TMD** as a ground for refusal to register a trade mark or as a ground on which to invalidate a registration. It is also a concept that is relevant to trade mark infringement. 'Unfair advantage' therefore plays an important role in both comparative advertising and trade mark law. The meaning of the phrase 'unfair advantage' was considered by Sharpston AG in her Opinion of 26 June 2008. Intel, the owner of the trade mark 'Intel', applied to invalidate the later mark 'Intelmark', registered in class 35 for marketing and telemarketing services by CPM. The 'Intel' mark was registered in classes 9, 16, 38 and 42 for computers and computer-linked goods and services. The UK courts noted Intel's strong reputation for the 'Intel' word mark in respect of computers and computer-related goods and services, even before 1997 when the 'Intelmark' registration took effect. The Court accepted that although the marks were similar they were applied to very different goods and services, so that use of 'Intelmark' did not suggest a trade connection with Intel, but hinted at the 'Intel' mark. The issue to be decided was whether Intel could rely on article 4.4(a) to invalidate the 'Intelmark' trade mark. Article 4.4(a) **TMD** provides that a trade mark shall not be registered, or if registered, shall be liable to be declared invalid, where and to the extent that:

> . . . the trade mark is identical with, or similar to, an earlier national trade mark . . . and is to be, or has been, registered for goods or services which are not similar to those for which the earlier trade mark is registered, where the earlier trade mark has a reputation in the member state concerned and where the use of the later trade mark without due cause would take unfair advantage of, or be detrimental to, the distinctive character or the repute of the earlier trade mark.

The High Court refused to invalidate the 'Intelmark' registration so Intel appealed to the Court of Appeal which determined that it required clarification of aspects of Article 4.4(a), and whether the facts were sufficient to establish unfair advantage and, if not, what factors the court should take into account.

In her opinion, Sharpston AG concluded that while the earlier mark has a huge reputation for certain specific types of goods or services, that those goods or services are dissimilar to the goods or services of the later mark, and is unique in respect of any goods or services – this was not sufficient to establish unfair advantage within the meaning of Article 4.4(a). She stated that in order to decide whether a case of unfair advantage (or free-riding) is established, the national court must take account of all factors relevant to the circumstances of the case. The national court should focus on the benefit gained by the later mark from being linked to the well-known earlier mark, rather than on whether the earlier mark is harmed by being linked to the later mark. Sharpston AG was clear that a claimant needs to establish some sort of advantage or boost given to the later mark by its link with the earlier mark. She further confirmed that if the connotations of the earlier mark have merely a neutral effect on the performance of the later mark, unfair advantage seems unlikely. By way of example, she referred to a range of expensive hand-made jewellery being sold under the mark 'Coca-Cola' which would not benefit the marketing of the jewellery unfairly (or at all) by using the Coca-Cola Company's trade mark. In substance, she was of the view that the mere fact that an earlier mark is unique and has a strong reputation does not mean a later mark necessarily takes unfair advantage of the earlier mark. However, it makes sense that the greater the reputation and distinctiveness of the earlier mark and the greater the similarity between the goods or services covered by the two marks, the more likely it is that the later mark will derive advantage from any link established between the two in the mind of the public. Further, if the later mark is to derive unfair advantage, the associations with the earlier mark must enhance the performance of the later mark. A final decision from the ECJ is imminent.

Finally, in the 'smell-alike' case of *L'Oréal v Bellure (2007)* the same issues arose. Bellure imported, distributed and sold products that 'knocked off' L'Oreal's luxury perfumes. However, the similarity was unlikely to mislead professionals. Even the public could clearly identify that Bellure's products 'knocked off' and were inferior products to those of L'Oreal. Bellure provided their retailers with lists which compared the scent of their 'knock off' product with that of the L'Oreal fragrance being imitated, in each case identified by reference to the word mark by which the L'Oreal fragrance was known. The sale of Bellure's inexpensive 'knock offs' had no impact on L'Oreals luxury perfume sales and it was accepted that no one was confused as to the origin of Bellure's 'knock off' fragrances. In proceedings in the UK, the judge at first instance held that Bellure's packaging amounted to an infringement under Article 5.2 **TMD**, as did the comparison lists. The 'honest practices' defence under the **TMD** advanced by Bellure was dismissed. Both parties appealed and the Court of Appeal referred several questions to the ECJ in October 2007. *L'Oréal v Bellure* is the first time the ECJ has been asked to interpret the concept of 'unfair advantage' under the CAD.

In June 2009, the ECJ held that article 5(2) of **TM Directive 89/104** must be interpreted as meaning that the taking of unfair advantage of the distinctive character or the repute of a mark, within the meaning of that provision, does not require that there be a likelihood of confusion or a likelihood of detriment to the distinctive character or the repute of the mark or, more generally, to its proprietor. The advantage arising from the use by a third party of a sign similar to a mark with a reputation is an advantage taken unfairly by that third party of the distinctive character or the repute of that mark where that party seeks by that use to ride on the coat-tails of the mark with a reputation in order to benefit from the power of attraction, the reputation and the prestige of that mark and to exploit, without paying any financial compensation, the marketing effort expended by the proprietor of the mark in order to create and maintain the mark's image. This interpretation favours L'Oreal. How can unfair advantage be proved? The ECJ stated that in order to determine whether the use of a sign takes unfair advantage of the distinctive character or the repute of the mark, it is necessary to undertake a global assessment, taking into account all factors relevant to the circumstances of the case, which include:

- the strength of the mark's reputation and the degree of distinctive character of the mark;
- the degree of similarity between the marks at issue and the nature and degree of proximity of the goods or services concerned.

The more immediately and strongly the mark is brought to mind by the sign, the greater the likelihood that the current or future use of the sign is taking, or will take, unfair advantage of the distinctive character or the repute of the mark or is, or will be, detrimental to them. Bellure had created a link, they had done so for commercial advantage and with the intention of creating an association with L'Oreal. This amounted to taking unfair advantage of L'Oreal marks. This means that the extent of exclusivity offered by a registered trade mark goes beyond a mark's essential function as an indicator of origin and is broader than how the English Courts have traditionally interpreted trade mark use. The ECJ has confirmed that the indicator of origin function is not the only relevant function for infringement purposes. Trade mark owners can prevent 'free riding' even when there is no loss of any sort suffered by the brand, if it can be shown that there is no due cause for the mark to be used.

In conclusion, as a result of the additional judicial guidance as to the scope of the concept of 'unfair advantage' it appears that the law that relating to the use of registered trade marks in comparative advertising now provides more protection for registered trade mark owners. Brand owners have increased opportunities to use their registered trade mark rights to prevent competitors from linking their well-known brands to the competitor's own products. Therefore, from the point of view of brand owners, the law is more fair.

◊ Question 38

Matelot et Cie is a clothing company incorporated in France in 1986. It registered the trade mark 'MATELOT' in the United Kingdom on 1 April 1996 and subsequently registered the company's distinctive logo in 1998. Miss Celia Crane, a British citizen and unrelated to the French company, registered a. com domain name on 1 April 2005. The registration was for the domain name MATELOT.com

During July and August 2005 there was inconclusive e-mail correspondence between Matelot et Cie and Miss Crane in which it sought to acquire the MATELOT.COM domain name for £1000. On 1 November 2005, Ms Crane or her agents registered the company name 'Matelot.Com Ltd'.

On 11 February 2006, Matelot et Cie trade mark agents Clerk & Marks (London, UK) wrote to Ms Crane setting out the grounds for a complaint. Ms Crane did not respond to this letter.

Advise Matelot et Cie.

Answer plan

This is a mixed question concerning a typical domain name dispute. It requires a knowledge of both the laws relating to trade marks and the Uniform Dispute Resolution Policy.

- Characteristics of registered trade marks;
- Legitimate registration of a domain name vs bad faith registration;

- Uniform Dispute Resolution Policy (UDRP);
- WIPO Arbitration and Mediation Center;
- UK jurisprudence.

Answer

The central issue of this problem question is whether securing UK registered trade mark automatically confers a right to use that mark as a domain name. Does the trade mark registration for MATELOT in the UK in 1996 by Matelot et Cie confer a right to use that mark as a domain name? Trade marks only grant national protection, whereas a domain name has global application. Because the same mark may be registered by different proprietors for different goods or services, someone else may also have legitimately registered the mark as their domain name. By contrast, a domain name must be unique. Once registered, a domain name is not tied to the owner's field of business as is a trade mark.

Domain names are registered on a 'first-come first-served' basis, and trade mark owners have no prior right to a domain name incorporating their mark. The rules for domain name registration are based on contractual agreement between the applicant and the registry. Domain name registries do not undertake trade mark searches before registering names. This has frequently led to disputes when the owner of a trade mark or business name is denied the use of that mark or business name as a domain name because another party has already registered it as a domain name. This is what has happened to the French company, Matelot et Cie.

A particularly difficult legal issue arises when the domain name registrant is not a 'cyber-squatter' but has a legitimate reason for registering the domain name. The facts relating to Ms Crane's registration of the domain name have to be explored to determine whether this is a case of a genuine dispute over a domain name or a case of cybersquatting (domain name piracy). However, in certain circumstances protection is afforded to trade mark owners through the courts and the WIPO dispute resolution procedures. Under the Uniform Dispute Resolution Policy (UDRP), Matelot may be able to secure a transfer of the domain name back to itself if it is able to prove that:

1. the domain name is identical or confusingly similar to a trade mark or service mark in which it has rights;

2. the third party has no rights or legitimate interests in respect of the domain name;

3. the domain name must have been registered by a third party and is being used in bad faith. Evidence of bad faith can be one of the following:

a. An offer to sell, rent or otherwise transfer the domain name to the owner of the trade or service mark, or to a competitor marketer of the owner of the trade or service mark, for valuable consideration.

b. An attempt to attract, for financial gain, Internet users to the domain name holder's website or other on-line location by creating confusion with the trade or service mark of the complainant ('passing off').

c. The registration of the domain name in order to prevent the owner of the trade or service mark from entering the market and corresponding domain name, provided that a pattern of such conduct has been established on the part of the domain name holders.

d. The registration of the domain name in order to disrupt the business of the complainant.

Most UDRP litigation takes place online and an action can be commenced through the World Intellectual Property Organisation's (WIPO) Arbitration and Mediation Centre, established in 1994 to offer alternative dispute resolution option for the resolution of international commercial disputes between private parties. The WIPO Centre is widely recognised as the leading dispute resolution service provider arising out of the abusive registration and use of Internet domain names.

The UDRP, however, is not designed to resolve disputes where each party has a legitimate claim to a domain name, nor is the UDRP intended to deprive the parties of their legal remedies and the parties to a domain name dispute can at any time litigate the issue in the courts.

However, as Matelot et Cie is unaware of the reasons behind Ms Crane's domain registration such that it is not able to currently assess whether she has registered the name in good faith or bad faith, a way forward for Matelot is to seek a UDRP panel decision. There has been frequent criticism that the UDRP panels have consistently made decisions that favour trade mark owners, especially in circumstances where trade mark principles would not have led to success (for example unregistered trade marks). This approach would tend to work in Matelot et Cie's favour. However, under the UDRP, the panel can only decide to transfer or cancel the domain name, or deny the complaint. It is not possible for the panel to make any monetary judgments.

Once a URDP panel decision has been made, it will not be implemented for 10 days, during which time either party may apply to a national court, if the claimant can substantiate the registered trade mark infringement or passing off. Any decision reached by the arbitration panel would be superseded by a court judgment. This approach will assist Matelot et Cie to discover the reasons for Ms Crane's registration and help it to determine whether it will need to pursue the matter in a UK court.

The UK courts take the view that any attempt to sell the domain name is prima facie an act of bad faith. In *Jeanette Winterson v Mark Hogarth (2000)* the respondent appeared to be a cybersquatter, having registered over 100 writers' names as domain names and offering to sell them to those writers. He claimed that he was setting up unofficial websites dedicated to information about the writers. The domain names jeanettewinterson.org.com and .net were all transferred back to her. Domain name registrars such as the UK's Nominet are still required to follow decisions of the courts. It is not clear that Ms Crane has made any offer to sell the domain name to Matelot et Cie. If Matelot could prove that such an offer had been made, its legal position would be much stronger. The fact that Ms Crane registered her company only after emails from Matelot et Cie could indicate bad faith, but further information is required. For example, Ms Crane could have been operating as a sole trader or in a partnership prior to registering as a company.

In conclusion, the number of domain name disputes filed with WIPO in 2006 increased by 25 per cent as compared to 2005. In relation to the quality of decisions by the UDRP, there has been criticism that they are not always consistent. In order to address this concern, WIPO has begun to publish its decisions. Further, WIPO acknowledges that the UDRP decision criteria must accommodate changing circumstances and new developments. For example, there is a new generation of techno-cybersquatters who use software to mass register domain names over every word available.

CHAPTER 8

PASSING OFF

In the United Kingdom, the common law tort of passing off enables an enterprise to protect its business's goodwill. Goodwill is intangible and this is why the subject falls within the intellectual property law regime. Passing off may apply in situations where trade mark protection does not apply. If a registered trade mark exists, the proprietor can sue both for trade mark infringement as well as for passing off. The concept for passing off derives from the ancient case of *Perry v Truefitt (1842),* which ruled that a trader must not 'sell his own goods under the pretence that they are the goods of another man'.

For example, Trader A will commit a tort against Trader B if he passes off his goods or business as those of B. Trader B need not prove that Trader A acted intentionally or with intent to deceive. Nor does Trader B have to prove that anyone was actually deceived, if deception was likely. Further, this cause of action does not require Trader B to prove damage.

The tort of passing off is usually carried out by imitating the appearance of the claimant's goods, or by selling them under the same or a similar name. If the name used by the claimant merely describes the goods, then generally no action will lie. It is not necessary for the defendant's trade to be identical to that of the claimant if there is sufficient similarity to mislead the public.

False advertising is not generally considered to amount to passing off, but it may in exceptional circumstances. Reverse passing off may occur when the defendant holds out the claimant's goods as his own: *Bristol Conservatories Ltd v Conservatories Custom Built (1989).*

There is an international obligation to assure effective protection against unfair competition under Art 10bis of the **Paris Convention**. Finally, the remedies for a successful claim of passing off include an injunction and either damages or an account of profits. Damages will reflect the lost profit plus loss of goodwill and reputation. A delivery up order is also available.

Question 39

Kensington Fashion Ltd has sold clothes under the 'Kensington Chick' label since the 1960s in their shops in Nottingham, Leeds and York but was refused trade mark registration. In 2007, another clothing manufacturing firm, Kensington Man Ltd, proposed to extend their business from men's clothing to womenswear and brought out their own 'Kensington Chick' clothing line. The line sold successfully in Leicester, Coventry and Northampton. Kensington Fashion Ltd has plans to open a fourth store in Leicester in 2008. Advise Kensington Fashion Ltd as to any cause of action they may have against Kensington Man Ltd. If successful, would the appropriate remedy be an injunction covering all of the UK and Wales?

Answer plan

This problem question focuses on the tort of 'passing off' as there are no registered trade mark rights. An action in passing off is a common law tort whereas other forms of protection (ie copyright, trade marks, design rights and patents) are statute-based rights. The facts of the problem are based on the case of *Chelsea Man Menswear Ltd v Chelsea Girl Ltd {1987} RPC 189*. Lecturers often re-configure the facts of an existing case usually designed to reward those students who have done the recommended reading on the topic. The question essentially has two parts.

- Introduce and define the common law tort of passing off;
- Outline the elements required for a successful action in passing off as established in *Reckitt and Coleman Products v Borden Inc {1990}*;
- Apply each element to the facts in turn and reach a conclusion as to KF's likelihood of success;
- Introduce the equitable remedy of injunction; and
- Consider the terms on which the Court might injunct KM from using the words 'Kensington Chick' in future.

Answer

As Kensington Fashion Ltd ('KF') have been refused trade mark registration they cannot rely on any registered rights under the *Trade Marks Act 1994*. Further, the UK has no law of unfair competition as in the EU and other civil law countries. However, KF may have a cause of action against Kensington Man Ltd ('KM') based on the common law tort of passing off which has its origins in the tort of deception. The tort of passing off is sometimes referred to as protection of the goodwill in a business or a concept and makes it possible for a trader to protect a business' goodwill. Goodwill is an intangible concept but is nevertheless a property right. According to Lord MacNaughten in *Inland Revenue Cmrs v Muller & Co's Margarine Ltd {1901} AC 217* the concept of goodwill means:

> Every positive advantage that has been acquired in carrying on the business which would give a reasonable expectancy of preference in the face of competition; the benefit and advantage of the good name, reputation, and connection of a business' and 'the attractive force that brings in custom.

In other words, the positive benefits that attract a consumer to prefer one business' products (or in this case, clothing line) over another.

The underlying basis for an action for passing off is found in the case of *Perry v Truefit (1842)* which held that 'A man is not to sell his own goods under the pretence that they are the goods of another man . . .'. Passing off may therefore be defined as a misrepresentation in the course of trade by one trader which damages the goodwill of another. In the context of the problem at hand, this means that KF may be able to bring an action for passing off against KM for their use of the words 'Kensington Chick' in connection with the KM clothing sold in Leicester and York.

Since the decision in *Perry v Truefit* in 1842 there have been several important cases that further developed the law of passing off including *Reddaway & Co Ltd v Banham & Co Ltd (1896)*, *Spalding & Brov AW Gamage Ltd (1915)*, *Bollinger v Costa Brava Wine Co Ltd (1960)* and *Warnink BV v Townend & Sons (Hull) Ltd (1980)*. However, the classic legal definition of passing off was established by the 'Jif Lemon' case. In *Reckitt & Coleman Products Ltd v Borden Inc {1990} All ER 1873 HL*, Lord Oliver reduced the elements to be proved in a passing off action to three. These three elements are now known as the 'classic trinity' formulation:

- Goodwill or reputation attached to goods and services (eg in claimant's goods, name, mark, get up etc);
- A misrepresentation made to the public (leading to confusion or deception) causing. . .
- Damage – actual or potential to the claimant.

Lord Oliver's classic definition of an action for passing off has since been endorsed in: *Consorzio del Prosciutto di Parma v Marks & Spencer Plc {1991} RPC 351*; *Harrods v Harrodian School (1996)*; and *BBC v Talksport (2001)*. The advantage of the 'classic trinity' formulation is that it is simpler and is preferred in practice. For KF to be successful in an action for passing off against KM, it must satisfy all three elements.

Firstly, does goodwill exist in KF's clothing label name 'Kensington Chick'? The words are descriptive in that 'Kensington' is a geographic word for the place known as Kensington in London and 'Chick' is slang for a young woman. In *County Sound plc v Ocean Sound Ltd {1991} FSR 367* the court found that the purely descriptive words did not attract goodwill. However, one could argue here that this case can be distinguished as KF have been using the two-word combination for more than forty years, whereas the use of descriptive words in *County Sound* was new use. Nevertheless, the length of time it takes to establish goodwill sufficient to bring an action for passing off is a question of fact in each case. However, in *Antec International Ltd v South Western Chicks (Warren) Ltd {1998} EWHC Patents 330* goodwill was established through use of a name for a period of ten years and in *Stennards Reay {1967} FSR 140* goodwill existed after just five weeks' use. We will assume for the sake of further analysis that a Court would find that a period of forty-plus years' use by KF of the name 'Kensington Chick' would attract sufficient goodwill to found an action for passing off against KM. KF must be careful to ensure that goodwill exists (ie there are actual customers for its Kensington Chick clothing line) and not merely reputation as there is strong authority that the law of passing off only protects goodwill and not reputation. Indeed, in *Harrods Ltd v Harrodian School Ltd (1996)* Millet LJ stated that ' . . . damage to reputation without damage to goodwill is not sufficient to support an action for passing off'.

Secondly, has KM made a material misrepresentation to the public (whether or not intentional), leading or likely to lead the public to believe that the clothing line sold by KM in Leicester, Coventry and Northampton are the clothing line of KF? In other words, is KM's Kensington Chick clothing line associated in the minds of the public with those of KF? The fact that the public may be confused as to the origin of the clothing line may not necessarily amount to a material misrepresentation: *Phones 4u Ltd v Phone4u.co.uk Internet Ltd (2007)*; *HFC Bank v HSBC Bank plc (2000)*. An initial misrepresentation which is corrected before the actual point of sale or contract may not amount to a material misrepresentation and therefore no actionable misrepresentation in passing off: *BP Amoco plc v John Kelly Ltd (2001)*. Further, customers will not be assumed to be 'morons in a hurry' to quote Foster J in *Morning Star Co-operative Society v Express Newspapers (1979)*. On the other hand, KM will not have a defence by asserting that the public would not have been misled if they were more 'literate, careful, perspicacious or wary': *Reckitt & Coleman (1990)*. As to whether KM has misrepresented a connection with the KF Kensington Chick clothing line, the court will assess the amount of attention a typical customer might be expected to exercise in purchasing the clothing, the type of shop in which the clothing is sold and generally the habits and characteristics of women's clothing consumers and how many customers have been misled. In relation to the number of customers deceived, KF will have to show that KM misled a substantial number of customers, but not all of the potential public: *Neutrogena Corp v Golden Ltd (1996)* per Morritt LJ. KF may wish to consider gathering survey evidence from customers and/or engaging an industry expert to give evidence to support its case.

Thirdly, the last element is damage (or the likelihood of damage) to KF's goodwill. KF must establish that there is a real likelihood of more than minimal damage to its goodwill: *Warnink BV Townend & Sons (Hull) Ltd (1980)*; *Harrods Ltd v Harrodian School Ltd (1996)*. Here, there is a strong likelihood of damage to KF's goodwill given (1) the damage by association caused by KM's misrepresentation that there is some connection between the parties; and (2) the damage caused directly through lost sales to KM, or (3) damage caused indirectly to the reputation of the Kensington Chick label.

KF may bring an action for passing off in the county court and the High Court. KF will want to know what remedies it will have if it is successful in its action for passing off against KM and in particular how to stop KM from using the Kensington Chick name as quickly as possible. KF will seek an order for an interim injunction against KM which would result in KM being stopped from continuing to sell its Kensington Chick clothing line until the issues were resolved at trial. In terms of an application for an interim injunction, only goodwill in the UK is relevant and while this does not present an issue for KF whose business is carried on in Nottingham, Leeds and York, one should consider the question of the geographical area over which KF's goodwill may be regarded as extending, as KF may have a reputation that is wider than Nottingham, Leeds and York. Further, KF have plans to open a fourth store in Leicester which would be in direct competition with KM's store. Here, it is likely that the defendants, KM, will argue that any injunction made against them should be confined to the areas of the claimants' (KF) pre-existing business, namely Nottingham, Leeds and York. However, a similar argument was rejected by the Court of Appeal in *Chelsea Man Menswear Ltd v Chelsea Girl Ltd,* a case in point, which allowed an injunction covering all of England and Wales. The Court of Appeal had regard to the fact that both people and goods move around the country, and also to the claimants' desire to extend their business in the future (although no specific plans appeared to have been made). Nourse LJ noted that *A. Levey v Henderson-Kenton (Holdings) Ltd {1974} RPC 617* was the only reported case to have imposed a geographical limit and only at the pre-trial stage. In *Levey*, the claimant who had run a department store business in Newcastle-upon-Tyne was granted an injunction at trial to prevent the defendant from opening a furniture and furnishing shop under the name 'Kentons' in Newcastle or the Newcastle area. The defendant group already operated 'Kentons' shops in the South of England. The desire of businesses to expand legitimately in the future may well make the *Chelsea Man* case the model for the future. There may nevertheless still be circumstances in which local goodwill exists and in which a geographically limited injunction is appropriate. The *Daily Mail* newspaper relied successfully on its goodwill in London and the south-east of England to stop the publication of a London evening newspaper under the name *London Evening Mail: Associated Newspapers, Daily Mail & General Trust v Express Newspapers {2003} FSR 51.*

Question 40

Janet Torvin is a former Olympic gold medallist ice dancer who turned professional when she joined a company that toured across Britain and overseas in the 1980s. In late 2008, at 48 years old, Janet lives in the UK and is preparing skating routines for a television ice dancing show, 'Ice Dancing Stars' which she is also producing. Earlier in the year, another TV production company, Winter Sport Productions Ltd (WSP), produced for sale in the UK a DVD entitled, 'Learn to Ice Dance Basics'. To illustrate the cover of the DVD, WSP used a picture of Janet from a photograph taken by a member of their staff while Janet was performing a routine in a live show at the Nottingham Arena in 2004. Janet is now suing WSP for passing off. Advise Janet as to the prospects of success of her action against WSP.

Answer plan

This problem question relates to celebrity image rights and passing off (the extended form of passing off).

- Introduce the notion of protection for personality and the legal recognition of image rights;
- In particular the issue of celebrity endorsement is relevant: *Irvine v Talksport (2002)*; and
- Consider whether the required elements of passing off are satisfied and any potential remedies Torvin may have against Winter Sport Production Ltd.

Answer

Some famous people, such as Janet Torvin, may be in a position to exploit their personality or reputation in a particular field by endorsing goods or services. Where a real person is concerned, the legal issues arising not only relate to commerce, but also to personal dignity and autonomy. In this case, the public may infer from Winter Sport Productions Ltd (WSP) representation that Janet Torvin is endorsing its ice dancing instructional DVD entitled 'Learn to Ice Dance Basics'. It is clear from the facts that Torvin did not authorise WSP to use her image on the DVD cover and that a cause of action may lie in passing off. Although not expressly stated, it would appear that Torvin would be more concerned with loss of commercial exploitation and profit than with damages for loss of dignity and autonomy, particularly as the market for the DVD is likely to be the same target market for her forthcoming 'Ice Dancing Stars' TV show. As an internationally known ice dancer, Torvin is likely to have significant commercial potential for exploiting her identity. Passing off resulting from a false impression that Torvin has endorsed a product may be determined on the basis of what she would normally charge as a fee for such an endorsement.

The law of relating to celebrity endorsement and passing off has developed in particular as a result of the decision in *Irvine v Talksport (2002)* which accepted that falsely implying that a celebrity was endorsing a product is actionable under the common law tort of passing off. For the first time, the UK courts acknowledged the right of celebrities to exploit their image and judicial notice was taken that celebrities do exploit their name and image through endorsements both inside and outside their own field. Justice Laddie indicated that the law of passing off had widened since the decision in *McCulloch v May (Produce Distributors) Ltd (1947)* to encompass celebrity endorsement. The *Irvine* case involved the Formula One racing driver Eddie Irvine and concerned the manipulation of his photograph used in an advertising campaign for radio station Talksport. The mobile phone Irvine had been holding when the photograph was taken had been replaced by a superimposed picture of a radio and underneath was the caption 'Talk Radio . . . We've got it covered'. In terms of Irvine's celebrity, he had since 1996 built up a worldwide reputation in the sport, which was accompanied by a growing business in endorsing products. Taking into account persuasive decisions from both Australia and New Zealand, Mr Justice Laddie found that the public can be misled if the likeness of a famous person is used to advertise a product without authorisation. It is necessary, however, that this person has built up sufficient goodwill and that the advertiser gives the impression that the person used really endorses the product. It would appear that although 'the man in the street' can still be used for advertising purposes without a licence, at least as far as the action of passing off is concerned, the same is not the case with a celebrity who may have image rights that need to be respected. Modern celebrities may have a reputation in their own field of endeavour which they may also use to endorse unrelated products for significant sums of money eg perfumes, clothing. Mr Justice Laddie found in favour of Irvine and held that a celebrity *did* have a monopoly over the use of his or her image. Laddie J stated, 'the endorsee is taking the benefit of the attractive force which is the reputation or goodwill of a famous person'. In order to be successful, Torvin will have to prove that:

- at the time the acts complained of occurred, she had a significant reputation or goodwill; and

- WSP's actions led to the false impression to a 'not insignificant section of her market' that Torvin had endorsed, recommended or approved WSP's actions.

The *Irvine* case clarified the law so that endorsement is definitely actionable where the celebrity in question has not consented to the use of his or her image. However, it could be argued that if a celebrity's image has been used without the implication of endorsement, the defendant may escape liability. This anomaly highlights the need for image rights *per se* to be legally protected. In some cases, it can also be defamatory to assert that a person has endorsed a product or service when this is not true. This is a matter of fact for the court.

Further, it is no longer the law that the parties must be in a common field of activity for passing off to occur, nor that damage will be confined simply to loss of sales. What is needed, however, is an association between the defendant's goods and the claimant. Clearly, where the parties do share a common field of activity it will be easier for the claimant to demonstrate that there has been a misrepresentation.

Accordingly, it would seem that Torvin's endorsement is indeed commercially valuable given her fame in the UK and internationally in the sphere of ice dancing. Although the endorsement on the 'Learn to Ice Dance Basics' DVD is unauthorised, a significant number of members of the public are likely to infer endorsement from WSP's representation. As such, Torvin has every prospect of success in relation to her action for passing off. Torvin will suffer the loss of earnings, both for this and for future endorsements so the appropriate remedy is an award of damages. How should damages be assessed in this type of case? In *Irvine v Talksport*, Laddie J held that the principles used to assess damages for patent infringement should be applied to celebrity endorsement cases. Irvine gave evidence that he would not have 'bothered to get out of bed' for less than £25,000'. Laddie J however assessed the damages as what would have been a 'reasonable' fee for Irvine's endorsement of the defendant's radio station. This was held to be the sum of £2,000. Irvine appealed and the Court of Appeal which took into account his evidence, awarded him £25,000 in damages. Accordingly, Torvin's claim for damages will be assessed by considering the licence fee she would have charged for the lawful use of her image for such an endorsement. In light of the authority, WSP may prefer to settle the matter with Torvin out of court by paying her a licence fee thereby avoiding the need to pay legal costs in addition to any damages award.

CHAPTER 9

GEOGRAPHICAL INDICATIONS

Legal protection is available for geographical terms when a valuable association has been created over time between a product and the region from which it originates, such as 'Parma ham' or 'Champagne'. Producers or traders from the region sharing the name may apply for either UK domestic legal protection or European Community rights. In the EU, this right is called a 'protected designation of origin' (PDO). A PDO is a sign used on goods and stating that a given product originates in a given geographical area and possesses qualities or reputation due to that place of origin. A PDO product must originate from a particular area, be fully produced, processed and prepared in that area and have qualities and characteristics which are exclusively due to a particular geographical environment. Only groups of producers may apply for a PDO to be registered.

Some of the first PDO registrations in the UK covered White Stilton and Blue cheeses, Orkney beef, Orkney lamb and Jersey Royal potatoes. An application is currently on foot to protect the Melton Mowbray pork pie as a PDO.

The criteria for a Protected Geographical Indication (GI) are less stringent. The geographical link must arise in at least one of the stages of production, processing or preparation. GIs may be used for a variety of products, particularly agricultural products.

At the international level, the **Trade Related Agreement on Intellectual Property Rights (TRIPS)** sets out the minimum standards of protection for GIs in Arts 22–24.

Further, the registration of a trade mark under the **Trade Marks Act 1994** for goods may be opposed on the ground that it contains a sign or consists of a sign which is a GI for goods originating in a country, region or locality other than that from which the relevant goods originated.

Question 41

Explain both the meaning and the legal protection (if any) afforded by:

(a) an indication of source;

(b) a geographical indication of origin;

(c) an appellation of origin;

(d) a protected designation of origin;

(e) a protected geographical indication;

(f) a certificate of special character.

Answer plan

This is a standard subdivided short answer question. Answer each sub-question in turn, clearly identifying the separate parts of the essay (a)–(f). Assume that each subdivision carries equal marks. Allocate equal time to each subs.

Answer

The core function of a trade sign such as a geographical indication, a name or a trade mark is to provide information to the consumer. With the increased mobility of goods since the industrial revolution and now globalisation, there is increased potential for confusion as to origin, including deliberate free-riding on the reputation of well-known geographical indications. In this field, there are many terms relating to geographical indications or GIs. The specific meaning of some of the key categories of GIs is set out below.

(a) Indication of source

An indication of source is simply an indication of provenance or origin. There is no legal requirement that there be any correlation between the characteristics or quality of a product and the place that the product came from. Examples include French perfume, Italian wine and German cars.

(b) Geographical Indication of Origin (GI)

Art 22(1) of the **Trade Related Agreement on Intellectual Property (TRIPS)** defines GIs as 'indications, which identify a good as originating in the territory of a Member, or a region or locality in that territory, where a given quality, reputation or other characteristic of the good is essentially attributable to its geographical origin'.

The **TRIPS Agreement** requires the geographic location to imbue the product with particular traits or characteristics. This extends beyond the quality of the product to include 'reputation or other characteristic of the good' (note the similarity with trade mark law). TRIPS defines general standards of protection of GIs for all kinds of goods (Art 22) and additional standards for wines and spirits (Art 23).

(c) Appellation of Origin

This is a specific type of GI. According to Art 2 **Lisbon Agreement for the Protection of Appellations of Origin and their International Registration of 1958** it is the 'geographic name of a country, region, or locality, which serves to designate a product originating therein, the quality or characteristics of which are due exclusively or essentially due to the geographical environment, including natural and human factors'. The geographic location must imbue the product with particular traits or characteristics. There must be a link between product and place. The concept of a GI encompasses appellations of origin.

(d) Protected Designation of Origin (PDO)

This is the term used to describe the designation of origin that has been registered under the 1992 EU Regulation on the protection of geographical indications and designations of origin for agricultural products and foodstuffs ('**PDO Regulation**').

A designation of origin is defined as the name of a region, a specific place, or country. It is also necessary to show that:

- the quality or characteristics of the product are 'essentially or exclusively due to a particular geographical environment with its inherent natural and human factors'; and

- the production, processing, and preparation take place in the defined geographical area.

A number of different products have been registered as PDOs in the UK: Cornish clotted cream, West Country Farmhouse Cheddar cheese, Jersey Royal potatoes, Shetland lamb, White Stilton and many others.

(e) Protected Geographical Indication (PGI)

This is the term that is used to describe a designation of origin that has been also registered under the **PDO Regulation**. GIs are defined as the name of a region, a specific place or, in exceptional cases, a country used to describe an agricultural product or foodstuff. To qualify for GI protection:

- A product must originate in that region, specific place or country.

- The product or foodstuff must also possess a specific quality, reputation, or other characteristic attributable to that geographical origin.

- The production, processing *or* preparation takes place in the defined geographical area (art 2(1) **PDO Regulation**).

149

A number of different GIs have been registered in the UK, including: Newcastle Brown Ale, Rutland Bitter, Whitstable Oysters, Scottish Beef, Welsh Lamb, Scottish Lamb, Welsh Beef, Dorset Blue Cheese, Exmoor Blue Cheese, Herefordshire Cider, Herefordshire Perry, Worcestershire Cider, Worcestershire Perry, Gloucestershire Cider, Gloucestershire Perry, Kentish Ale.

In the famous case of *Consorzio del Prosciutto di Parma v Asda Store Ltd* (2002) involving Parma ham, Lord Hoffman said, 'a PGI is similar to a PDO except that the causal link between the place of origin and the quality of the product may be a matter of reputation rather than verifiable fact.'

(f) Certificates of Special Character (CSC)

This is the term given to traditional foods and recipes registered under the **1992 EU Regulation on certificates of specific character for agricultural products and foodstuffs (the Traditional Foods Regulation).** Specific character means the 'features or set of features which distinguishes an agricultural product or a foodstuff clearly from other similar products or foodstuffs belonging to the same category'.

For a name to be registered to obtain a certificate of special character, it must:

- be specific;
- express the specific character of the foodstuff or product;
- be traditional or established by custom (Art 2(1)).

As well as granting property rights over use of the registered name, registration to obtain a Certificate of Special Character also enable producers to use the designation Traditional Specialty Guaranteed (TSG) and the accompanying logo.

In conclusion, GIs as a general concept are understood by consumers to denote the origin and quality of products. Many of them have acquired valuable reputations which, if not adequately protected, may be misrepresented by dishonest commercial operators. False use of geographical indications by unauthorised parties is detrimental to consumers and legitimate producers. The former are deceived and led into believing to buy a genuine product with specific qualities and characteristics, while they usually in fact get a cheaper imitation. The latter suffer damage because valuable business is lost and the established reputation for their products is damaged.

Question 42

The **TRIPS Agreement** requires additional 'indication of origin' protection for wines and spirits. Discuss by reference to relevant legislation, case law and illustrate with examples. Should this level of protection be afforded to other types of goods, for example Swiss watches or other non-foodstuffs?

Answer plan

- Introduce the concept of a GI as a form of intellectual property;
- **Trade Related Agreement on Intellectual Property** (Arts 22–24);
- Higher-level of protection for wines and spirits;
- Interim solution of bilateral agreements.

Answer

In the House of Lords' decision in *Consorzio del Prosciutto di Parma v Asda Stores Ltd (2002)* Lord Hoffmann said that a protected designation of origin (PDO) is a form of intellectual property right. Both the UK courts and the ECJ recognise GIs as intellectual property. He further said that 'a PGI is similar to a PDO except that the causal link between the place of origin and the quality of the product may be a matter of reputation rather than verifiable fact'. The basis for a GI is that there is an exclusive link between the product and the place. The members of a collective group from the region control and share the GI rights.

At an international level this was firstly acknowledged in the **Paris Convention for the Protection of Industrial Property**, followed by the **Madrid Agreement for the Repression of False or Misleading indications of Source on Goods** and the **Lisbon Agreement for the Protection of Appellations of Origin and their International Registration**. TRIPS is the most important international agreement in this area mainly because of its broad membership and the fact that it was most recently signed in 1994.

Art 22(1) **TRIPS** defines geographical indications as 'indications, which identify a good as originating in the territory of a Member, or a region or locality in that territory, where a given quality, reputation or other characteristic of the good is essentially attributable to its geographical origin. This requires the geographic location to imbue the product with particular traits or characteristics. It extends beyond the quality of the product to include 'reputation or other characteristic of the good' (this shows a similarity with trade mark law).

Presently, GIs are protected beyond the EU by member states who have signed the **TRIPS Agreement. TRIPs** has very broad membership and requires member states to provide legal means for interested parties to prevent:

(i) use of any means in the designation or presentation of a good that indicates or suggests that a good originates in a geographical area other than the true place of origin in a manner that misleads the public as to the geographical origin of the good; or

(ii) any use that constitutes an act of unfair competition within the meaning of Art 10 of the **Paris Convention 1967**.

Note that the **TRIPS Agreement** applies to all products, not just foodstuffs.

Higher level of protection for wines and spirits

TRIPS provides for higher levels of protection for wines and spirits than for other agricultural products. Art 23 requires member states to provide protection even where the true origin of the goods is indicated, the geographical indication is used in translation, or is accompanied by the expression such as 'kind', 'type', 'style', 'imitation', or the like. The case of *J Bollinger v Costa Brava Wine Co Ltd (1960)* in the Chancery Division of the High Court provides a good illustration. It also requires member states to determine the status of homonymous names.

Art 23(4) provides that the TRIPS Council should undertake negotiations for the establishment of a multilateral system of notification of registration for wines. Art 23 sets out certain exceptions (for example in relation to overlap between GIs and trade marks).

Despite protests from the US and the other WTO members, at the 2001 WTO Ministerial Conference in Doha a group of WTO members, led by the EU, succeeded in increasing the likelihood that the current regime of GI protection would be revised.

In particular, the Doha Declaration set a mandate for the negotiation of a multi-lateral system of notification and registrations of GIs for wines and spirits, and the possibility of extending the higher level of protection currently given to wines and spirits under Art 23 **TRIPS** to all agricultural products. Basically, the EU members proposed that the EU standard of GI protection should be the global standard.

The proposals to amend **TRIPS** met with a negative reaction from the former British Colonies who have little to gain directly from these changes. This attitude was entrenched when the EU members put forward a list of 40 names that were to be given absolute protection. It is unlikely that this matter of amending **TRIPS** will be settled in the near future as there is much disagreement. As a result, the EU has entered into several bilateral agreements to protect wines and spirits with the following countries:

- Australia–EU Agreement on Wine (1994);
- EU–Chile Association Agreement on Wine, Spirit Drinks and Aromatised drinks (2002);
- EU–Mexico Agreement on Spirits (1997).

In conclusion, in future negotiations as to whether it would be beneficial to extend **TRIPs** s 23 protection to all kinds of goods, several matters will need to be carefully considered, namely:

- the extent to which traditional producers face a threat to their livelihood and cultural heritage from foreign competition;
- the costs and incentives for competing producers to establish their own geographic brand;
- the consumer benefits from improved information about differentiated products;
- the consumer costs of premium GI protected brands; and
- the costs of establishing an administrative structure for protecting GIs.

CHAPTER 10

CONFIDENTIAL INFORMATION AND KNOW-HOW

Confidential information is the riskiest form of intellectual property in which to deal because of its nature. There is no registered right to evaluate or assess. It is not like patents, copyright or designs where a particular 'thing' is afforded protection. Rather, know-how or certain information is valuable precisely because it is confidential and not in the public domain. The extent of the confidential information or know-how is usually difficult to establish with certainty. In the UK, an action for breach of confidence may lie in equity, or contract or at common law. The legal doctrine of confidential information is a set of principles developed over centuries by the courts. It is the application of those principles to particular fact situations which determines whether the information is confidential or not. To achieve fairness, broad legal principles have been developed to permit considerable flexibility. The fundamental legal principle that forms the underlying basis of the law of confidence is that a person who has received confidential information from another will not take unfair advantage of it or profit from the wrongful use or publication of it.

Essay questions will usually expect the student to focus on the elements of the action for breach of confidence and the defences. Problem questions often arise in a commercial or employee/employer context.

Question 43

For the past two years, Paul, a consultant aviation engineer and former airline pilot has been independently developing an innovative highly geared by-pass fan (HGBF). Paul has been careful to keep his innovation confidential and has not disclosed the details to any other third party. However, in January 2009, he attends a preliminary meeting at the London head office of Orion Aerospace and meets with the Research and Development director, Dr Gunn. At the beginning of the meeting Paul states that the subject matter of the meeting is confidential as between the two men. Dr Gunn nods in agreement and Paul proceeds to tell him about the details of his invention. Paul also shows Dr Gunn a technical drawing of the fan but retains this when he departs the meeting. Dr Gunn confirms Paul's innovation is of interest to Orion and that they should meet again to discuss proposals for the manufacture of a new aircraft HGBF. Two further meetings are held in February. However, after some disagreements between Paul and Orion Aerospace regarding the terms of a potential licence agreement and in particular the royalty rate, negotiations break down. In June 2009 Orion proceed to manufacture their own new aircraft by-pass fan, the Orion X2009. In July 2009 Paul becomes aware of Orion's new development when he reads an article in an aeronautical engineering trade magazine which features a photo of Dr Gunn and two other members of his team standing beside the X2009 fan. Paul is livid and suspects that Orion has used at least some of the information he disclosed to Dr Gunn earlier in the year. Paul seeks your advice as to whether he has a case for breach of confidence. In particular, he is concerned that he did not insist that Dr Gunn sign a written non-disclosure agreement and enquires whether this will affect his legal rights.

Answer plan

A straightforward question concerning breach of confidence set in a commercial context. The issues to be considered are:

- The implication of oral agreement and lack of a formal contract between the parties and the impact this may have on bringing an action for breach of confidence;
- Whether the facts establish the elements of the action for a breach of confidence as set out in *Coco v AN Clark (Engineers) Ltd (1969)*:
  (1) the information must have a necessary element of confidentiality
  (2) the information was communicated in circumstances of an obligation of confidentiality
  (3) the information is used in an unauthorised way [possibly] to the detriment of the party communicating it;
- If Orion Aerospace have any relevant defences it can rely on?
- The remedies available to Paul.

Answer

While Paul has taken the prudent step of verbally stating to Dr Gunn that the information he will disclose regarding his new highly geared by-pass fan (HGBF) is confidential, he has not required Dr Gunn or Orion Aerospace to sign a written agreement including terms to protect his confidential information, namely, the 'know-how' or 'trade secret' related to his HGBF, nor have the parties entered into a formal licence agreement. The difficulty for Paul will be to prove that an oral agreement exists, and while not impossible this could be problematic. Fortunately, the law of confidence is often used to protect economically valuable commercial information such as Paul's HGBF design and his industrial 'know-how' (although it may apply equally to any information that has the necessary quality of confidence). Orion Aerospace and its employee Dr Gunn have possibly breached the law of confidence by designing their own HGBF if they have used any of Paul's information without his consent. Accordingly, Paul should consider initiating an action against Orion Aerospace relying on the doctrine of confidential information. To clarify, this means that the equitable doctrine of breach of confidence will operate as a stand alone action regardless of any contractual relationship between the parties: *Prince Albert v Strange (1849)*; *Morrison v Moat (1851)*. This is because an action for breach of confidence has its roots in Equity on the basis that it involves a breach of trust between the parties: *Coco v AN Clark (Engineering) (1969)*; *Naomi Campbell v Mirror Group Newspapers (2004)*. The law of confidence can operate as a stand alone cause of action in its own right or as a supplementary action or for example, supporting an action for patent infringement or breach of contract. The court can act independently in equity even in the absence of proof of an oral agreement between Paul and Dr Gunn that the information disclosed by Paul directly to Dr Gunn would remain confidential. Indeed, in *Saltman Engineering Co Ltd v Campbell Engineering Co Ltd (1948)* Lord Greene MR stated that 'If a defendant is proved to have used confidential information directly or indirectly obtained from the [claimant] with the consent, express or implied, of the [claimant], he will be guilty of an infringement of the [claimant's] rights.' He further stated that the obligation to respect confidence is not limited to cases where the parties are in a contractual relationship.

English law does not distinguish between types of information that may be protected against breach of confidence. In the ancient case of *Morrison v Moat (1851)* a recipe for medicine was protected via the doctrine of confidential information. There is a wide range of protected information which may include trade or technological secrets and know how and commercial records: *Robb v Green (1895)*. It is clear therefore that Paul's HGBF design information is the type of information able to be protected via the doctrine of confidential information. Finally, in *Seager v Copydex Ltd (1967)* the Court of Appeal confirmed that the court would act independently of the law of contract. The facts of *Seager v Copydex Ltd (1967)* are a case in point here. During preliminary negotiations with the defendants, the claimant revealed secret information to them about a carpet grip he had invented. After the negotiations had broken down, the defendants produced a carpet grip of their own which apparently made use of the claimant's information. There was no contract between the parties. In his judgment, Lord Denning MR stated:

The law on this subject does not depend on any implied contract. It depends upon the broad principle of equity that he who receives information in confidence shall not take unfair advantage of it. He must not make use of it to the prejudice of him who gave it without obtaining his consent.

Prima facie Paul has an action against Orion Aerospace for breach of confidence. The three elements of an action were established by Megarry VC in the seminal case of *Coco v AN Clark (Engineers) Ltd (1969)* as follows: (1) the information must have a necessary element of confidentiality; (2) the information was communicated in circumstances of an obligation of confidentiality; and (3) the information is used in an unauthorised way (possibly) to the detriment of the party communicating it.

Paul's action for breach of confidence against Orion Aerospace will fail unless the essential elements for a successful action in breach of confidence are shown. Each element of the test for breach of confidence will be considered in turn below.

First, for Paul's HGBF design information to be 'confidential' it must not be public property or knowledge. Specifically, in *Saltman Engineering v Campbell Engineering (1948)* Lord Greene MR stated that information must have 'the necessary quality of confidence about it, namely it must not be something which is public property and public knowledge'. It is clear that Paul's information is valuable technical information and is not mere 'trivial tattle'. The facts do not suggest that Paul's information has entered the public domain. However, Paul's design information and know-how must be shown to be clearly identifiable and sufficiently well-developed so as to be capable of realisation: *De Maudsley v Palumbo and Others (1996)*; *Lock International plc v Beswick (1987)*. This could be done by referring to specific documentation such as Paul's technical design drawing and his research notes which clearly confirm the HGBF technical information and suggest it was not merely an idea, but rather was sufficiently developed. It would be very helpful if such documentation was marked with the words 'confidential information' or the like and dated. If Orion Aerospace has reproduced the documentation, in particular if they have reproduced a technical design drawing incorporating Pauls' information, an action may also lie for breach of copyright.

Second, the next question is whether Paul's HGBF information was communicated in a way that obliged Dr Gunn and Orion Aerospace to keep the information confidential? Dr Gunn, employed as the Research and Development director for Orion Aerospace, expressly agreed with Paul his HGBF information confidential at their preliminary meeting in January 2009. The objective test formulated by Megarry J in *Coco v Clark* is clearly satisfied:

If the circumstances are such that any reasonable man standing in the shoes of the recipient of the information would have realised that upon reasonable grounds the information was being given to him in confidence, then this should suffice to impose upon him the equitable obligation of confidence.

Dr Gunn will have the expertise and experience in the field to realise that Paul is disclosing the information on a confidential basis. Dr Gunn (and therefore his employer Orion Aerospace) has a clear obligation to keep Paul's information confidential and not to use it without Paul's permission. The second element of the action for breach of confidence is made out.

Third, has Orion Aerospace used the information in an unauthorised way to Paul's detriment ? This is not clear on the facts. We are told that Dr Gunn and his team at Orion Aerospace have developed their own HGBF known as the Orion-X2009. It may be that Orion Aerospace has used Paul's confidential HGBF technical information to its advantage as a 'springboard'. Paul will require further evidence as to the nature of the Orion-X2009 and its development process in order to establish this third element of the action for breach of confidence. In his favour, Paul has not placed his HGBF in the public domain such that the information is accessible by the public, so Orion Aerospace will have to explain how it developed its Orion-X2009. As Roxburgh J stated at 392 in *Terrapin v Builders Supply*:

> A person who has obtained information in confidence is not allowed to use it as a *springboard* for activities detrimental to the person who made the confidential communication, and springboard it remains even when all the features have been published or can be ascertained by actual inspection by any member of the public . . . The possessor of the confidential information still has a long start over any member of the public.

If Paul is able to prove that Orion Aerospace has used his confidential information to assist it to develop its Orion-X2009 then an inference of breach of confidential information could certainly be drawn on this point. There are many examples of cases where suppliers or manufacturing companies take the original inventor's ideas and manufacture their own products. For example, the new carpet grip invented by Mr Seager, which Copydex 'unconsciously' used after licensing negotiations with Mr Seager broke down: *Seager v Copydex Ltd (1967)* as mentioned earlier. See also *EPI Environmental Technologies plc v Symphony Plastic Technologies plc (2004)*.

Orion Aerospace does not appear to have any relevant defence. Paul's technical HGBF information is not in the public domain, nor has there been any undue lapse of time, nor does a 'public interest' argument arise on the facts.

In *Coco v Clark*, Megarry J questioned whether the claimant must show that he has or will suffer detriment by the breach of confidence. In *A-G v Guardian Newspapers Ltd (1989)*, the ' Spycatcher' case, Lord Keith made the point that detriment is usually present in commercial cases. Here, it would be a very straightforward matter for Paul to show financial detriment by Orion Aerospace's unauthorised use, especially given the negotiations between the parties as to a licence agreement and royalty rate in February 2009. He could also rely on the time he spent and expenses incurred in developing the fan.

In conclusion, Paul has a strong case against Orion Aerospace for breach of confidential information. Paul should immediately apply for an interim injunction to restrain any further publication of the detailed technical HGBF design information and know-how pending a full hearing of an action for breach of confidence, in order to preserve the status quo for as long as possible. However, Paul's action must be for damages (*Seager v Copydex Ltd (No 2) (1969)*) and not simply for restraint. In *Dowson v Mason Potter (1986)*, the Court of Appeal set out that damages should be based on the market value between a willing seller and buyer. In a case where the claimant would wish to have retained the information, a loss of profits calculation would be entertained: *AG v Blake (1990)*. Further, an award of an account of profits may be available where, although the information has passed into the public domain, the defendant is set to gain financially by breaching his obligation of confidence. In future, Paul should be advised to seek a confidentiality agreement in writing before he discloses commercially valuable confidential information to another party.

Question 44

In 2002, Karen Leaver, no longer challenged by her job as Business Development Manager for a City law firm, establishes her own consultancy firm 'Leaver Legal', giving advice on client service and retention to small law firms. She hires a close-knit team of employees to work for her. Leaver Legal sets up a helpline for its clients and is very successful. On 15 November 2006, the executive staff, including star employee Jessie Jump, meet to discuss its new strategic initiative, namely, to target clients in the Leeds city centre and a list of prospects is produced at the meeting. It is understood that the discussions and documentation from the meetings are to be kept confidential as competition in the industry is fierce.

Two weeks later Jessie decides to end her employment with the consultancy after three years of employment. Jessie sets up her own private legal consultancy, Jump & Co, based in Leeds. Several customers that were included on the Leaver Legal list of prospects for Leeds receive a brochure from the newly formed Jump & Co. Leaver Legal believes that Jessie has taken a copy or memorised the list of its prospective customers and are concerned that she will use her acquired knowledge in direct competition against them.

Advise Leaver Legal on their position.

Answer plan

This is a typical breach of confidential information problem question involving an ex-employee, which requires a discussion of the relevant case law, including *Faccenda Chicken v Fowler (1986)*.

- Protection of Legal Leaver's confidential information in (1) its prospective customer list; and (2) its strategy for Leeds;
- *Faccenda Chicken v Fowler (1986), CA* and the three classes of confidential information.

Answer

Confidential information is unlike other forms of intellectual property. It is not excised from the brain of one person when disclosed to another. Rather like a snail, even after it has been removed to a new home, its trail remains over everything it has touched.

After an employment relationship ends, it is likely that the interests of the parties will conflict in relation to the ex-employee's use of the employer's confidential information.

Here, Jessie Jump has been made privy to certain confidential information by her former employer, Leaver Legal, namely, its plans to engage in new business in Leeds as well as a prospective customer list for that city. The question is whether Jessie has used any part of the Leaver Legal's confidential information as the basis for launching her new business in Leeds and whether it is unlawful.

Equity protects confidential information on the basis that it is unconscionable for a person to have acquired confidential information to release it without permission from the proprietor. A wide range of categories of information is protectable by the doctrine, including commercially valuable customer lists: *Faccenda Chicken v Fowler (1986)*.

However, it is not established on the facts whether Jessie has taken a copy of the Leaver Legal's prospective customer list or made a copy from memory. Generally, when employees leave a company, they have a right to take with them the skill, experience and ideas they acquired during the period of employment. Many companies have entrance and exit interviews with employees who will be exposed to confidential information and require the employees to sign non-disclosure and non-competition agreements. These agreements, however, are often difficult to enforce.

As an ex-employee, Jessie will therefore be subject to a less strict duty of confidentiality to her former employer. In *Faccenda Chicken*, the court divided confidential information into three classes: (a) trivial of publicly available information; (b) information of a confidential nature but becomes part of the employee's own skill and knowledge; and (c) certain information that is highly confidential and cannot be disclosed to third parties. In relation to (b), information will be confidential as long as Jessie is an employee, but her obligation ceases on termination.

The facts of the *Faccenda Chicken* case are on point in that Mr Faccenda hired Mr Fowler as sales manager for his poultry business in Northampton. Over seven years, Mr Fowler built up a sizeable part of the business, although not the biggest part. Mr Fowler resigned when he was charged with stealing some of his employer's chickens and during the next year set up a competing business. The court decided that Fowler had used the following *Faccenda Chicken* information, but that none of the information was entitled to protection after termination of employment:

- customers' names and addresses;
- the most convenient routes to reach customers;
- customers' usual quality and quantity requirements;
- the days of the week Faccenda called on customers; and
- prices charged to individual customers.

The rationale seems to be that 'mere' confidential information is mostly inseparable from skill and knowledge.

In relation to Jessie's situation, the knowledge that she possesses in relation to Leaver Legal's strategy for Leeds and its list of prospective clients, seems to be information that she may retain and use after she leaves Leaver Legal's employ. It is not an actionable breach of Jessie's duty of fidelity to her former employer to make plans or preparations for when her employment with the firm ends. *Hivac Ltd v Park Royal Scientific Instruments Ltd (1946)* provides that legitimate preparation to compete is permitted. Jessie has a right to use her general skill and knowledge, which can include 'mere' confidential information of her ex-employer, such as knowledge of the prospective client list and for that matter, Leaver Legal's strategy to enter the Leeds market. Neither item of information carries an obligation of confidence once her employment has ceased.

However, it would be a breach of her duty to her former employer to conspire to injure Leaver Legal by soliciting its existing customers. The soliciting would be unlawful because in taking the employers' business it would be a breach of the Jessie's duty of fidelity.

In future, Leaver Legal should ensure that its existing and future employees sign employment contracts containing a suitably drafted (that is enforceable) anti-compete covenant and/or restraint of trade clause to cover the markets in which they conduct business. The employment contract is the key to ensuring an employee's obligations after termination.

Question 45

Critically analyse the pros and cons of relying on the doctrine of confidential information to protect an invention as opposed to applying for a patent.

Answer plan

This essay question requires a high level of critical analysis and the development of a strategy for good decision-making following analysis of the legal protection afforded by the two regimes. One should not forget, however, to refer to relevant legislation and case law where appropriate.

- Nature of patent protection under the **Patents Act 1977**;
- Nature of confidential information protection;
- How to choose between confidential information and patent protection.

Answer

All technology begins with ideas, information and know-how. While the proprietors generally wish to let others know that the new technology is effective, they also want to keep other information confidential in order to secure a patent or other intellectual property right, or because there is no other form of intellectual property right available for that information. For example, certain know-how may not be protected by the claims of a patent specification.

A patent is a legally recognised 20-year monopoly which the government grants in exchange for a complete disclosure of how to make and use an invention: **Patents Act 1977**. Confidential information, on the other hand, covers a wide variety of categories of information such as personal secrets (*Argyll v Argyll (1967)*); commercial records (*Anton Piller KG v Manufacturing Processes Ltd (1976)*); trade secrets (*Seager v Copydex (1967)*); and government secrets (*AG v Guardian Newspapers (1990)*). To be protected, the information must have 'the necessary quality of confidence about it, namely, it must not be something which is pubic property and public knowledge' per Lord Greene MR in *Saltman Engineering Co Ltd v Campbell Engineering Co Ltd (1963)*.

Tension frequently exists between the options of keeping an invention confidential or filing a patent application which discloses the invention. Relying on the equitable doctrine of confidential information may eliminate any possibility of ever being able to patent an invention if the secret is later disclosed and enters into the public domain. That said, the publication of a patent destroys any confidential information which it discloses. Sometimes, the choice to patent an invention or to maintain it as confidential information is clear. Usually, however, the decision involves a balancing exercise between the various commercial and legal factors.

Because of the disclosure requirements of patents and the secrecy requirements of confidential information, these two forms of intellectual property cannot usually co-exist for any one particular technology. A choice must be made either to patent or to keep the invention confidential.

How to choose between confidential information and patent protection

In deciding whether to proceed with a patent, many factors must be considered. Several factors weigh strongly in favour of patenting. Other factors weigh strongly in favour of maintaining the invention confidential. Other considerations are less clear in favour of one alternative or the other and require a balancing of several factors.

The critical factor is to assess how realistic it is to keep the information confidential and for how long.

- If the information can be kept confidential for approximately as long as the commercial life of the products made using it, patent protection may not be required.
- Equally, if the information can be kept confidential for even longer than the 20-year patent term, then the information might be best protected as confidential information.

However, the duration of confidential information is uncertain. The protection for the confidential information can be lost overnight if the secret is publicly disclosed, even if the disclosure was not intentional.

The need-to-know factor and ex-employees

In relation to a typical business, if only a few people need to know about the invention, secrecy may be a viable option. The difficulty arises when employees leave. The ex-employee may be subject to a contractual restraint of trade obligation, but this is limited in duration and scope. In other words, an ex-employee cannot be restrained from using every 'secret', especially if it is their stock in trade.

Reverse-engineering

Another consideration is whether the information can be kept secret after the product has been made available to the public – can the product be easily reverse-engineered? Confidential information does not protect against reverse-engineering which is lawful unless patent-protected. Accordingly, it is of no use to protect a product which can be reverse-engineered. In this situation, a patent is the only option.

A classic example is the formula for Coca-Cola, which has not to date been reverse-engineered. If the formula had been patented when it was first used in 1886, the formula would have been in the public domain a century ago and would now be free for anyone to use. However, by maintaining the formula as a trade secret, Coca-Cola has continued to dominate the worldwide soft drink industry.

Independent Invention

Similarly, the equitable doctrine of confidential information is of little use when dealing with an invention that is likely to be independently invented by another. In fact, this situation presents the dangerous possibility that the second inventor may file for and obtain a patent on the invention. The second inventor may then prevent the proprietor of the confidential information from practising the invention. Therefore, filing a patent application is the clear choice in this situation, especially where the proprietor is in a race with competitors to invent.

Market life of the product

It is important to consider the nature of the invention; a product with a short market life, such as an electronic children's game design to be updated annually may be adequately protected by confidential information giving the proprietor a good 'head start' in the market. However, compare this with an invention for an X-ray airport security system that may become a worldwide standard for many years.

If the major competitive advantage is by being 'first-to-market' or if the technology will be obsolete in less time than it would take for a patent to issue, then a patent is of little or no use.

The need to grant licences

For the invention to be licensed out, a licensee may be more willing to pay for an invention that is patented. Licensees may worry that their rights are less clearly defined by the doctrine of confidential information and that the value of a licensed invention may be abruptly lost if the licensor fails to maintain the secret.

Patent applications remain confidential until publication

The decision to file a patent application is not irrevocable. The act of filing a patent application does not result in loss of confidential information rights. In the United Kingdom, patent applications are kept confidential and are generally published eighteen months after the initial filing date. Therefore, if a patent is not granted on an application, or if the application is abandoned, the confidential information disclosed in the application will not be published and secrecy can be maintained.

Therefore, one effective strategy may be to file a patent application and also to continue to maintain confidential information during the application process. This will provide a substantial delay for the need to decide whether to abandon confidential information status in favour of a patent.

Cost

A further advantage of confidential information over patents is that there are no official prosecution costs or maintenance fees in order to establish confidential information or to keep it in force. Patenting costs may amount to several thousand pounds or more. These costs are not incurred if an invention is maintained as confidential information.

However, this does not mean that there are no costs involved in maintaining confidential information. Quite the opposite, in some circumstances, confidential information can be expensive to maintain. For instance, there may be costs associated with physically preventing the public from learning the confidential information. These costs may include: physical plant construction to restrict access to the grounds and buildings; checking on repair and service people; restricting information to individuals in the company who need to know; fragmenting information so that no single individual has access to complete confidential information; labelling containers so that process variables and ingredients are not shown; marking documents confidential; using encryption technology. There may also be legal costs for the preparation of contracts which clarify the existence of confidential information and the duty not to disclose. These contracts may have to be signed by suppliers, licensees, customers, consultants and others with whom the proprietor does business, such as those considering engaging in a joint venture or to include restraint of trade terms for employees leaving the organisation.

The costs and difficulties encountered in maintaining confidential information can be significant to the extent that this consideration is enough to tip the balance in favour of patenting, despite the fact that other considerations might favour relying on the doctrine of confidential information.

Freedom of Information and the public interest

Another difficulty with maintaining an invention confidential may occur whenever documents are submitted to the government. Due to the UK's **Freedom of Information Act 2000**, it can be problematical to prevent information contained in these documents from being discovered by competitors or litigants who make freedom of information requests under the Act. This is because the government can argue that a public interest excuses its use or disclosure of the information.

Conclusion

Whether to seek or rely on the doctrine of confidential information is a complex matter that needs to be considered on an individual case basis by examining the specific facts related to the case.

In at least two situations, patents are a clear choice over maintaining an invention confidential. If an invention can be reverse-engineered or independently developed, if there is a need to disseminate information about the invention, or if the invention is a technology for which a licensee will only pay if it is patented, then the choice is clearly in favour of patents. On the other hand, if the information or know-how is not patentable, if it provides an advantage which is of a shorter duration than the time that it would take to obtain a patent, or if the information will be valuable for a very long time and secrecy can be maintained during that time, then the choice is clearly in favour of confidential information. For the most part, the choice is not black and white, so the various commercial and legal considerations must be carefully weighed up in order to arrive at a reasoned and practical decision.

Question 46

A major chink in the armour in the law's protection of confidential information is created by the public interest defence. Discuss.

Answer plan

The law related to confidential information is judge-made law which has generally protected confidental information subject to disclosure in the public interest. A good answer will cover the following key cases on the subject of the public interest defence:

- *Lion Laboratories Ltd v Evans (1985)*;
- *W v Edgell (1990)*;
- *R v Chief Constable of the North Wales Police, ex p AB (1998)*.

Answer

Under UK law, where an obligation to keep information confidential arises, it will not extend to preventing disclosure of the information where a serious risk of public harm exists. The permitted disclosure will only be to the extent necessary to prevent such harm. In other words, a disclosure of confidential information made in the public interest will only avoid being a breach of the obligation of confidence if the disclosure is limited to those who need to know to prevent the harm. For example, this may involve disclosure of certain confidential information to a regulatory body or to the police. Originally, this defence as termed the 'iniquity' rule (*Gartside v Outram*

(1856)) but it is now framed in terms of defence of the public interest. The key issue is what nature of public interest justifies the breach of obligations of confidence?

A classic example is the case of *Lion Laboratories Ltd v Evans (1985)* where the claimants were manufacturers of the intoximeter device used by the police for measuring blood alcohol levels by road users. The defendants were ex-employees of the firm and they disclosed to the press, documents obtained while still in employment. The documents showed the intoximeters to be variable in their results and therefore unreliable. The employer's action against the ex-employees for breach of confidence failed, based on the public interest exception. The Court of Appeal held that the defective intoximeters represented a serious threat to the fair administration of justice and it was essential to publicise the inaccuracy of the evidence provided by the devices. The *Lion* case was the first in which the public interest defence succeeded where an iniquity was not involved; however, a wide public interest could be identified.

Lord Justice Stephenson set out the three guiding considerations for the court to analyse:

(1) the public may be interested in matters which are not their concern;

(2) the media has its own interest which may not reconcile with that of the public; and

(3) the best recipient for information may not be the police or other responsible body.

Another example is the Court of Appeal's decision in *W v Edgell (1990)*. W was a mental patient convicted of multiple manslaughter who had been examined by the defendant, a doctor. The doctor's concern at W's condition led him to send a copy of his report to the Home Secretary. W sued the doctor, alleging breach of confidence, founded on the doctor–patient relationship. However, the Court of Appeal favoured the public interest over the interests of the patient and held that the doctor was justified in disclosing the report to reduce the risk of W being freed and possibly carrying out further attacks against members of the public.

The approach in *W v Edgell* was confirmed in *R v Chief Constable of the North Wales Police, ex p AB (1998)*. The Court of Appeal agreed that confidential police information concerning paedophiles who had completed their prison sentences could be disclosed to a campsite owner to enable him to take protective steps to safeguard the children arriving at the campsite for the Easter holidays. The interests of the public were found to prevail over the police's obligation of confidence.

It is clear from these cases that a significant degree of harm must be established in order to justify or excuse the breach of confidence. The courts do not appear to shy away from subordinating the confidentiality to the public interest in certain circumstances. Indeed, the decision in *W v Edgell (1990)* shows that the rights of the public can take priority, even over one of the longest established fiduciary relationships of confidence in the English legal system, that between doctor and patient.

However, just because information is of interest to the public does not mean it is in the public interest to know it. The purpose for which the confidential information will be used is clearly a relevant consideration. As we have seen, the court will excuse the disclosure of confidential information if it is motivated by civic responsibility rather than selling for personal gain.

More recently, in *London Regional Transport v Mayor of London (2003)*, the Court of Appeal held that its role was to balance competing interests, taking account of the proportionality of the restraint upon freedom of expression.

In conclusion, for many years the courts have shown that a claim of public interest may excuse a breach of the obligation of confidence. It is fair to say that while the availability of the public interest defence has increased, it does not create a major chink in the law's protection of confidential information; rather the development is a sensible improvement to the law's ability to the public's best interests.

CHAPTER 11

CHARACTER MERCHANDISING AND MALICIOUS FALSEHOOD

Character merchandising refers to the use of fictitious characters devised for a book, film, television series or a computer game. There are many famous examples including: the Disney characters, the Teletubbies, the Flower Pot Men, Bob the Builder, Spiderman, the Simpsons, etc. Such characters are commercially valuable because they can be licensed for use on a variety of products in return for a flat fee or a royalty. Character merchandising also covers living personalities as well, such as famous sportspeople and celebrities. Famous people allow their name to be used for promotional purposes or to endorse products and services, for example J-Lo perfume. The law has attempted to protect character merchandising through passing off (when copyright and trade mark protection are not available).

Malicious falsehood is a tort that is related to passing off. It arises when a person publishes information maliciously, that is capable of damaging an enterprises position or reputation. However, this tort is not limited to commercial activities and has been used in a variety of ways to prevent the spread of malicious falsehoods. In some cases, there is an overlap between malicious falsehood and defamation. Nonetheless, for a successful claim of malicious falsehood the statement must only be false, not defamatory.

Question 47

A children's production company, Norse Gods Ltd, has developed a new television series based on the Viking sagas aimed at children aged 6–10 years. The characters are derived from the Viking Sagas of the dark ages, depicting them as children growing up in Scandinavia. The stories revolve around the Blood Axe clan and their adventures. The three main characters are Erik Bloodaxe, Valkyrie and Harald Bluetooth. The television show proves to be a great success and the programmes are licensed to numerous international stations. A full-length feature film is produced and within a year the characters are famous around the world. The company enters into many lucrative character merchandising licence agreements to generate additional revenue. Another firm, the Hi Chin Cho (UK) Ltd (HCC), produce an 'Unofficial Blood Axe clan spellbook' currently for sale in several large bookstores. Advise Norse Gods Ltd as to the nature of the legal protection they can rely on to enforce their rights over their fictional characters against unauthorised use.

Answer plan

The issues to be considered are:

* The availability of copyright and trade mark protection;
* Passing off;
* *Reckitt and Coleman Products v Borden Inc (1990)*;
* *Mirage Productions v Counter-Feat Clothing (1991)*.

Answer

How can Norse Gods Ltd protect the Blood Axe clan characters it has originated? Surprisingly, fictitious characters per se are not protected under English law. However, copyright, trade mark laws and passing off afford some protection.

Copyright and trade mark protection

Copyright protects the words and the form in which ideas are expressed, not the ideas or characters themselves. The type of unauthorised use traditionally envisaged by the **Copyright, Designs and Patents Act 1988 (CDPA 1988)**, copying chunks of original text, is not what happens when someone misappropriates a famous Blood Axe clan character's name or catchphrase for their bed linen or T-shirt.

It may be possible to protect the scripts or text of the Blood Axe clan series as literary works, if they can truly be shown to be original, but not usually a television format. Names do not attract copyright protection, as they are considered too short to be a literary work. They can, however, be protected by trade mark law. For example, *Peter Rabbit* is registered as a trade mark which would be infringed if an unauthorised person published a Peter Rabbit book.

The Blood Axe clan characters are presumably illustrated, so it may be a little easier to protect them as artistic copyright works: s 4 **CDPA 1988**. The original drawings will attract copyright and any new works which use a substantial part of any of those drawings will infringe Norse God Ltd's rights. Pictures or three-dimensional objects which bear a remarkable resemblance to the Blood Axe clan characters will also be infringements. Illustrations can also be registered as trade marks, but this does not protect the character as a concept, only each specific image. In 1993, copyright protection over Beatrix Potter's pictures expired and each image was then registered as a trade mark. Now, each individual picture now has the (registered symbol against it, indicating it is a registered trade mark ((denotes a trade mark that is not yet registered). Although the trade mark registration process is expensive it has the great advantage that trade marks can be renewed every ten years, so protection can be perpetual.

Passing off

If the Blood Axe clan characters are not protected by copyright or trade mark, Norse Gods Ltd may still be able to prevent unauthorised use through the law of passing off, which is intended to stop someone trading on another's reputation. Passing off applies if someone is confused into thinking that the new goods were designed or licensed by the original author. In *Reckitt and Coleman Products v Borden Inc (1990)* the House of Lords summarised the three elements to be proved in a passing-off action, now known as the 'classic trinity' formulation:

1. goodwill or reputation attached to goods and service (for example in claimant's goods, name, mark, get-up etc.);
2. a misrepresentation made to the public (leading to confusion or deception) causing . . .
3. damage – actual or potential to the claimant.

Norse Gods Ltd could claim damages in passing off if the public thinks the Blood Axe clan characters had been licensed to HCC to use. This is because Norse Gods Ltd have actually created merchandising products and goodwill can therefore attach to the Blood Axe clan characters for merchandising purposes: *Mirage Productions v Counter-Feat Clothing (1991)*. However, as the book is called the '*Unofficial* Blood Axe clan spellbook', there might be little that Norse Gods Ltd can do. By calling it 'unofficial' HCC makes it clear that the book has not been endorsed by Norse Gods Ltd, so there is unlikely to have been a misrepresentation to the public.

In conclusion, passing off is not actionable. If HCC has not used substantial chunks of the text or the illustrations in the 'Unofficial spellbook' there will be no copyright infringement. The only possible cause of action that remains is if the unofficial spell book amounted to derogatory treatment of the original in some way by damaging the integrity of the work or damaging the authors' reputation. Although the law relating to character merchandising is still at an early stage of development in the UK, other jurisdictions such as the United States, most of continental Europe and Australia have laws against unfair competition and may be more promising in terms of the legal protection provided for fictional characters and character merchandising activities.

Question 48

Critically analyse the elements of the common law action for malicious falsehood.

Answer plan

The issues to be considered are:

- Falsity and malice as the basis for the action;
- *Schulke & Mayr UK Ltd v Alkapharm UK Ltd (1999)*;
- *DSG Retail Ltd v Comet Group plc (2002)*.

Answer

Malicious falsehood (or injurious falsehood or trade libel) is primarily concerned with redress for loss caused as a result of malicious false statements regarding a business's reputation or its goods. The tort may be applied in a wide range of situations and related to passing off. For example, Trader A may state untruthfully that Trader B's goods are counterfeit. The statement may be made orally or in writing (*Ratcliffe v Evans (1892)*). The tort may be combined in an appropriate case with an action for defamation or trade mark infringement. Accordingly the action often arises in comparative advertising cases which are dealt with under s 10(6) of the **Trade Marks Act 1994**. The tort of malicious falsehood is not however limited to commercial activities. Malicious falsehood actions will be tried before a single judge and not with a jury as is the case with libel actions.

Establishing malicious falsehood

According to the modern malicious falsehood case *Schulke & Mayr UK Ltd v Alkapharm UK Ltd (1999)*, in order to succeed the claimant must show all of the following:

1. The defendant has published an untrue derogatory statement of fact. The statement must refer to the claimant, his goods or services.
2. The defendant published the words maliciously.
3. The words have caused the claimant pecuniary loss as a natural and direct result of the publication.

The claimant carries the burden of proving all three elements which makes the claim more difficult than a libel claim. 'Malice' has the same meaning as it does in defamation law. The claimant must show either:

(a) that the defendant did not have a positive belief in the truth of the statement (where he is reckless as to whether a statement is true or false, he will be treated as if he knew that it was false); or

(b) that the defendant's *dominant motive* in making the statement was dishonest or improper. If a statement is made maliciously, it must be made with the *dominant* object of injuring the claimant's business. The mere fact that the statement has damaged the claimant's business will not in itself be sufficient to prove malice: *Dunlop Pneumatic Tyre Company v Maison Talbot (1904)*.

The court has to decide as a matter of fact whether the defendant's belief was genuine and if genuine, whether it was one a reasonable man might hold: *Atkins v Perrin (1862)*. If the defendant proves that he honestly believed the statement made was true, when it is actually false, no malice is established and the action for malicious falsehood will fail. Where the defendant makes a derogatory statement carelessly and lacks an intention to harm the claimant, no action will lie: *Balden v Shorter (1933)*.

It is immaterial whether the untrue statement causes damage to the claimant's reputation. A statement may be actionable as malicious falsehood even though it is not defamatory. However, the fact that the untrue words are also defamatory will not exclude a claim being made in malicious falsehood, although the courts will not allow the claimant to recover damages for both defamation and malicious falsehood for the same loss: *Joyce v Sengupta (1993)*.

In *DSG Retail Ltd v Comet Group plc (2002)*, Owen J reviewed the principles of malicious falsehood. Curry's had been running two press campaigns offering 10 per cent discounts and £10 off local Comet prices. Comet put up in-store posters stating that their products were cheaper than competitors offering such deals, with the Curry's advertisements affixed to the poster. Curry's complained that the obvious inference of the poster was that Comet was referring to Curry's offers and the claim that Comet's products were cheaper was incorrect. They sought an injunction to stop the Comet campaign. Owen J confirmed that the following questions were relevant to the facts:

• whether the defendant's advertisements were directed at the claimant;
• whether the meaning in the advertisements was false;
• whether the advertisements were intended to be taken seriously;
• whether the advertisements had been published maliciously; and
• whether there was a likelihood that the claimant would suffer actual damage.

It was held that Curry's had successfully proved each of the above and judgment was made in its favour.

This decision further clarifies the legal principles underlying a malicious false-hood action. Whereas in an action for passing off, the test is whether a substantial number of people would be deceived, this is not the test for actionable malicious falsehood where the 'one-meaning' rule is used. The judge must decide a single and natural meaning of the defendant's statement and determine its falsity on the basis of that meaning.

Falsehood

The false statement must be a statement of fact and the claim must prove this to the court's satisfaction. Equally, if the statement is true, the claimant is not entitled to any remedy, no matter how damaging it may be: *Danish Mercantile v Beaumont (1950)*.

Consequently, several types of statements are not actionable for malicious falsehood. Advertising puffs will not, on their own, amount to malicious falsehood nor will statements of opinion or vulgar statements. In *Hubbuck & Sons Ltd v Wilkinson, Heywood & Clerk Ltd (1899)* the defendant published a statement that its zinc paint had a slight advantage over the claimant's paint. This was held not to amount to malicious falsehood even if the statement had been made maliciously. A statement of opinion is unlikely to give rise to a claim in malicious falsehood, provided that it is clear from the statement that it is an expression of opinion and not a statement of fact: *Emaco v Dyson Appliances (1999)*. In *British Airways v Ryanair Ltd (2001)* Ryanair created comparative advertisements comparing its prices with those of British Airways under the headings 'EXPENSIVE BA. . . . DS!' and 'Expensive BA'. Justice Jacob said that British Airway's malicious falsehood claims '[did] not get off the ground'.

Proof of damage caused by the malicious statement

As with other torts, the claimant must prove that pecuniary loss has been suffered and that the loss is attributable to the defendant's statement.

The second limb of this test is often difficult to satisfy. It will not usually be sufficient to show there was a downturn in sales at about the time that the statement was made, unless the claimant can also show that the downturn could not be attributable to other factors such as a seasonal downturn or the economic climate generally.

Where the words are published in writing or other permanent form, the claimant does not have to show *actual* loss. It is sufficient to prove that the untrue words were likely to cause pecuniary loss: **Defamation Act 1952**, s 3(1)(a).

Where the untrue words are likely to cause pecuniary damage to the claimant in respect of any office, profession, calling, trade or business held by or carried on by him at the time of publication, it will not be necessary for the claimant to prove actual damage: **Defamation Act 1952**, s 3(1)(a).

The loss or likelihood of loss must be a natural and probable consequence of the falsehood. This was not the case in *Stewart Brady v Express Newspapers (1994)* where the convicted murderer, Ian Brady, brought proceedings for malicious falsehood against the *Express* newspaper over an allegation that he had assaulted a female prison visitor. It was held that Mr Brady did not have a reasonable cause of action as he could not show that the publication was likely to cause him financial loss.

In *Khodaporast v Shad (2000)* the Court of Appeal awarded damages for distress as aggravated damages. It was emphasised that in order to recover such damages, the claimant must, as a precondition, be able to show that it has suffered pecuniary loss as a natural and direct result of the publication.

Injunctions

Often, claimants in malicious falsehood cases are anxious to restrain repetition of the alleged falsehood as a matter of urgency and will seek an interim injunction to restrain repetition during the period of the trial. However, in most instances, an interim injunction to restrain publication of the falsehood will be an interference with the defendant's freedom of expression. Under the **Human Rights Act 1988** the claimant must demonstrate a likelihood of obtaining relief at trial and consideration must also be given to the importance of the right to freedom of expression.

Where the statement in question is not obviously untrue or where the defendant indicates on oath that it is intending to prove the truth of the statement at trial, the rule in *Bonnard v Perryman (1891)* will apply. This means that no injunction will be granted unless the court is satisfied that the defendant will not be able to prove the truth of the statement: *Boscobell Paints v Bigg (1975)*. In *Microdata v Rivendale (1984)* the Court of Appeal indicated that the rule in *Bonnard v Perryman* ought not to be extended any further than is necessary to preserve 'the fundamental right' of free speech.

A final injunction will normally be awarded at trial to restrain further publication of the malicious falsehood.

The limitation period

The limitation period in relation to malicious falsehoods is one year from the date that the cause of action arose, although the court has discretion to extend the period in appropriate cases: **Defamation Act 1952**, ss 5–6. The same position applies in defamation cases. The Act also provides for the defendant to make amends by offering a suitable correction, apology and compensation under s 2(1).

CHAPTER 12

IMAGE RIGHTS

Legal protection for valuable celebrity 'image', 'personality' or 'publicity' rights does not exist per se in the UK. Protection is based on a number of statutory common law rights, none of which are specifically designed to protect the unauthorised use of a personality's image.

Without a general right of publicity or right of personality (as exists in other common law countries such as the US, Canada and Australia), a celebrity has to rely on passing off, trade mark infringement, copyright infringement, libel, malicious falsehood and the **Trade Descriptions Act 1968**.

The closest the UK courts have come to recognising a 'celebrity right' was racing driver Eddie Irvine's success against Talksport in the High Court in March 2002. This decision was consistent with existing principles; it simply recognised the commercial value of personal endorsements.

Celebrities argue that they should have legal control over their own image and that this amounts to a valuable intangible right that 'belongs' to them. Consequently, they should be the one to commercially benefit from it. On the other hand, others argue that a celebrity's image is a public property as part of popular culture and should not be protected as a private property right.

Question 49

The English courts appear to be developing the law to give celebrities protection against the misappropriation or unauthorised use of their images. Discuss the development of the UK case law.

Answer plan

The law related to image rights in the UK is judge-made law. A good answer will cover the following key cases and law:

• *Irvine v Talksport (2002)*;

- *Arsenal Football Club Plc v Reed (2003)*;
- *Niema Ash v Loreena McKennitt (2006)*;
- *Articles 8 and 10 of the European Convention on Human Rights.*

Answer

The customary position is that English law will not afford protection to celebrities, on the basis that they have voluntarily invited publicity and so they should accept that their name and reputation be used as public property and should not be subject to legal control. However, this attitude on the part of the courts has been slowly evolving since 1930.

In the UK, the first case relating to use of a celebrity's image arose in *Tolley v Fry (1930)*, which involved a celebrity endorsement and defamation claim. Cyril Tolley was a well-known golfer. When chocolate manufacturer Fry's used a caricature of him playing golf with a Fry's chocolate bar sticking out of his pocket for its advertising, he sued for defamation. Such use, he said, implied that he was endorsing a product, not suited to his status as an amateur sportsman.

Traditionally, the law of publicity has always been closely linked to the concept of privacy. Whereas privacy involves being left alone and having some private space, publicity rights are concerned with protecting the celebrity's projected image and focuses on protecting that rather than their individual and private right. In jurisdictions where image rights do subsist, the development of the law has usually followed that of a privacy law. The first step is the creation of an actionable right to privacy, followed by the development of an economic right whereby a celebrity's image or personality can be exploited economically. These privacy and publicity rights are usually set in the context of existing regimes of copyright law, performer's rights, trade mark law, trades description legislation, data protection provisions and the laws of defamation, which can also, to an extent, protect creative works, performances, trade and personal reputation.

In the United Kingdom three recent court decisions have considered the concepts of 'privacy' and 'personality'. They have, variously, through the use of the law of passing off, a reinterpretation of trade mark law, and recent moves to embrace a new 'law of privacy', developed what might possibly be called a 'fledging' image right. These three important cases are:

- Eddie Irvine's successful action against Talksport Radio for passing off in *Irvine v Talksport (2002)*;

- Arsenal's trade mark action against the seller of 'unofficial' Arsenal merchandise in *Arsenal Football Club Plc v Reed (2003)*; and

- *Niema Ash v Loreena McKennitt (2006)* which involved folk singer Lorna McKennitt's action for breach of confidence against a former friend and confidant (this followed on from Naomi Campbell's action against Mirror Group Newspapers and Michael Douglas and Catherine Zeta-Jones' action against *Hello!* Magazine).

The leading case on the subject of image rights is *Irvine v Talksport (2002)*. Although the issue in this case centred on a false endorsement, the matter was litigated under the head of passing off. For the first time, the UK courts acknowledged the right of celebrities to exploit their image and judicial notice was taken that celebrities do exploit their name and image through endorsements both inside and outside of their own field.

The case concerned the manipulation of a photograph of the Formula 1 driver Eddie Irvin for an advertising campaign for Talksport in which a mobile phone he had been holding when the snap was taken had been replaced by a superimposed picture of a radio, under which was the caption 'Talk Radio . . . We've got it covered'. Mr Justice Laddie heard the case and found in favour of Irvine. He held that a celebrity *did* have a monopoly over the use of his or her image. The claimant had to prove that:

- at the time the complained of acts occurred, he had a significant reputation or goodwill; and
- the defendant's actions led to the false impression to a 'not insignificant section of his or her market' that the defendant's actions had been endorsed, recommended or approved by the claimant.

The *Irvine* case clarified that false endorsement was actionable under English law where the celebrity in question had not consented to the use of their image. However, it could be argued that if a celebrity's image had been used without the implication of endorsement, the defendant may escape liability. This anomaly highlights the need for image rights per se to be legally protected.

More recently, however, two decisions by the Court of Appeal in *Arsenal Football Club plc v Reed (2003)* and *Niema Ash v Loreena McKennitt (2006)* together appear to provide the foundation for an actionable 'image', 'personality' or 'publicity' right.

In the *Arsenal (2003)* case, the Court of Appeal found that where a third party used in the course of trade, a sign that was identical to a validly registered trade mark on goods which were identical to those for which the trade mark was registered, then the registered owner could prevent this third party use. It can be argued that the *Arsenal* decision applies to more than just trade mark matters, for example, music group names and artists' names as brands.

The case of *McKennitt v Ash (2006)* concerned efforts by Canadian folk singer Loreena McKennitt to prevent publication of parts of a book about her life by a former friend and confidante, Niema Ash. The Court of Appeal held that in order to find the rules of the English law of breach of confidence it had to look to the jurisprudence of Arts 8 and 10 of the **European Convention on Human Rights (ECHR)**. Those articles are now not merely of persuasive or parallel effect but, according to Lord Woolf, are the very content of the domestic tort that the English court has to enforce. Accordingly, where the complaint is the wrongful publication of private information, the court has to determine two things. First, is the information private in the sense that it is in principle protected by Art 8? If the answer is no then that is the end of the case. If the answer is yes, the second question arises: in all the circumstances, must the interest of the owner of the private information yield to the right of freedom of expression conferred on the publisher by Art 10?

In summary, the combination of these three cases may just be tipping the balance and turn a 'right to privacy' into a quasi-commercial right – a 'right *of* privacy'. By way of analogy, s 16(1) of the **Copyright Designs and Patents Act 1988** allows for the exploitation of copyrights by allowing the owner to restrict the uses made of a copyrighted work and now a celebrity, by being able to control and prevent the publication of private information and photographs can in turn use these 'restricted acts' to allow for the economic exploitation of the self same texts and pictures. However, it is important to note that none of these three aforementioned cases have been tested in the House of Lords.

Having considered the fact that image rights should be protected, it is important to recognise the potential dangers inherent in a complete prohibition of third-party usage of a celebrity's image. What is the position vis-à-vis freedom of expression for reporting purposes, an area of law given much media attention in the context of the private lives of Naomi Campbell (*Naomi Campbell v Mirror Group Newspapers (2002)*) and Gary Flitcroft (*A v B plc and Another (2002)*)? In both cases, the courts essentially ruled that, although much information about the private lives of celebrities does enter the public domain, often through self-promotion, it does not necessarily follow that every detail of a celebrity's private life is open to being turned into frontpage news by journalists.

While the freedom of the press remains protected by Art 10 of the **ECHR**, schedule to the **Human Rights Act 1998**, reporting by the press has to be justified and celebrities, in spite of living in the public eye, are still entitled to a certain amount of privacy. This right is supported by both the *Data Protection Act 1998* and Art 8 of the **ECHR**.

In conclusion, the existence of image rights has been recognised by the judicial systems in the US, Canada, Germany and France. A person's name, voice and likeness are all protected by the law. Yet the UK law remains somewhat backward on this matter and consequently, celebrities have no option but to continue to try to claim infringement of their fledgling image rights using other heads of law which are not always particularly well-suited to the types of action being brought. In the UK, the court in the *Irvine* case gave a clear indication that it was prepared to grant celebrities a greater degree of control over how their images are used. However, it has yet to endorse image rights as a new form of intellectual property per se.

CHAPTER 13

FRANCHISING AND INTELLECTUAL PROPERTY RIGHTS

There is no specific legal definition of a franchise. The concept of franchising is a business format that is licensed to a franchisee by the franchisor. The franchisee pays for the use of an established business format and associated intellectual property rights (for example the latter's name, reputation and get-up), which is usually controlled and supervised by the franchisors. The advantage to the franchisee is that s/he does not have to reinvent the wheel and the franchise network usually helps to reduce the risk of business failure. The public also benefit in that they come to recognise and associate the franchise trade names with a certain quality of product of service. Successful franchised businesses include well-known enterprises such as Thornton's chocolatiers, the Body Shop, McDonald's, Starbucks, etc.

As the use of images, logos, trade marks and copyright material is central to the franchised business format, intellectual property issues arise in connection with the full spectrum of intellectual property rights (for example copyright, trade marks, passing off, design, know-how, confidential information, patent law) and competition law.

Question 50

Analyse the intellectual property issues that arise in modern franchising.

Answer plan

- Explain the concept of franchising and associated intellectual property rights;
- Franchising and trade marks, copyright and design law;
- Franchising and passing off;
- Franchising and confidential information, know-how or patent law;
- Franchising and competition law.

Answer

Franchising is a system of marketing goods or services. It usually involves close collaboration between separate undertakings, each being legally and financially independent companies. The franchisor owns the business concept including substantial intellectual property rights to that concept. This may include a portfolio of trade marks, copyright, confidential information and know-how and/or patents. While the franchisee has an opportunity to own his own business, he agrees to pay the franchisor a royalty on all goods sold or services provided by the franchisee and licenses the business concept and associated intellectual property.

A successful franchise operation depends on the existence of a relatively sophisticated legal system that defines and protects the rights and obligations of both the franchisors and franchisees. As there is no specific legislation governing franchising operations in the UK, such rights and obligations are included in a detailed franchise agreement. The franchise agreement sets out the obligations of the parties to each other, and as franchising is essentially intellectual property driven, it importantly includes intellectual property matters. Both parties to the agreement need to be aware of the package of intellectual property rights relating to trade marks, trade names, shop signs, designs, copyrights, know-how or patents and confidential information.

First, it is essential that the franchisor effectively controls the use of the intellectual property by the franchisee. The franchisor will need to clearly and precisely fix the terms by which the franchisee may lawfully use the franchisor's intellectual property assets. This is crucially important in order to retain the goodwill that attaches to the franchised business. Trade marks usually are the most important and valuable intellectual property assets and it is vital that any trade marks are registered in the name of the franchisor. The question of revocation for non-use by the franchisor can be dealt with by s 25 of the **Trade Mark Act 1994 (TMA 1994)** which provides that revocation of a mark is not possible if the mark has been genuinely used by the proprietor or with his consent. Further, ss 28 and 29 **TMA 1994** permit the franchisor to grant the franchisee an exclusive licence to the trade mark. If this occurs, the licence transaction for the franchisee to use the mark should itself be registered under the Act.

Secondly, central to the franchise relationship lies the concept of goodwill. The tort of passing off protects goodwill. The issue that arises is, 'to which party does the goodwill belong?' The Privy Council decision of *JH Coles Pty Ltd v Need (1934)* confirms that the franchisor is the owner of the franchise goodwill. However, an authority on the franchisee's rights of action in passing off is lacking.

Thirdly, the franchise agreement must set out who owns the copyright in a number of works that may be shared by both parties, such as business plans, manuals, architectural plans, websites, etc.

Fourthly, it is important to protect any confidential information or know-how by adopting a confidentiality policy that will apply to franchise employees as they are likely to share information for the purpose of running the business. In relation to patent rights, if involved, these will usually be retained by the franchisor but licensed to the franchisee to use.

In terms of enforcing intellectual property rights against third parties, usually the franchisor is responsible for prosecuting these rights. Franchisees, however, are equally concerned to ensure that the franchisor has done everything that is reasonably possible for him to protect the intellectual property rights in question. It follows therefore that the franchisee will be anxious to ensure that in the event of infringement, the franchisor has taken sufficient steps to safeguard his ownership in his intellectual property rights so that he can protect the reputation of that brand for the benefit of the franchise network.

Finally, UK and EU competition laws seek to limit anti-competitive practices, including any practices as between franchisors and franchisees to create monopoly businesses. The **Competition Act 1998** implements the EU's rules on competition and in particular, Art 81 EC, which applies to franchise agreements. The decision of the ECJ in *Pronuptia de Paris v Schillgalis Case 161/84 ECR 353* involved the franchisor, Pronuptia, suing its franchisee Mrs Schillgalis (the franchisee for Hamburg, Oldenburg and Hanover) because her royalty payments were lower than required by the franchise agreement. Mrs Schillgalis counterclaimed that Pronuptia could not rely on the agreement because it contravened Art 81 and was therefore void. However, the Court concluded that the restrictions contained in the agreement to maintain common standards and to protect intellectual property rights did not fall within the scope of Art 81(1). As such, the terms of the agreement did not restrict competition and Mrs Schillgalis's argument failed.

Ultimately, the European Commission drafted a 'block exemption' for certain types of franchise agreements in 1988. Since May 2000, however, franchise agreements have been covered by the **Block Exemption Regulation** which covers vertical agreements containing intellectual property rights (IPR) provisions if five conditions are fulfilled:

1. The IPR provisions must be part of a vertical agreement, that is an agreement with conditions under which the parties may purchase, sell or resell certain goods or services.

2. The IPR must be assigned to, or for use by, the buyer (franchisee).

3. The IPR provisions must not constitute the primary object of the agreement.

4. The IPR provisions must be directly related to the use, sale or resale of goods or services by the buyer or his customers. In the case of franchising where marketing forms the object of the exploitation of IPRs, the goods or services are distributed by the master franchisee or the franchisees.

5. The IPR provisions, in relation to the contract goods or services, must not contain restrictions having the same object or effect as vertical restraints which are not exempted under the **Block Exemption Regulation**.

The key limitation of the block exemption is that the franchisor/supplier's market share must not exceed 30 per cent of the relevant market on which the contract goods or services are sold: Art 3. If the franchise agreement nevertheless unduly restricts competition, even though the regulation is complied with, the benefit of the regulation can be withdrawn by the Commission.

In conclusion, the franchising model has been very successful both in the UK and abroad and a large number of well-established enterprises are conducting business profitably. However, franchises require a careful consideration of intellectual property rights issues and competition law.

CHAPTER 14

IP LAW EXAM TECHNIQUE

Prior preparation and practice prevent piss-poor performance.
The 'Seven Ps' – an old Royal Navy saying

(1) Well before your exam, read your syllabus or module pack and confirm precisely what is examinable.

(2) Ensure you have all the materials you need to study (for example textbook, lecture notes, tutorial questions, marked assignments, up to date copy of the relevant statute, etc).

(3) Draw up a study timetable and stick to it.

(4) Prepare and revise the examinable material. Reread and condense your notes, don't write more notes. Use visual aids such as colour coding, diagrams, flowcharts or mind maps to condense information into one page summaries of each topic.

(5) Practise answering past exam questions set by the course co-ordinator in previous year(s).

Do not endlessly revise, only to apply your hard-won knowledge for the first time in the exam. You wouldn't run a race without training.

Law exam questions assess your ability to critically analyse and discuss issues within a limited time, so it is sensible to practise this skill before the exam. Students are still required to write law exams in longhand. If you are used to using a computer keyboard to type assignments and notes, don't forget to practise writing out your answers. You will be surprised how much harder it is to write a good answer without being able to cut and paste, delete, format, etc.

(6) Ensure you are familiar with the format, style and duration of the examination.

(7) Avoid 'question spotting' or adopting the risky study strategy of selecting a minimum number of topics to concentrate on. The odds are against you.

(8) Confirm which materials will be permitted to be brought into the exam, if any, for example unmarked statute books, textbooks, etc.

(9) Plan your answer before you start to write. Use the answer plans in this text as a guide.

(10) Answer every part of the question. Answer the whole question.

(11) Do not ramble, keep your answer on point.

Essay Questions – allow for flexibility to include the knowledge you have acquired and to adapt it to the question. After completing an answer plan, include a brief introduction, use headings to signpost the issues being discussed to the examiner, and end with insightful concluding remarks. Underline or highlight relevant cases to assist the marker.

A good approach is to:

• Define and explain the key terms included in the essay question itself;

• Compare and contrast;

• Critically analyse the social, economic and political circumstances that impact on the development of the relevant law;

• Identify any areas ripe for reform;

• Suggest possible reforms;

• Summarise the key points you have covered in a sentence or two followed by your concluding remarks.

Students should avoid adopting an overly 'journalistic' style or writing an answer with 'too much opinion and not enough law'.

Throughout the essay, students should ensure that they refer to relevant statutory provisions and leading cases, and highlight any controversial issues they are aware of from their wider reading.

Problem Questions – problem questions largely determine the structure of answers. An appropriate answer can be structured by legal issue or by party, as required.

It is good advice to question the significance of all the information provided in the question. Dates, acts, events are usually all relevant, although occasionally an examiner will plant a red herring.

The facts of leading cases are regularly adapted for use in problem questions. If this happens, ensure you mention the similarity in the factual situations and analyse the decision in the relevant case – will it be followed or can it be distinguished?

In the exam

Bring all required materials with you, for example your student ID, sufficient pens, pencils, erasers, highlighters, rulers, tissues and a bottle of water (if permitted).

Use the reading time to work out which questions you will answer, in what order.

Keep an eye on the clock – work out a strategy for writing your exam answers based on the length of time and the number of questions to be answered. If you give yourself 40 minutes per question then stick ruthlessly to your plan. You will achieve a better mark for completing all questions rather than not having time to attempt one.

If all else fails – if you are stumped or are running out of time, try to at least write a paragraph or two on the general topic of the question. This way you may get 10–30 marks for the answer. These extra marks you gain could mean the difference between an overall pass or fail.

CHAPTER 15

INTELLECTUAL PROPERTY EXAM CRAM GUIDE

Type of IP Right	Key Attribute	Subject Matter	Procedure	Right Created	Duration
Copyright	Originality	Literary, dramatic, musical and artistic works ('LDMA' works), sound recordings, films and broadcasts, etc.	Statutory right arising automatically under the **CDPA 1988** No registration	Exclusive rights of reproduction, distribution, public performance, broadcasting, including in a cable program, adaptations (except fair dealing)	Variable. Maximum of the life of the author plus 70 years.
Moral Rights	Rights of author-creator vs those of the entrepreneur who exploits the work Originates from Art 6 **Berne Convention** See also Art 27 of the **Universal Declaration of Human Rights**	Literary, Dramatic, Musical and Artistic Works Moral rights do not apply to: • computer programs • where ownership of a work originally vested in an author's employer • where material is used in newspapers or magazines • reference works such as encyclopaedias or dictionaries	Statutory right under the **CDPA 1988** which are personal to the author No registration, but must be asserted	There are five: (1) Right to Paternity (2) Right of Integrity (3) Right to object to false attribution (4) Right to privacy for photographs and films (5) Artist's Resale Right	Right of integrity and paternity last for the same period as the relevant copyright. The right to false attribution exists for 20 years from the death of the person subject to the false attribution.

Patent	New invention	Requirements: – Novelty – Inventive Step – Capable of indus- trial application – Not excluded	Statutory right under the **Patents Act 1977** obtained by being granted a patent by the Patent Office	To exclude all others from making or using the sub-ject matter	A maximum of 20 years
Registered Design	Novelty and individual character	Protection for the: – Aesthetic or func- tional aspects of the appearance of the whole or part of a product	Statutory right under the **Registered Designs Act 1948** obtained by the grant of a registered design by the Designs Registry of the Patent Office	Use of the design in any product, importation or distribution	A maximum of 25 years
Unregistered Design Right	Not commonplace	Subsist automatically over certain aspects of the shape or con-figuration of articles	A statutory right under the **CDPA 1988** which arises from the date on which the design is recorded. No registra-tion is required	Copy the design (causal: not accidental re-creation) importation; distribution (but compul-sory licence)	A maximum of 15 years
Registered Trade Marks	Distinctiveness	Requirement: A distinctive sign capable of being represented graphically	Statutory right under the **Trade Marks Act 1994** by the grant of a registered mark by the Trade Marks Division of the Patent Office	Exclusive use of mark Can license	Will exist for as long as the trade mark registration continues to be renewed by the owner

Passing Off	Trade confusion	Protects against mis-representations that damage the goodwill of an enterprise	A common law tort	Exclusive use of the unregistered mark	Will exist until the goodwill of the enterprise ceases
Confidential Information	Trade secret know-how or other non-public information	Information possess-ing the necessary quality of confidence or secrecy	Enforced by relying on equitable principles and/ or con-tractual terms relat-ing to disclosure	Exclusive use	Will exist until the information passes into the public domain and is no longer confidential

CHAPTER 16

USEFUL WEBSITES

	http://
ACID Anti Copying in Design	*www.acid.co.uk*
Alliance Against IP Theft	*www.allianceagainstiptheft.co.uk*
Brand Enforcement	*www.brandenforcement.co.uk*
Chartered Institute of Patent Attorneys	*www.cipa.org.uk*
Community Plant Variety Office	*www.cpvo.eu.int*
Community Trade Mark/Design Office	*www.ohim.eu.int*
Copyright Licensing Agency	*www.cla.co.uk*
Department of Trade and Industry	*www.dti.gov.uk*
DTI Office of Science and Innovation	*www.dti.gov.uk/science/*
European Commission	*www.europa.eu.int/comm*
European Court of Justice	*www.curia.eu.int*
European Free Trade Association	*www.efta.int*
European Patent Office	*www.epo.org*
Esp@cenet	*www.european-patent-office.org/wbt/espacenets/#*
European Union	*www.www.europa.eu.int*
Federation against Copyright Theft	*www.fact-uk.org.uk*
Federation Against Software Theft	*www.fast.org.uk*
HM Stationery Office	*www.opsi.org.uk*
Judicial Protection of IPR in China	*www.chinaiprlaw.com*
ICANN	*www.incaa.org*
IFPI (Recording Industry)	*www.ifpi.org*
Institute of Trade Mark Attorneys (ITMA)	*www.itma.org.uk*
Intellectual Property Owners Association	*www.ipo.org*
IP Bar Association	*www.ipba.co.uk*
IP Europe	*www.ip-europe.org*
IP and Media ADR Group	*www.ipandmedia.co.uk*
IP Law firms Database	*www.intellectualpropertylawfirms.com*
Intellectual Property Institute	*www.ip-institute.org.uk*
International Intellectual Property Institute	*www.iipi.org*
Office of Fair Trading	*www.oft.gov.uk*
Managing IP	*www.managingip.com*
OHIM	*www.oami.europa.eu*

Society for Computers and Law	*www.scl.org*
UK Government IP Site	*www.intellectual-property.gov.uk*
UK Patent Office website	*www.patent.gov.uk*
UK Plant Varieties Office	*www.defra.gov.uk/plant/pvs*
United Stated Patent and Trade Mark Office	*www.uspto.org*
World Intellectual Property Organisation	*www.wipo.org*
World Trade Organisation	*www.wto.org*

INDEX

account of profits 148
Anti-copying in Design (ACID) 24
Anton Piller orders
  see search orders
artistic works 37–9
  sculptures 37–9

biological inventions 92, 94–6, 110–13
breach of confidence 8
  see confidential information

character
  malicious falsehood 171, 174–7
    injunctions 177
    limitation period 177
  see passing off
  merchandising 171–3
confidential information 155–69
  employees 155–60, 160–3
  patents 155–60, 163–7
  public interest 159, 166, 167–9
  reverse-engineering 164
  type of information protected 155, 157–8, 162
consumer protection 6
copyright
  artistic works
    architecture 47
    photographs and incidental inclusion 46–8
    public display 48–9
    sculpture 37–40, 46–7
  database 52
  de minimus principle 51
  economic rights 32
  expression 49–52, 58
  see fair dealing

graphic work 39, 47
ideas, protection of 33, 49–52, 58
infringements
  primary 29, 40–2, 55
  secondary 29
lectures 40
literary works 40–3, 58
lyrics 44
masthead 51
material form
  see moral rights
musical works 44–6
  lyrics 44
  sampling 44–5
names 51
photographs 46–8
plagiarism 43
public lending rights scheme 32
  see remedies
restricted acts 29
translations 43
strap-line 49, 51
subsistence 37–38, 40–3, 49–51
substantial copying 45–7
symbol, copyright 33, 40
computer technology 57–72
  adaptation right 57
  see databases
  decompilation right 67–9
    reverse analysis or engineering 67–9
  fixation 59
  literal copying 58–60
  literary works 58
  non-literal copying 58–60, 64–7
  programs 57, 58

reproduction right 57
software 57
technological protection measures (TPMs) 57,
    61–4
counterfeiting 22
HM Revenue & Customs 23

damages 21, 22
celebrity endorsement 146
confidential information 148
proof 176
databases 52, 69–72
Department of Trade and Industry (DTI) 22, 24
National IP Enforcement Report 25
design
design right 74, 77–83
    commonplace 73–6
    duration of protection 83
    originality 84
    ownership 79
    surface decoration 77–8
industrial design 74
original 73–5
registered design 80–3
    duration of protection 83
    grace period 81–2
    novelty 81
    originality 83
    reform 81–2
domain name dispute 134–7
Uniform Dispute Resolution Policy 135–6

Eco Patent Commons 10, 12, 13
essential medicines 17

fair dealing defence 34–5, 39, 42, 43
acknowledgement 36
criticism and review 35, 42
incidental inclusion 48
permitted acts 35, 48
private study 35
reporting current events 36, 43
research 35
Federation Against Copyright Theft (FACT) 24
Federation Against Software Theft (FAST) 24
franchising 187–6

geographical indications 7, 147–53
appellation of origin 148, 149
certificate of special character 148, 150
homonymous names 152

indication of source 8, 147, 148
protected designation of origin 147, 149
protected geographical indication 147–9
goodwill 8, 79, 139, 141–2
Gower's Review of Intellectual Property Report
    1, 85, 92
Green Channel vii, 10, 11, 12
Group of Eight (G8) 19–20

Hegel, Georg Wilhelm Friedrich 4, 5, 53

idea-expression dichotomy 33, 49–51
see copyright
image rights 179–82
injunction 21, 23, 24–7, 140–3, 177
American Cyanamid 26–7
balance of convenience
final 165
interim 23, 25–6, 148
International Centre for Trade and Sustainable
    Development 19

Labour theory
John Locke 4, 5, 110–11
licences
literary works 40–8, 53
Locke, John 4, 5, 110–11

malicious falsehood 171, 174–7
medical treatment patents 92, 93, 105, 106
misrepresentation
see passing off
moral rights 31, 32, 34, 37–9, 52–5
artist's resale right 33–34, 53, 55
commissioner of a photograph 53, 55
damages 39
derogatory treatment 39, 53–5
droit de suite 53
false attribution 33, 38, 53–4
integrity 33, 39, 53
paternity 33, 53–5
privacy in photos or films 33, 55
musical works 44–6
lyrics 44
sampling 44–5

natural rights 4, 5
negative rights 4

Olympics
Association Right 14, 15

Games' marks 13–16
London Olympic Games 12 –15

passing off 8, 139–43, 143–6
  character merchandising 139–46
  common field of activity 132–3, 136
  damage 140–3
  endorsements 144–6
  false advertising 139
  fictional characters 132
  goodwill 79, 139, 141
  image rights 144–6, 167–70
  misappropriate of personality 132
  misrepresentation 142
  protection of personality 144–6
  reputation 141–2
  reverse passing off 139
  unfair competition 139
patents
  application 87–9, 103–5
    examination 89
    filing 87, 89
    grant 89
    priority date 87, 89
    procedure 87, 88
    publication 89
    search 12, 89, 90
  computer programs 57
  confidential information 151–5
  disclosure to the public 90
  duration 88, 90, 91
  Eco Patent Commons 10, 12, 13
  employee inventors 106–10, 152
    amount of compensation 108–9
  Gower's Report on Intellectual Property 1, 85, 92
  Green Channel vii, 10, 11, 12
  harmonisation 104, 105
  industrial application 85, 87, 88, 103
  infringement 107
  invent around 90
  inventive step 85, 87, 88
  licence 153
  litigation 108
  medical methods 92, 93
  monopoly 103
  novelty 85, 87
  patentability 85, 87, 102–6
    biological inventions 92, 94–7, 102–6, 108–11
    business methods 92

  claims 90, 97–102
  computer programs 57
  databases 92
  discovery 104
  DNA 110–11
  doctrine of equivalents 100
  excluded inventions 102–6
  Human Genome Project 108
  mechanical devices 105
  medical methods 92, 93, 105, 106
  person skilled in the art 99, 10
  purposive construction 99, 101
  Swiss claim 93
  Windsurfer test 86, 88
  prior art 87, 88
  specification 90, 91
  state of the art 88
Patents County Court 21, 29
personality theory 4, 5
piracy 23
plant varieties 105–6
Public Lending Rights Scheme 32

remedies
  account of profits 21, 23, 148
  civil 21, 23
  criminal 23, 24
  see damages 21, 23, 146, 148
  declaration of non-infringement 23
  delivery up and destruction 23, 39, 139
  see injunctions
  self-help 24, 29
  see search orders

search orders
  aims 29
  Anton Piller Order 29
  counterfeiting 29
  discretionary 30
  drawing up the order 30
  execution 30
  ex parte 29
  pre-requisites 29
  safeguards

technology transfer 6
TellPat Database 22, 25
Think Kit
  UK Patent Office 1
trade marks
  colour marks 117, 119–22

Community trade mark 115
comparative advertising 122–7, 127–34
copycat products 122–7
domain name dispute 134–7
grounds of refusal 116–18
infringement 122–7
knock offs 122–7
Olympic Games' marks 121–2
see passing off
registered trade marks 115–22
scent marks 115, 118, 119–22
slogans 118
trade secrets
see confidential information

TRIPS Action Network (TAN) 19

United Kingdom Patent Office 1, 10, 11, 22
esp@cenet patent database 70
United Nations Conference on Trade and
Development (UNCTAD) 19

World Business Council for Sustainable
Development 10, 12
World Health Organization (WHO) 18
World Intellectual Property Organization
(WIPO) 10, 11, 25
Advisory Committee on Enforcement 25
World Trade Organization (WTO) 10, 11, 16

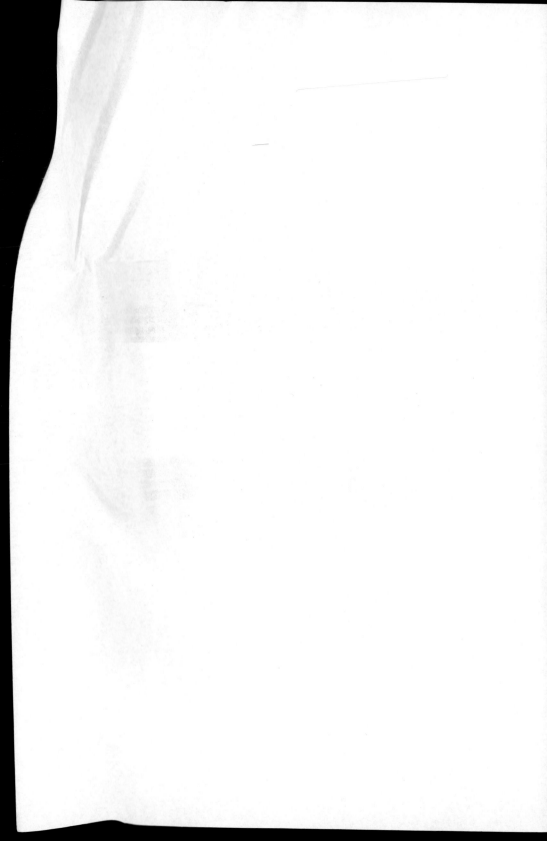